BISON
BOOKS

Covered Wagon Women

Diaries and Letters from the
Western Trails
1854–1860

Volume 7

Edited and compiled by
KENNETH L. HOLMES

Introduction to the Bison Books Edition
by Shirley A. Leckie

University of Nebraska Press
Lincoln and London

⊚ The paper in this book meets the minimum requirements of American National Standard for Information Sciences—Permanence of Paper for Printed Library Materials, ANSI Z39.48-1984.

First Bison Books printing: 1998

Library of Congress Cataloging-in-Publication Data
The Library of Congress has cataloged Vol. 1 as:
Covered wagon women: diaries & letters from the western trails, 1840–1849 / edited and compiled by Kenneth L. Holmes; introduction to the Bison Books edition by Anne M. Butler.
p.   cm.
Originally published: Glendale, Calif: A. H. Clark Co., 1983.
"Reprinted from volume one . . . of the original eleven-volume edition"—
T.p. verso.
"Volume 1."
Includes index.
ISBN 0-8032-7277-4 (pa: alk. paper)
1. Women pioneers—West (U.S.)—Biography.   2. West (U.S.)—History.   3. West (U.S.)—Biography.   4. Overland journeys to the Pacific.   5. Frontier and pioneer life—West (U.S.)   I. Holmes, Kenneth L.
F591.C79   1996
978—dc20   95-21200   CIP

Volume 2 introduction by Lilian Schlissel.
ISBN 0-8032-7274-X (pa: alk. paper)
Volume 3 introduction by Susan Armitage.
ISBN 0-8032-7287-1 (pa: alk. paper)
Volume 4 introduction by Glenda Riley.
ISBN 0-8032-7291-X (pa: alk. paper)
Volume 5 introduction by Ruth B. Moynihan.
ISBN 0-8032-7294-4 (pa: alk. paper)
Volume 6 introduction by Linda Peavy and Ursula Smith.
ISBN 0-8032-7295-2 (pa: alk. paper)
Volume 7 introduction by Shirley A. Leckie
ISBN 0-8032-7296-0 (pa: alk. paper)

Reprinted from volume seven (1987) of the original eleven-volume edition titled *Covered Wagon Women: Diaries and Letters from the Western Trails, 1840–1890*, published by The Arthur H. Clark Company, Glendale, California. The pagination has not been changed and no material has been omitted in this Bison Books edition.

Introduction to the Bison Books Edition

Shirley A. Leckie

By 1852 information about overland travel had become so widely known that a ten year old in Monroe, Michigan, recorded advice in her diary. Elizabeth (Libbie) Bacon, the future wife of George Armstrong Custer, overheard a neighbor tell her parents that on the Overland Trail "the plains were . . . a burying place of the dead." The neighbor also noted that "the emigrants feel so burdened with baggage they throw it away, so that the plains are covered with clothes."[1] The message was clear; overlanders should pack as lightly as possible.

By 1854, when Sarah Sutton made her journey to Oregon Territory and Anna Maria Goodell and Elizabeth Austin traveled to Washington Territory, the tide of emigration, after a falling off, had resumed more heavily than ever. In addition to wider dissemination of knowledge, travelers benefited from the organized relief efforts now spearheaded by California and Oregon newspapers intent upon assuring the continual flow of new settlers to the Pacific coast. Moreover, trading posts, often run by former trappers with Indian wives and métis children, were more abundant. Those heading for California found Salt Lake City a comfortable way station, although prices for labor and supplies were generally high. Perhaps most important to the majority of covered wagon women, who were young and in their childbearing years, the nearly two-thousand-mile trek across the continent could be completed in about five months rather than the six or so required a decade earlier.[2] Nonetheless, whether one describes a diary from the 1840s or 1850s, the most frequent and important notation referred to the miles traveled each day.

How an individual woman experienced emigration, however, depended largely on her age, health, and circumstances beyond her control. Pregnancy, childbirth, nursing children, the death of oxen, the disappearance of cattle, the spread of disease, accidents, or unseasonably cold, hot, wet, or dry weather were factors that often rendered covered wagon travel arduous and dangerous. Moreover, new trails, such as the one residents of Washington Territory carved out in 1853 over the Cascades to connect Fort Walla Walla with Puget Sound, might still prove extraordinarily difficult.[3] Diarists Anna Maria Goodell and Elizabeth Austin experienced that fact a year later.

Forty-eight-year-old Sarah Sutton from western Illinois was older than most covered wagon women. Undoubtedly, she represented a valued source of wisdom and experience for the younger members of her party. Moreover, by moving with her children and their families she avoided the alternative of saying good-bye to them, probably forever. And if Oregon land was as fertile as her husband reported, not only would the couple benefit but their children would probably stay in the region. That meant that the larger extended family would remain relatively intact, something that no longer held true in many places. In New England, for example, family holdings were often too small to parcel out among heirs and the soil was far less fertile.[4]

Harriet Augusta Stewart, Sarah's sixteen-year-old daughter by a former marriage, welcomed the move to Oregon for other reasons. Earlier her mother had described her as "not well," but poor health was no reason to stay home. Oregon was viewed as a healthier climate when compared with the ague- and fever-ridden Mississippi River Valley.[5] In addition to her extended family, Stewart noted that neighbors from the area of Beardstown, Illinois, were accompanying them, "all pleased with the Idea of going to oregon" (24).[6] Personally she wanted "to see the curiositys and get gold for sewing & to see the buffalo and to hear the wolves howl" (24). In other words, in addition to an exciting adventure, she looked forward to living where female labor brought greater remuneration. Within a year, however, like so many other young women who arrived in Oregon, she was married.

If the trail had become, on the whole, safer for emigrants, it had become more dangerous in one important respect. Although the Native peoples were never the threat portrayed in later Hollywood sagas or even in the reminiscences of pioneers, the emigration westward brought them new hardships. Between 1840 and 1880 the buffalo herds, on which the Plains Indians depended, almost disappeared. Although changes in tribal relationships, new patterns of trade, and periods of drought played a role in this catastrophe, emigrants contributed their share. The overland trains of the 1840s and the smaller parties a decade later included oxen, horses, mules, and other livestock that spread diseases to the buffalo herds. Moreover, the emigrants' livestock consumed much of the pasturage that sustained the bison. That, along with the diminishing of other game, such as the elk mentioned in Sutton's diary, exacted a heavy toll on the food supply and material well-being of Native peoples.[7]

Moreover, tribal people suffered severely from cholera and other diseases the emigrants brought westward. When Sarah Sutton's diary is

read carefully, it is obvious that the Native peoples her party encoun-
tered along the Platte River and in the area of Independence Rock were
in dire straits. A kind woman, Sutton commiserated with them, but she
had no inkling that she and her family were contributing to their calamity.

In addition to their misunderstanding of the hardships facing Native
peoples, covered wagon women such as Sutton and Goodell disdained
the Euro-American traders (often of French ancestry) and their Indian
wives whom they met along the trail. They referred to these women as
"squaws," an ethnocentric term that conveyed the idea that Indian women
were "beasts of burden" without honor among their own people and
subject to maltreatment from husbands, whether Native or white.

More recent historical investigation reveals, however, that fur traders who turned to merchandizing or ranching after both the large supply of beaver and the European market for beaver pelts disappeared
enjoyed marriages with Native women that were similar to those of
other Americans in stability, number of children, and presumably degree of affection. Moreover, given the role Indian wives had played in
helping these men forge crucial alliances with various tribes, they were
important assets as well as companions.[8]

Finally, of course, the long accepted idea that Indian women were
"beasts of burden" has been challenged. Catherine Price, for example,
notes that among the Oglala gender roles were "complementary with
women and men performing quite different but equally valuable roles
(*okicicupi*)." By serving as seers, curers, members of the Medicine Society, or preparers of medicine for war or by becoming expert
craftswomen and artisans, Oglala women achieved honor and distinc-
tion among their people.[9]

Families on the Overland Trail, having little comprehension of any
of these realities, clung to their prejudices, in part because those prejudices justified their migration. Sutton, for example, saw herself and her
family as similar to the Chosen People of the Old Testament. Her belief
that God had laid out the trails to lead her family to the Promised Land
gave her an unfailing sense of their right to settle in Oregon Territory.

Moreover, she and other overlanders believed that they would use
the land more productively than the original inhabitants. When Indians
arrived to trade salmon for a shirt, as she and her party were camped on
the Boise River on August 2, 1854, she penned a notation in her diary.
Noting that the river bottomland around her was fertile and well treed,
she dismissed it as "to far away in an uncivilized land among the sav-

age indians who know no more about work than the grasshoppers and never saw such thing as a garden vegetable grow here" (70).

Yet despite evidence of deeply rooted ethnocentrism, diaries of the covered wagon women tell us that once they came in contact with the individuals of various tribes, they often saw them as people rather than stereotypes. Sarah Mousley, for example, was immensely comforted when the Sioux, both adults and children, visited her younger sisters, Martha and Wilhelmina, after they were injured during a cattle stampede. When the Indians kept watch all night by her suffering sisters' bedside, she wrote the next day, "Oh how I love their society and although so ignorant of their language I love to behold them" (179).

Overall, covered wagon women were a hardy lot. Who can forget Ellen Hundley's description of her hardships during her family's trip from Utah to Texas. "I suffered a heap of fatigue walking and carrying my child and trying to catch the waggons" (138). Days later she wrote, "we started again and traveled over bad road sometimes having to make it as we went crossed several dry creeks and deep ravines still a barren sandy desert; we traveled on 30 miles and not a drop of water for our horses we still come on till 11 oclock at night and still no water" (140). Overall during that twenty-four-hour period, she covered fifty miles with her seven-month-old son, another two year old, and six children from her former marriage.

In part, women such as Sutton, Hundley, and Mousley were steeled by religious fervor, an outcome of the earlier Second Great Awakening. That evangelical movement of the nineteenth century had brought many unchurched Americans into religious denominations. At the same time, it had lifted female self-esteem, since clergymen turned to women as conduits of grace. Once converted they could be relied on to encourage their husbands and children to join the Baptists, Methodists, Congregationalists, or Presbyterians or the more recently established Disciples of Christ or Seventh-Day Adventists.[10]

In one instance, however, a denomination had appeared that affected female converts in a singular fashion. For members of the Church of Jesus Christ of Latter-day Saints, or Mormons, one scholar notes that "the highest degree of glory in the celestial kingdom, the attainment of Godhood, was reserved for those who had entered into polygamous relationships."[11] Moreover, although the majority of men did not take multiple wives, such unions were the ideal for Mormon leaders by the 1850s.

That ideal, according to Lawrence Foster, should be placed in the context of an America in which the market revolution had left many individuals disoriented and cut off from older traditions and social relationships. Thus the adoption of polygamy was "part of a larger effort to reestablish social cohesion and kinship ties in a socially and intellectually disordered environment."[12] Certainly, in nineteenth-century America, those who entered into plural marriages cut themselves off irrevocably from the larger society. In the process they tied themselves more securely to the Mormon faith.[13]

But polygamy served another function as well. Among their religious duties, prominent men were expected to serve as teachers, missionaries, and members of the priesthood. In that light, marriage to more than one woman weakened the intense bond between husband and wife and threw plural wives on their own resources, emotional and otherwise. Not surprisingly, many became more independent, especially if they were part of a truly extended family, which often included sisters.[14] (As Kenneth Holmes notes, Sarah Mousley later became the first wife of Angus Munn Cannon, the same day that he married her sister, Ann Amanda Mousley.)

The impact of polygamy on Mormon women is not easily summarized, although one diarist in this volume, the feisty and assertive Hannah Keziah Clapp, was certain she knew. She characterized them as "miserable slaves." She had no inkling that many of them, given their husbands' long absences in service to the church, managed farms and businesses with ingenuity and skill. Nor did she see the advances women had achieved in Utah. The territorial university, established as the University of Deseret, admitted females as soon as it opened its doors in 1850. At that time, Oberlin College was the only coeducational institution of higher education in the United States.[15] Moreover, in Utah unhappily married wives could win divorces more easily than in the East, since Brigham Young and other leaders saw affection as the only means by which a marriage could be sealed for "time and eternity."[16] Although these advantages did not give Mormon women equality, they tell us that the status of women in Utah was not as "degraded" as eastern critics maintained.

The economic and social changes in the United States during the 1840s and 1850s raised many questions about the role and status of women. Only a small minority of women and men supported the woman's rights movement emanating from Seneca Falls in July 1848, but American views on female potentiality were slowly changing. As Glenda Riley observes, although the "capable" woman had appeared in literature several decades earlier, she was a more popular figure in works published in the decade before the Civil War.[17]

Julia Archibald Holmes, like Hannah Clapp, had internalized a sense of herself as innately competent, largely as a result of her involvement in the woman's rights movement. Influenced by transcendentalists, such as Ralph Waldo Emerson, who stressed self-reliance, and wearing her bloomer costume despite criticism from both sexes, Archibald Holmes, like other young, childless women in this volume, experienced her trip to the Colorado mining camps as an exhilarating adventure. Imbued with the common belief that contact with nature improved health, she saw the trip as an opportunity to test her stamina and improve her endurance levels. In that sense, her ascent to the top of Pike's Peak on August 5, 1859, as the first woman on record, was simply the culmination of her trail experience.

Six months after the diarist Martha Missouri Moore arrived in the Honey Lake Valley of northern California in October, 1860, the United States was involved in the Civil War. Although the war ended in 1865, sectional reconciliation was not complete until the turn of the century. Here the West played a significant role since Americans, both North and South, celebrated their common pioneering heritage in this region.[18]

The odyssey of families migrating westward in covered wagons emerged as a valued but often mythologized part of that shared heritage. Unfortunately, Native peoples were often presented as bloodthirsty savages and a barrier to be removed as intrepid male pioneers protected the weaker sex and carved out a home for themselves in a western Eden. Today, thanks to historians such as John Mack Faragher, Lillian Schlissel, and the late John D. Unruh, among others, historians have a far more realistic view of those who emigrated on the various trails between 1840 and 1860. The late Kenneth Holmes added immeasurably to that understanding by searching for obscure diaries of women and reprinting them as close to their original form as possible. With female voices telling their story from their viewpoint, the record is now fuller, although the history that emerges is far more complicated than the earlier version.

One day perhaps it will become even richer and more complicated. The Native peoples have their own oral traditions and accounts of how the arrival of these emigrants affected their lives. Although they had made a world together with trappers and traders earlier, largely because these Euro-Americans had found it necessary to adapt to their customs in order to succeed in their ventures, the permanent settlement of Euro-American women and their families altered that world irrevocably.[19]

Somewhere, one hopes, another pioneer, in the spirit of Kenneth Holmes, is compiling Native traditions and oral history accounts. If their voices can become part of the historical narrative, all will gain a truly panoramic view of what migration meant to families, both those who crossed the continent in covered wagons to Oregon, Utah, and California and those who were already there and called the land their home.

NOTES

1. Elizabeth Clift Bacon journal, 8 April 1852 to 31 December 1860, gift of Marguerite Merington to Western Americana collection, Beinecke Rare Book and Manuscript Library, Yale University, New Haven, Connecticut. Quotes from entry for 8 September 1852.

2. John D. Unruh, *The Plains Across: The Overland Emigrants and the Trans-Mississippi West, 1840–60* (Urbana: University of Illinois Press, 1979), 79–85, 307; Lillian Schlissel, *Women's Diaries of the Westward Journey* (New York: Schocken, 1982), 118.

3. Unruh, *Plains Across*, 351.

4. Charles Sellers, *The Market Revolution: Jacksonian America, 1815–1846* (New York: Oxford University Press, 1991), 17–19.

5. John Mack Faragher, *Women and Men on the Overland Trail* (New Haven: Yale University Press, 1979), 17.

6. Virginia Scharff has noted that Euro-Americans moving westward were, in one important respect, similar to the Native peoples they were replacing; both groups were often "traveling villages." "Gender and Western History: Is Anybody Home on the Range?" *Montana, The Magazine of Western History* 41 (spring 1991): 62.

7. Elliot West, *The Way West: Essays on the Central Plains* (Albuquerque: University of New Mexico Press, 1995), 52–83.

8. William R. Swagerty, "Marriage and Settlement Patterns of Rocky Mountain Trappers and Traders," *Western Historical Quarterly* 11 (April 1980): 159–80.

9. Catherine Price, *The Oglala People, 1841–1879: A Political History* (Lincoln: University of Nebraska Press, 1996), 19.

10. Glenna Matthews, *The Rise of Public Woman: Woman's Power and Woman's Place in the United States, 1630–1970* (New York: Oxford University Press, 1992), 103–19; Sellers, *Market Revolution*, 227–29.

11. Klaus J. Hansen, *Mormonism and the American Experience*. Chicago History of American Religion (Chicago: University of Chicago Press, 1981), 165.

12. Quoted by Hansen, *Mormonism*, 161.

13. Hansen, *Mormonism*, 157–58.

14. Lawrence Foster, "Polygamy and the Frontier: Mormon Women in Early Utah," *Utah Historical Quarterly* 50 (summer 1982): 268–89. For a discussion on "sister wives," see page 279.

15. Foster, "Polygamy and the Frontier," 280–81. By contrast, the University of Michigan barred women for another twenty years, until state lawmakers, determined to save the state the expense of establishing a separate institution for women, demanded their admittance. See Rosalind Rosenberg, "The Limits of Access: The History of Coeducation in America," in *Women and Higher Education in American History: Essays from the Mount Holyoke College Sesquicentennial Symposia*, ed. Jack Mack Faragher and Florence Howe (New York: W. W. Norton, 1988), 110.

16. Foster, "Polygamy and the Frontier," 284–85; Carole Cornwall Madsen, "'At Their Peril': Utah Law and the Case of Plural Wives, 1850–1900," *Western Historical Quarterly* 21 (November 1990): 430–32.

17. Glenda Riley, *Women and Indians on the Frontier, 1825–1915* (Albuquerque: University of New Mexico Press, 1984), 27.

18. Robert Athern, *The Mythic West in Twentieth Century America* (Lawrence: University Press of Kansas, 1986), 165.

19. Robin Fisher, "The Northwest from the Beginning of Trade with Europeans to the 1880s," *The Cambridge History of the Native Peoples of the Americas* vol. 1, pt. 2, ed. Bruce G. Trigger and Wilcomb E. Washburn (Cambridge: Cambridge University Press, 1996), 148–51.

Contents

EDITOR'S INTRODUCTION 9

A TRAVEL DIARY IN 1854, by Sarah Sutton
Introduction 15
Family Letters 23

THE VERMILLION WAGON TRAIN DIARIES, 1854
by Anna Maria Godell and Elizabeth Austin
Introduction 79
The Diaries 86

FROM UTAH TO TEXAS IN 1856, by Ellen Hundley
Introduction 133
The Diary 136

DELAWARE TO UTAH, 1857, by Sarah Maria Mousley
Introduction 157
Sources and Family Members 158
Persons Named in Diary 161
The Diary 163

TO PIKE'S PEAK AND NEW MEXICO, 1858,
by Julia Anna Archibald [Holmes]
Introduction 191
The Letter 193

FROM ASHTABULA TO PETALUMA IN 1859,
by Harriet Booth Griswold
Introduction 217
The Diary 218

A SALT LAKE CITY STOPOVER, JULY 1859,
  by Hannah Keziah Clapp
  Introduction 245
  The Letter 247
THE TRIP TO CALIFORNIA, 1860,
  by Martha Missouri Moore
  Introduction 259
  The Journal 263

Illustrations

ELIZABETH [AUSTIN] ROEDER 78
ELLENOR HUNDLEY 132
JULIA ARCHIBALD HOLMES 190
HANNAH KEZIAH CLAPP 244
MARTHA MISSOURI MOORE 258

Introduction to Volume VII

> The most striking new developments were prompted by the way station requirements of overland stagecoaching (to Denver and Pike's Peak country as well as to Salt Lake City and California) and Pony Express. When coupled with the rapidity of rural and urban settlement west of the Missouri River, east of the traditional California and Oregon destination points, and on all sides of Salt Lake City, the net result was an overland trip which resembled the pioneering ventures of the early 1840s in name only. For in 1859 and 1860 there were literally hundreds of supportive facilities en route. Rarely did the emigrant travel more than twenty-five or thirty miles without encountering at least one habitation.   Paul D. Unruh, Jr., *The Plains Across*.[1]

The above quote from one of the finest of all books about the ways west gives a picture of trail life in the late 1850s and 1860 — the period with which our present volume deals. There was a tapering off of overland travel in the early and mid-1850s, and then there was a build-up in 1859 and 1860.

There were some pertinent events or activities that relate to the experience of women travellers who wrote during the 1850s.

This was first of all, the decade of intense activity in the rise of the feminist movement in the United States. It had its beginnings in up-state New York, especially in Seneca Falls.[2] The major symbol was the "Bloomer Costume," named for Amelia Bloomer, an active person in the woman's movements of the day. This has been mentioned in the diaries we have already published of women during the early 1850s. (See

---

[1](Champagne, Illinois, 1979), p. 298.

[2] Miriam Gurko, *The Ladies of Seneca Falls: The Birth of the Woman's Rights Movement* (New York, 1974), *passim;* Margaret Hope Bacon, *Mothers of Feminism* (San Francisco, 1986), *passim.*

especially Volume IV, pp. 13-15,) Women traveling overland
seem to have been even more active in wearing this costume
than other American women for two reasons. They found it
more comfortable to wear on the overland journey, and they
could stride a horse and not be limited to riding side-saddle.
These women on the western venture were also more
independent and intellectually adventurous than those who
remained in the east. Two of the women in this volume were
active feminists: Julia Archibald (Holmes), who chose at
times not to use her new surname and wore the "American
Costume" during a journey to the Colorado gold fields in
1858. She became the first white woman of record to climb
Pikes Peak — this in her bloomer costume. She also insisted
on standing watch during the night the same as the men of
the wagon train. The men resisted this. The other woman
who was active in the movement of that day was Hannah
Keziah Clapp, who told in a letter published in the following
pages of wearing a bloomer dress on her overland journey
and added drama by carrying a revolver at her side.

The late 1850s were also a time for driving large herds of
cattle and flocks of sheep from Missouri to the Pacific Coast,
particularly to California. There were herds of as many as
800 to 1,000 cattle. The numbers of sheep were phenomenal.
One of our diarists, Martha Missouri Moore, records the
herding of a drove of 5100 sheep. They sold off 1,000 of
them along the way and drove the rest over the Lander Road
to the Red Bluff area of northern California, where James
Preston Moore had already laid a claim, having driven 4,500
across in 1853. Other droves of sheep were significant:
Colonel W.W. Hollister herded 9,000 from Ohio, and
several others drove flocks of smaller size.[3]

---

[3] The classic work on sheep drives is Edward Norris Wentworth, *America's Sheep
Trails* (Ames, Iowa, 1948), pp. 138, 169. See also Paul W. Gates, *California Ranchos
and Farms, 1846-1862* (Madison, 1967), pp. 33-37, also p. 190 for reference to James
Preston Moore.

In the third place, the 1850s were also a time of road surveying and building by the Interior Department of the Federal Government. It might well be called the Frederick West Lander decade, for he was the surveyor who mapped out five overland transcontinental routes.[4] The one most important to the California pioneers was the road that led from Fort Kearney to South Pass and down the Humboldt across present Nevada to Honey Lake on the eastern boundary of northern California. The western leg of the way became known as the Lander Wagon Road.

He recommended that "All stock drivers should take it at once. All parties whose stock is in bad order should take it, and I believe the emigration should take it, and will be much better satisfied with it, even the first season, than the old [California] road."[5] That was the way followed by the Moores with their large flock of sheep in 1860.

Fredrick Lander's report to the Department of Interior in 1859 indicated that "over sixty-two thousand cubic yards of earth and rock have removed, eleven miles of willow, and twenty-three miles of heavy pine timber cleared from the roadway."[6] This would indicate that for the purposes of wagon travel the great natural roadway was adequate.

For those who have not read the introduction to the first volume of this series, we reiterate some salient points which have been used to guide the editorial hand. It is a major purpose to let the writers tell their own story in their own words with as little scholarly trimming as possible. The intent in this publication of primary sources is to transcribe

[4]"Lander, Frederick West," *Dictionary of American Biography*, X (New York, 1933), pp. 569-570; E. Douglas Branch, "Frederick West Lander, Road-Builder," *Mississippi Valley Historical Review*, XVI (September, 1929), pp. 172-187; Peter T. Harstad, "The Lander Trail," *Idaho Yesterdays* (Fall, 1968), pp. 14-28.

[5]Branch, *Opus Cit.*, p. 184.

[6]*Pacific Wagon Roads, Letter from the Secretary of the Interior, House Executive Document No. 108*, 35th Congress, 2nd Session, 1859, p. 7.

each word or phrase as accurately as possible, leaving mis-spellings and grammatical errors as written in the original.

Two gestures have been made for the sake of clarity:

1. We have added spaces where phrases or sentences ended and no punctuation appeared in the original.

2. We have put the daily journals in diary format even though the original may have been written continuously line by line because of the writer's shortage of paper.

There are numerous geographic references that are mentioned over and over again in the various accounts. The final volume in the series will include a geographical gazetteer, in addition to an index and bibliography to aid the reader.

The scarce and unusual in overland documents have been sought out. Readily available accounts are not included, but they will be referred to in the final volume along with the bibliography. If the reader knows of such accounts written while on the journey, please let us know. Our goal is to add to the knowledge of all regarding this portion of our history — the story of ordinary people embarked on an extraordinary experience.

KENNETH L. HOLMES

Monmouth, Oregon, 1988

The Diaries, Letters, and Commentaries

A Travel Diary in 1854

⸹ Sarah Sutton

INTRODUCTION

> 4 of our wagons are not covered in the yard   we have a light two
> horse wagon for myself and some of the least children to ride
> in   the girls are very busy in washing and cooking every day as
> we have a great deal of company and a large family, and it is a great
> trouble to get rid of our things.   we have to give away a great deal

With such words written to a niece in an undated letter did
Sarah Sutton describe the beginning of a long journey from
Illinois to Oregon with her large family. And large it was: There
were eight children of hers by her former husband, Joel Stewart,
from whom she had been widowed on June 1, 1847. There were
four more children by John Pierce Sutton and his first wife,
Nancy McCall Sutton. Sarah and John, a widower, had been
married sometime in 1848. There was one small boy, age 4, named
Walter, who was the son of Sarah and John Sutton.

In the same letter Sarah wrote "Augusta is not well." There is
a family tradition that Sarah made a shroud for 16-year-old
Harriet Augusta to wear in case of her death on the long journey.
There was no need. The daughter lived a long and rich life. The
men probably prepared clean boards and laid them on the floor of
one of the wagons before loading it. These would be the material
for a coffin in case it was needed. In this case the shroud and coffin
makings were not used for Augusta, but for her mother, Sarah,
the writer of the journal, who died sometime in September in the
Tygh Valley, just east of Mount Hood in eastern Oregon. Sarah
did not reach the promised land. The children later remembered
how the wagons were driven back and forth over the new-made

grave so that it would not be molested. The wagon train did not reach the Willamette Valley until October 2, 1854.

Your editor assumed at first that Sarah Sutton died soon after the last entry was written on August 15. That, however, was not the case. She had loaned her glasses to a woman in a neighboring wagon train, and did not get them back. Hence, she could not see to write.

Sarah (Thurston) Sutton, (b. Jan. 12, 1806, in New Bedford, Ohio), was not one of those who wrote routinely about the finding of grass, water, and fuel every day. She shared her inner thoughts, her hopes and fears, her treasuring of every beautiful scene and those not so beautiful. She was deeply religious, writing down quotes often from the ancient hymns of her day. She knew her King James Bible intimately and made references to it often.

John Pierce Sutton (b. Sept. 20, 1805, Roane Co., Tennessee) and his three oldest sons, James McCall, Solomon Henry, and Asahel (Asa), traveled west over the Oregon Trail in 1851. They settled on a land claim near Holmes Hill, some 10 miles as the crow flies west and a little north of Salem in Polk County. Their neighbor to the east was a farmer named Horatio Nelson Viscount Holmes. They were near the "Old California Trail," now Highway 99 W. they were right on the edge of Baskett Slough, the winter home of thousands of Canadian geese.

John and James McCall Sutton, father and son, returned to Illinois, arriving September 26, 1853, and they all began to get ready for the overland journey the next year described in Sarah's journal. Solomon Henry and Asahel stayed on in Oregon. What the Illinois folks did not know until the end of their journey in October was that Asa died in July while they were on their way west.

It was on April 25, 1984, that the editor of this set of books spoke to a retired teachers group at the Salem Y.W.C.A. He told about how the project was generated and discussed the number of documents that had been found in the hands of private parties. After the presentation Mrs. Thelma "Rita" Clement came forward to say that a friend of hers, Howard B. Giesy of Aurora possessed the diary of an ancestor who had crossed the plains. A phone call opened up the channel to Giesy, and a few days later we held the precious hand-written document in our hands. This diary of Sarah Sutton is one of the treasures of American history, and we are fortunate to be able to publish it to be used for all time forward as a basic source on travel overland.

The letters included with the diary are from the collection of Sutton papers in the hands of Mrs. Laura Krantz Johnson of Eugene, Oregon. She has been most gracious, even enthusiastic, in sharing them with us. Mrs. Johnson is a Sutton descendant.

Other descendants, direct or indirect, who have helped in our research on Sarah and John Pierce Sutton and their families are Pauline Sullivan of Langlois, Oregon; Don and Lillian Larson, Waldport; Mrs. Justine Jones, Salem, and Mrs. Zahna Z. Rainboth, Gold Beach.

Members of the Party in 1854
Children of Joel and Sarah Stewart

(Five of Sarah's children had died at an early age before 1854.)

Laura Ann (Stewart) Carter, b. Apr. 14, 1829. She married Joseph Carter, date unknown. Sarah Stewart in an April 1847, letter to her mother said, "Laura & Joseph did not agree long and she has been home for six months   He kept her & bedclothes &c and we cannot get them." This quarrel seems to have been patched up by 1854, for he traveled with the overland party. They are listed as husband and wife in the 1860 and 1870 Polk Co., Oregon, censuses. They had three small children with them during the crossing, six more through the years in Oregon.

Ann Elizabeth Stewart, b. Oct. 3, 1832. She was listed as a single woman in the Oregon 1860 census.

Amos Kendall Stewart, b. Mar. 24, 1836. He is the one nicknamed "Doc" in the overland journal. In the 1860 census he is listed as a farm worker, living in Polk Co. By 1870, according to census records, he was living with his brother, Frank, in Port Orford, Curry, Co., on the southwest Oregon coast, keeping saloon.

Harriet Augusta Stewart, b. Apr. 13, 1838. She was married to Aaron Zahniser in Marion Co., Oregon, on April 9, 1855. He was a Pennsylvanian by birth. They lived in Marion Co. for several years, he working at his trade as a tanner. In later years he had a leather shop in Portland.

Melissa Stewart, b. Jan. 20, 1840. Marriage records for Marion Co. tell of her marriage to Samuel Smith on Apr. 6, 1856. They lived most of their married lives in Portland.

Hanna Jane Stewart, b. Aug. 22, 1841, Illinois. She was listed in the 1870 census of Marion Co. as the wife of John F. Smith, a Bavarian farmer. They became parents of a large family.

Alexander Franklin (Frank) Stewart, b. Jan. 25, 1842, Cass Co., Illinois. He and Hattie M. Riley were married on Jan. 25, 1867. she died soon afterwards. He lived with his brother, Amos Stewart in Port Orford, Curry Co., Oregon, for a while before he married Laura E. Riley in 1872. He continued there as a school teacher. He later served as county treasurer, superintendant of schools, state legislator, and collector of customs in Coos Bay. There is a biography in Orvil Dodge, *Pioneer History of Coos and Curry Counties* (Salem, 1898), p. 85. See also *Pen Pictures of Representative Men of Oregon* (Portland, 1882), p. 54.

Susan Stewart, b. Feb. 5, 1845. She became the wife of John Reynolds, a house painter in Portland. According to a descendent today, "They were never well off. She died in poverty."

Children of John Pierce and Nancy (McCall) Sutton:

James McCall Sutton, b. June 29, 1830; d. Oct. 21, 1878, Ashland, Oreg. He went west with his father and two brothers in 1851; returned to Illinois with his father, and was a member of the 1854 party. He married Mary Jane Shook in Jacksonville,

Oreg., Feb. 14, 1867. He is noteworthy in Oregon history as the person who named Crater Lake. As editor of the Jacksonville *Oregon Sentinel* he led a party into the lake in July and August, 1869. Twelve persons, including his father, John Pierce Sutton, packed in with pre-cut timber with which to construct a small boat. They carried the pack down to the shore of the lake and were soon paddling over to Wizard Island. That night around the campfire they discussed what the lake should be called. They had all come to the conclusion that the mountain was volcanic, so they dubbed the body of water "Crater Lake." The details of this episode are described in the *Sentinel* in its August 21 and 28 issues for 1869. An easily accessible reference is Howard and Marian Place, *The Story of Crater Lake National Park* (Caldwell, Id., 1974), pp. 24-26.

Solomon Henry Sutton was 19 years old when he traveled overland with his father and two brothers in 1851. He remained in the Northwest. His later years were spent in Montana, where he died in the town of Stanford on July 25, 1916.

Asahel Sutton was listed as being 16 years old in the 1850 Cass Co., Illinois census. He was an overlander in 1851 with his father and two brothers. The 1854 party was shocked when they arrived in the Willamette Valley to find that he had died the previous July.

Margaret Jane Sutton, b. Dec. 1838; d. Oct. 24, 1904, Jackson Co., Oreg. She and Benjamin Franklin Miller were married on May 14, 1857, in Polk Co., Oreg. He was a nurseryman. They moved to become pioneer settlers in the Rogue River Valley of southern Oregon. Ben Miller had been a member of the Sutton wagon train of 1854. In the years of their married life they were blessed with six children, three of whom died at an early age.

Mary Emily Sutton was an 11 year-old in 1854. She and Thomas Curry were married in Jackson Co. on Oct. 15, 1863, according to official marriage records of that county. Sarah Sutton wrote in a letter (undated) just before leaving for the west that "Mr. Suttons Beautiful little Mary came here and staid three or four

hours with us . . . and was dressed as fashionable as a butterfly."
Melinda (often spelled Malinda) A. Sutton was listed in the
Jackson Co. Census of 1860 as a 20-year-old. She and Elizar
Kimball were married in Polk Co., on Jan. 23, 1856. They soon
moved to Jackson Co., where they lived out their lives.

Child of John Pierce and Sarah Sutton:

Walter Sutton, b. Dec. 20, 1849, Cass Co., Ill. In 1860 his father
moved from Polk Co., Oreg., to Sam's Valley in Jackson Co.
Walter and Louisa Schmitt, an Iowa woman of German descent, were married on Feb. 14, 1877. He became a well-known
newspaper editor and publisher. His first training in this field
was as a compositor in the plant of the Portland *Oregonian.*
Most of his years were spent in southern Oregon where he was
associated with several newspapers over the years. There are
several references to his career: Orvil Dodge, *Pioneer History of
Coos and Curry Counties,* (Salem, 1898), *passim:* George Turnbull, *History of Oregon Newspapers* (Portland, 1939), pp. 374-
75. The *Curry County Reporter, Progress Number* (Gold
Beach, Oreg. Aug. 1926) gave him full billing.

Roster of non-family members in the Sutton Diary

Joseph Carter. See Laura Ann (Stewart) Carter above.

Mr. Chamberlain was David Chamberlain, who settled in Lane
Co. in the Eugene area. His land claim (No. 452) indicates that
he was born in Oneida Co., N.Y., in 1819. He arrived in
Oregon in Aug. 1854, and settled on his claim on Jan. 12, 1855.
The *Oregon Statesman* of Salem reported his wedding to Martha
A. Cooper the following June 19 in Lane Co. in its issue of June
30, 1855.

Three Chapman brothers were members of the party. One was a
single man, Addison B., born in Giles Co., Va., 1829. The
other two brothers were George, age 32 and his wife, Eliza
Jane; and John H., age 29, and his wife Martha M. They
settled in Douglas Co., Oreg. All of them were from Iowa.
They are recorded in land titles and censuses.

William Chapman (no relative of the above) and his wife, Mary
   Ann, were with the overland party. They were both born in
   Devonshire, England. They had arrived in the United States
   in May 1841, and traveled west to settle in Illinois. The
   Oregon land records indicated that they had been granted
   citizenship in Cass Co., Ill., in the Circuit Court in Oct. 1849.
   In Oregon they settled in Josephine Co., in Kerby precinct, on
   a stream which William dubbed "Chapman Creek." There
   they raised livestock.

Thomas L. and Harriett J. Cook and their two little boys arrived
   in Oregon on Oct. 1, 1854, and settled on a claim in Polk Co.,
   on June 8, 1855. They had been married on Sept. 13, 1850, in
   Cass. Co., Ill. They farmed in the Willamette Valley for 25
   years. Their life is summarized in Joseph Gaston's *Centennial
   History of Oregon*, II (Chicago, 1912), pp. 377-78. Over the
   years they had ten children.

Jacob "Missouri" Cook and his wife, Jane Ann, settled on a claim
   in Lane Co., Oreg., on Feb. 14, 1855. He had traveled west
   from Rockingham Co., Va., to Dale Co., Mo., where he and
   Mary Jane were married on December 23, 1845. They had
   three Missouri-born children with them on the overland journey, one of them a tiny baby.

William Dunbar is only one of several of that name in early
   Oregon. So-far he is unidentifed.

Gov. Gaines was John P. Gaines, appointed by President Zachary
   Taylor to be the second governor of Oregon Territory. He
   served three years. His biography is in George Turnbull's
   Governors of Oregon (Portland, 1954), pp. 22-23.

Mr. Gray was Joseph Gray, who, with his wife, Mary, accompanied the party overland. They settled on a claim in Polk Co., on
   Sept. 29, 1854. He was 20 years old, and she was 17 when they
   traveled west from Morgan Co., Ill.

Reuben Thurston Lockwood was a delightful 30 year-old teacher
   from Ohio. He had traveled overland in 1852, but the long wet
   Oregon winter discouraged him, and he went east again via the

Panama route. At home in Ohio the bitter winter of 1853-54 discouraged him again, so he returned to Oregon in 1854 with the Sutton wagon train. He married a young widow, age 25, named Mary C. Bryant, who had a daughter, Nancy Ann, b. 1850. This Oberlin educated young man studied the law on his own and was admitted to the bar in 1858. Over the years the family moved often as he taught in such disparate places as Oregon City, The Dalles, Petaluma, Ca., and several Washington schools. His story is well told in Fred Lockley's "Impression and Observations of The Journal Man" in the *Oregon Journal* of Portland of July 16 and Aug. 16, 1936, in interviews with Lockwood descendants.

William Marlett (correct spelling, Marlatt) died on the trail after leaving the Sutton train. His widow, Mary, remarried a French Canadian named Joseph Bashaw and became a Marion Co., settler.

Miller, Benjamin Franklin. See Margaret Jane Sutton, above.

Meshach and Elizabeth Tipton, both born in Tennessee, traveled overland with the Sutton wagon train with five strapping sons. They settled in Douglas Co., Oreg., near Scott Mountain close to present Sutherlin.

W. Turnham is so-far unidentified. There had been an earlier notorious character in Oregon named Joel Turnham, but he was killed in a gun fight in 1845.

The Widow Waldo was Avarila Waldo. There is a deposition in the Oregon land records which reads, "Waldo, Avarila 'a widow lady,' Douglas Co; b. 1810, Spencer Co. Indians; Arr Ore 17 Sept 1854; SC settled claim 29 Nov 1855; m John B. Waldo. 5 Feb 1856 Avarila Waldo gave off that her husband, John B. Waldo, left Mo 20 April 1849 with intention of coming to Ore, by way of Cal for the purpose of taking a land claim, they arrived in Cal 23 Sept 1849, that her husband died of Diahria on the Makson River 5 Nov 1849, deponent returned to the States in the year 1850. Deponent came across the plains to Oregon in 1854 and arrived in Territory 17 Sept

1854, & that she has no children living." Mrs. Waldo settled on claim No. 667 in Douglas Co., in southern Oregon. What happened to the "7 Negroes" mentioned in the diary is not known. See *Genealogical Material on Oregon Donation Land Claims*, III (Portland, 1962), p. 45.

FAMILY LETTERS

The following letters in the original manuscript belong to Mrs. Laura Krantz Johnson, of Eugene, Oregon, a descendant of John Sutton.

[Stewart/Sutton Family Letter. The first three paragraphs below were written by Harriet Augusta Stewart who was 15 years old at the time.]

Nov. 26, 1853

Dear Coussin,

I now sit down to address a few thoughts to my far distant Coussins, you must consider this as written to you all,   with pleasure we received your letter which gave us great pleasure.   we are sorry to heare of your sickness and the Death of Coussin Ella. I am glad you sent one of her yellow locks   we expected to hear bad news from there and glad it is no worse, for of such is the kingdom of heaven. — We take the papers; & we hear from there every week ever since the yellow fever Commenced; I am glad we were out of the reach of yellow fever but it has been quite Sickly   some have died   tell Elen old Mrs. phelps is Dead; we have had some ague but nothing worse,   I must stop for to night   it is now after eight O Clock   Mar [Ma] has gone to bed   Par [Pa] has gone a Coon hunting   we have heard them shoot twice since dark;

Here I am again after dark   you ought to be here to see the girls   there is more here then you could Stir with a stick.

Margret Sutton is here now; Melissa and Margret and I are all of a size and are a wild Set   Mar trys to keep us all to work but she cant come it   we have some bad boys as well as girls   james Sutton & dock [Amos] and frank are as bad as the[y] can be; dock wishes Wm. was here to help him carry cranes and brants he kills two at one shoot   he fetches in ducks and quailes most every day   we feel like thumping them for it for we have them to pick; we have 30 tame geese to pick   we will pick them once more and then sell them   we shall take with us 6 feather beds to oregon

we are all pleased with the Idea of going to oregon; two of our nearest neighbors are fixing to go with us   one is Jo Grey; I want to go to see the curiositys and git gold for sewing & to see the buffalo and to hear the wolves howl.

I Margaret Sutton wants to go because the rest is a going and to meet my brother at the end of my journey.

I Mary Melissa want to go for the fun of travling and to ride a pony or an ox to drive cattle for my kind father, to help us get away from this sickly country.   excuse my poor writing. If ever I write better my cousins shall hear from me.

I Amos Stewart want to go to drive A team and hunt the buffalo and antelope, and let the wolves, and Indians, alone if they will be so good as to let me alone — for give my poor writing   I will let you have enough when I learn to write better. Amos K. Stewart

I Franklin A. Stewart, want to go to see the Journeys & cross the rockey mountains and the cascade mountains and see the tall fir timber and smell the sea breese   if I live to get there I will go to school some more.   Franklin A. Stewart

I Jim Sutton want to go to Oregon to find a place where I can get rid of these troblesome ge-hals [girls?], for they are more torment to me than forty head of stray *ducks*,   they tease me from the time they open there eyes in the morning till they close there eyes to snore me a tune of peace.   they beat me with rotten aples, bang me over the head with the dishrag. — If I do nothing but tear up an old dirty apron, although it may have a dozzen holes in it my poor head pays for it at the rate of twenty cts a yard. O! misrable being that I am!   when shall my troubles have an end — All that read my tale of sorry pitty me   Written by request and beaten for it at that.   Yours truly   J.M. Sutton

Monday evening   I have waited for the rest to git through there nonsence and nonsence it is; James Jackson wife, Joseph Carter Sister died yesterday morning   father and mother and joseph and Laura and Margret and I all went;   tell Elen and francis and Cordelia that I have not forgoten them yet and never shall. I want them to write to me and tell me where the[y] all are and how the[y] are doing;   dad and Jim got in such a hurry the other day to go to oregon the[y] sacked up there beans and peaches and sewed them up   the[y] wanted to sack up the apples, and we told them they were not quite ready to go yet and to let them lie in the barrels; we have been making A good many sack and have A bout forty more to make; we have to sack every thing we take even our cloathes;   I have to come to a close for want of something to say.   give our respects to uncle John; you must write as soon as you recieved this   Mar [Ma] wrote your mother a letter not long ago   did you git it.   from your cousin H Augusta Stewart to Miss Perkins

Written by Sarah Thurston Stewart Sutton: Number 1

Dec. 20th [1853]

Dear Brothers Sisters Nephews & Neices
    You see that I am A going to trouble you once more with A few lines, and expect to while you and I are inhabitants of this present evil world, while there is but few of us spared to corispond with each other.   the others tho as good have not

been permited by our Father in heaven to remain but a short
time upon earth, I hope they are sleeping now like Lam[b]s,
upon their saviors breast, where the weary are to rest, and
there we all shall meet and never part again.   you know we
never hear any good news, but we want to run and tell our
friends, to come to see or hear, and this has been the case with
me, ever since Mr. S returned although it is nothing to
interest you, but I want to tell you how providence has
smiled upon us and spared us both to meet once more, for he
tells us we will acknowledge him in all of our ways and he will
direct our steps & I dare not do any other way so you see I
fear him, and cannot live with out his assisting aid. Mr
Sutton arived safe hom the next saturday night about
midnight after I wrote that last letter to you, was from the
first of July to the 26 of september coming hom the overland
route   he says he was so anxious to get hom it appeared as
tho he would never get here again   I think he suffered as
much with homesick and anxious to get home as I did with
anxiety to see him come   he came across one of our old
neighboars some distance of   he told him he was going
home with him   they rode up and hallowed. I got up and
went to the window saw two men.   the moon shone
bright.   the man wanted to know if Mrs Sutton lived
here   said he had come to tell me that he had heard from
Mr Sutton lately & he was well and doing well   said I your
George Mac, and I ve heard that myself. I guess you have got
him along; I could see Mr S. sitting on his horse saying
nothing   I says Gorge you had better put up your horses
and stay all night.   he looked at Mr S says sposin we do, at
that both jumped of and came in   I lit a candle   he took it
and ran to the bed to look at Walter first, and then into the
other room to the rest.   they were all right up and slept no
more that night.   he rode home a mule and James came next
day about noon with four more three of them packed coming

before them without bridles.   it was quite a show, with their oregon sadles belt spurs, whips 5 colored blankets, shotgun holster pistols, revolvers, butcher knives and durks [dirks] he gave me an oregon gold dollar, and a fifty dollar gold whach [watch] I had never seen before. I have no doubht but you have seen them. they were a great curiosity here.   they paid 125 dollars apeice for their mules in oregon   we have them all yet   he would sell them at 100 dollars apeice   as you may suppose as the word got out they swarmed here   in every direction   men and women for a good many miles around.   he could hardly get a chance to walk out on the farm for two weeks coming to hear about the country, and their friends that are there and he met on the way   he met Ira Kimball   they had lost a little girl 5 years olds   Henry had gone to the mines and he left Ira to go to school until he returns   we have received a good letter from him. Ira had arrived there safe and was well pleased   they are all glad that it ever fell to their lot to go to oregon.   they all got rid of the Illinois ague along the way & have become perfectly healthy. James staid but A few days at home.   his Uncle came and told him it would be the best thing he can do to go to illinois Colledge and get A finished education, and he would go with him and fetch his mule back   they did so   He is a Methodist preacher & has a circuit & has come back with the mule.   we have had 3 pretty letters from Jim   I am a going to send William one some time   Jim fetched one of his sisters with him that lived in Dosha [Meredosia] and we sent amos right of for another that lived near.   they made a good visit and returned home Melissa lives so far of he has not seen her yet   he says he has seen so much better country than this that he can never be satisfied to stay here any longer than to fix to get away   if he knew he had but two years to live he would take the children there to leave them in a healthy land   there is warm winters and the

easyest country in the world to make a good living in   he
took a claim and worked three weeks on it, and sold it for 400
dollars.   he took a notion to come home and did not go to
the mines at all   people thinks he done well to make enough
to get hom on   it cost them a good deal when they got to St
Jo in missouri   they went in to a barber shop and got
sheared and scraped   bought new cloathing and dressed up
fine and throw others away   a great [unreadable word]   Mr
Sutton is very [anxious] to get of next spring but it is not
certain yet as we dont know yet if he intends to and leave the
farm   it will take 3 wagons at least for our family   a good
many here a going in the spring and want him to go with
them as he is acquainted with the way and the diferent tribes
of indians   although the indians were very numerous and
troublesome they molested them in the least   Joes family
are all well and doing very well   they are all here to day. I
will send you a lock of Daniels yellow curls   this leaves us
all well and hope this will find you all well   we received
your letter and all of the papers — I was pleased that you
sent me susans letter.   the girls insist I send in a letter A
specimen of their flower paintings   Augusta and Melissa
are nearly grown   Augusta will be 15 in April   she stays
the most of the time with Laury.   she is weaving this
winter.   tell [unreadable word] that Doc is pleased that his
dad has got home, that he will not be obliged to kill sheep or
any thing else alone   he is feeding catching quail and sells
them for 50 cts per dozen and ocasionaly hauls a load of corn
to Beardstown for [?] cents per bushel for a neighbor.   how
is Nancy and John getting along   how easy they might do
well if they would   I wish she loved her husband as well as
you and I do ours   they could not get a quarel out of me   I
am writing this so as to send you one of Mr Suttons letters to
me that you may hear more from oregon than I can tell you,
and I have none to present you   they are gone   two of

them are [unreadable words]   Mr S is very anxious to get letters from all of you and watches every mail & has provided me with a pack of envelopes united states postage wafers steal pens and so forth   got another letter yesterday from James   is anxious to get back to oregon, if it is god's will for us to go we shall leave it altogether with him to do as he thinks that it is best for us   farewell though oceans wide between us mother it never can divide this union of the souls   unto us be given to meet on that blest shore amidst the bliss of heaven.   write soon   tell Nan to write and tell us all about the things there. I would be glad to hear good news from them and to see them. Write to Doc from you know who

S & J Sutton

Letter written by Sarah Thurston Stewart Sutton: Number 2

March, 1854

Dear Brother and Sis,

   I am scarcely able to write a few lines to you, to let you know what we are about. We are within one week of taking our last look of our old residence where we have lived and died for this last 21 years. I think I told you before that we sold our farm for 20 dollers per acre, and not one of the family sorry for it yet. For one I ought to be glad. I have had the ague most all winter. Have missed it of late, and took the areciples in my eye. The Doc lanced my cheek and corner of my eye in three places. It is getting well fast but my fingers and eyes are too week to be writing. We had our last sale day before yesterday and they are striping us pretty fast of our furniture. We have 3 new wagons in the yard painted red and green, get another this week. Come and help us make the covers and tent and see what a confusion we are in and the company that is coming all the time. We [have] a young man

that is buying up cattle and turning in with ours. We have
about a hundred head and Ira Kimball has sent for Mr.
Sutton to bring 20 head of heifers bought with his money and
we shall have half. When we get through.   we are a going to
take them. His son is buying them up, and feeds them till we
start. They are a hundred dollars a head in Oregon. We take
Ira a two horse carriage and use it through. The Lord only
knows what luck we shall have but you will hear if I live. We
have great news from our neighbours that went through last
year. They said they were there just as well pleased as they
could be and the children went to school the next day after
they got there, and they had went to preaching every sabbath,
and it was easier to drive his stock all the way to Oregon to
winter them on grass than it was to raise a crop and feed it to
them here.

                                            March 15th
    We have set the 20th of March to start. We have covered
to of the wagons and the boys made their bed in them last
night for the first. We shall have 6 covered wagons this week,
one is Jo Carters and one William Marlets, the young man
that is going with us. He·has two hands and we have three,
take them for their work through. I have written to Jane but
believe I shall not have time to write to Susan. I want you to
write to her and tell her about us. I will write to her after we
start. We will probely lay by a few days at St. Joseph to brand
stock and so forth. We have bought a five dollar sheet iron
cook stove and a great lot of tin ware and 20 little flat pans to
drink coffee in. Shall have 19 in family. Mr. Grey and family
goes out with us. Our eggs and vegetables through the
summer will be beans, dried fruit, rice, and so on. We
received your children's letters with great pleasure. Our
children will not have a chance to write but you must write to
Oregon and direct your letter to Cincinnati, Polk County,

Oregon T. You can have a letter there against we get there, so no more for want of time. Oh may we meet in heaven.

Sarah S.

THE TRAVEL DIARY

From Beardstown Cass County [Illinois] crossing the Illinois river at Meredosia, and from thence to Quincey there crossing the Missisippi river on a steam ferry boat and landing in the slave state, Missouri. leaving our old residence the 21st day of March 1854, bound for Oregon on the western shores of America. We much regret leaving behind us our good neighbours and kind friends to see their faces no more on earth. but we were bound to search for a healthyer and milder clime, than Illinois to spend the remainder of our days, let them be many or few, for our own satisfaction, and the benefit of our many children. I do not in the least regret leaving the sickness and cold, sand piles and lakes of that region behind, and are looking forward for the time to arrive when we may all get settled safe at our place of destination. passing through Missouri, I could not help meditating on the wonderful works of God. the wide missisippi river is stretched as a line, deviding the level country, from the Mountainous Missouri he has formed it hilly from the one river, clear into the other, to let us notice his handy work and the wide perraries waving in regular green hills are admirable, and reminds us of the poet. Wherever in all creation wide — We chance to turn our eye. We see inscribed on every side. There is A God on high Tis written on the boisterous wave in the heathen land. And on the clear blue sky. Tis writen in the lonesome cave, there is A God on high.[1] most of the hills are long

---

[1] The poetic quotes in Sarah Sutton's journal seem to have been mostly from old hymns, although she may have written some of the lines herself.

and gradualy discending, and acending the same way, and
very good roads, when dry.   we passt numbers of fine towns
through Missouri

There are hours long departed, which memry bring like
blosoms of Eden — to twine round the heart   And as time
rushes by — On the might of his wings   They may darken
awhile, but they never depart

[In margin:] I wrote 8 letters at St. Jo, and sent diferent ways
to our friends

we came on in sight of St Joseph and campt for 3 or 4 days to
rest our stock, and lay in the balance of our fit out.   here one
of our oxen died of murren [murrain], and a great many are
gathering here for california and Oregon.

April saty 22   came into town this morn early, to cross the
river with about 100 head of loose cattle, nine wagons and 10
head of horses, and 36 souls.   we were detained untill after
dark before all got over.   the ferry boat was an old steam
boat with the under part cleared out to take cattle in.   they
took the Cattle 5 wagons and family all on at once.   we
camped on the bank, and felt very thankful that we were
landed there safe.   we had some oats to feed our horses, but
the cattle had nothing to eat.   we felt a little doughtful that
night, it being the first we spent in the indian nation, and so
many strangers was tented near us. St. Jo is not a large
town   the situation is hilly clear into the river, and some of
the streets dug through hills, and the river is very ugly, and
mudy and the banks very steep,   some buildings from the
town have caved into the river

April 23   Sabbath as it is.   we were obliged to travel about
5 miles back to find grass for our cattle   we passed 3 or 4
white families, that were clearing a wide road through this 5
miles of heavy timber   here we found good grass, and
plenty of water and a good place to camp, in the edge of the
plains, and laid buy one day for the sake of our cattle.   here

3 indians come to see us   they were a great curiosity   our
boys put up a hat for one to shoot at with his bow and arrow
and he hit the mark.   they gave him the hat, he put it on his
head and went off.

April 24th   we started this morn and came about 12 miles
and found a creek and good place to camp, and stoped   saw
none of the red men.   the plains are only plain one way yet,
there is no timber but as hilly as Missouri up one hill and
down on the other side, and when we come to the branch
there is A few scatering trees.

April 25th   we come on A few miles and were stoped by
indians   they had built A bridge acrosst a creek where they
always had forded it.   we parley'd A long time not knowing
what to do.   our men went and made a bargain with them to
all go over for 5 dollars and a half.   there was 13 gay indians
at the bridge wraped in red, green, & blue and white
blankets.   we went across and went about A quarter and
stoped.   several come to see us, their heads were shaved all
but a narrow strip from the crown of their head back and that
stood strait up, and their head and temples painted red, and
they wore heavy ear rings, and beads on their neck and rings
on their wrist. I think they were fixed in their sunday best, to
see the Emegrants, and get all they could of them.

April 26   came on 4 miles to the mission,[2] 25 miles from St.
Jo   here is a farm A school, a store, and so forth, among the
indians   we come on a mile past to a branch and campd.
here we have to wait a day or two for W Turnham to catch up
with us.   here we were again stoped by indians.   they have
a bridged A small branch, and fell two trees across the ford,
and want 25 cents for each wagon.   our cattle drinked at the

[2] This was the Presbyterian Iowa, Sac & Fox Mission in present Doniphan Co.,
Kansas. Louis Barry, *The Beginning of the West* (Topeka, 1972), p. 1162. The Nemaha
Indian Subagency was also situated there on the St. Joseph route to the west. John D.
Unruh, Jr., *The Plains Across* (Urbana, 1979), p. 482.

branch and went over no thanks to them   with a little work they have fixed the ford, so some wagons have crossed.   we did not know but it would make war with the indians,   the two days that we have stoped here, we have had some of the blanket men to take dinner with us

April 26 [date repeated]   our friends came on last night after dark, and we started soon this morn   paid the indians 10 cents for crossing on the bridge   he come along very earley this morn, and come to us for his breakfast. Nathan brown knew him   he was raised by Richard Johnson of kentucky, and had lived at George Finches in Meredosia he could talk as well as any person and could read.   but I suppose chose to come and live among those of his own nation and wrap in his blanket.   he was bareheaded   had on A calico shirt, blue blanket, and mocesons, and no ornaments as the most of them have.   the holes in his ears had torn out, by wearing heavy rings.   we came about 2 miles to a little bridge about 6 feet across it   here set 3 indians, wanting pay.   our men told them they was not A going to pay them any thing, and they could not get a word out of them   they gave them A dime apiece and we all went on, and A piece farther on was 5 more indians on ponys.   we see narrow hard beaten paths every direction where they ride their poneys, and often see 20 little paths at each side of the road. the perrarie to day [h]as been up hill and down, but not too steep to cultivate, and at the foot of nearly all the hills was a mud hole.   our horse wagon has mired down twice to day we had to hitch oxen to it to pul it out   we stoped for the night   sun about two hours high,   here we found a mans skull and bones, and a bullet hole in the forehead, and A short distance from it found his cloathing, an oil coat and some shirts and 2 or 3 pounds of tobaco, a knife, a pair of gogles, ink stand and soforth.   we think if indians killed him they would have taken his things, but the circumstance

is unknown to us at present.   it is 16 miles from any house
or timber.   every day brings with it something new, and the
lord only knows what new discoverys we shall make
tomorrow.   traveling is pleasent when the weather is good
and the company are in A good humour

April 29   we have traveled over a high rich roling prerrarie
far better than Illinois and well waterd but no timber but a
few scattering trees along the creek   enough for the
wandering Emegrant to make a fire, to warm themselves,
and cook their dinner, but they cannot fence theire fields
here and must pass over the rich land, and leave it behind for
beasts of prey, and men as fierce and wild as they,   for we
have seen both the savage indians, and the wild wolf the
inhabitants of this region.   the time has been when Elk
were plenty here, but have been scared off by the passing
emegration   we see some of their horns nearly every
day.   we have had to drive about A mile off[f] the road to
camp this eve.

April 30th Sun.   how calm comes on this holy day although
we are traveling.   there is a sensation in the looks and
apearance of things, makes it seem diferent from another day
to the reflecting mind   we this eve came to the Nimehow
[Nemaha] river.   had to pay 50 cents a wagon for crossing
on the new bridge.   here is a new settlement of 18 families
some just building their little cabin, and some have wintered
here, and have not fenced any yet[3]   here is high roling rich
land as was ever seen, with A strip of timber along the
creek.   we have seen about 20 wagons before us and herds of
cattle bound for California   we are now 100 miles from St.
Joseph and the bridge keeper tells us that there is 10,000
head of cattle before us, and 100 and 18 wagons.

---

[3] This community at the crossing of the Nemaha in present Nemaha Co., Kansas, was
founded and a bridge was built by William W. Moore, and known as Moorestown. It
was very short lived. Barry, *op. cit.*, p. 1224.

May the 1th   we have come about 15 miles to day   on
account of it being rainy we have stoped about 3 oclock, for
the night   providence has formed this country delightful
for the weary traveler.   here it has the apearence of never
ending prairie.   still every day when we feel like stopping
we find a branch of water, and A few trees surrounding it,
and without both together we should be in a poor situation.
there is about 1000 head of cattle in sight of us at this time &
they remind me of the 50th psalm if ever there were cattle on
a thousand hills, it must be now on these plains.   there is no
timber on them, and very hilly.   we have paid our money
for our cattle, and call them ours, but God says every beast of
the forest is mine, and the cattle upon a thousand hills. I
know all the fowls of the mountains, and the wild beasts of
the forest are mine. If I were hungry I would not tell thee: for
the world is mine, and all that is in it, but call upon me in
time of trouble, and I will deliver the out of the hand of thy
enemies.

May 2nd   this is very cool morn   froze ice over the pans of
water   have traveled about 20 miles to day, and seen a great
many wagons and droves of cattle   had to drive a mile off of
the road to camp.   passed over beautiful land as ever was
seen but no timber.

May 3rd   started soon this morn and when we got to the
road there was too droves, one just before us, and the other
behind   we got between them and still remain so we came
on about 3 miles onto big blue river, in the Nebraska
territory.   here is a boat, but the river being low we forded
it.   here is one white family.   35 miles from the last house
and A postoffice, and store and here you can get a comon pie
for 25 cents.   we are passing along with 10 wagons in
company, and all well, and are able to get out and look at the
graves of others, that have found their last resting place
along this road and disappointment was their doom.   drove

about a mile of the road to camp   found A big spring deep
enough to dip a bucket full of water and made quite a large
creek below it

May 4th   came about 15 miles to day   saw 5 droves before
us and A great many wagons.   grass is not near as good as it
was a week back.   have again drove off of the road, on
account of so many camping near the ford.

May 5th   traveled to day about 20 miles, crossed otter
creek and came about A mile and half off of the road   found
good water, and wood, and a delightful situation to stop, and
grass pretty good.

Saturday May 6   have not started to day   concluded to
stop a day or two, to let our cattle rest & eat grass, and do up
our washing and clean up our rooms, and put our beds out to
sun and we are all well, and lively, with about 40 souls in
company, and hope and pray this will be our good fortune all
the way through our long pilgrimage.   the men are repairing
for their summers work, doctoring their Cattle greasing their
wagons, and thinking they are doing the easyist way to
winter their stock, driving them all the way to Oregon.   to
winter themselves on grass is easier than raise a crop and
winter them here

May 7th   have traveled about 22 miles to day and camped
again on little blue.   we got up it but not cross it   there was
about 30 wagons in sight at once, and about 1000 head of
cattle   there apeared to be a string A mile long.   we are in
the pawnee nation but have not seen an indian for a week and
half

May 8th   have traveled about 20 miles to day   we have a
new train in sight.   those that were in sight yesterday, have
gone on out of sight or fell back behind, and the roads are
crowded with others   have camped again on little blue, and
a great many campers and droves are near us now.   nothing

of importance has occured to day.   the roads are very hard and dusty.

May 9th   have come about 16 miles and stopt again on little blue   we dont cross it at all but go up it several days travel.   the wind blew so hard and such a fog of dust its to bad to travel   we stoped A while on acount of it, and our boys kill an antelope   fish and squiril for supper.

May 10th   came about 15 miles to day and there being no water for 25 miles we stoped   have left the beautiful stream little blue, and expect to get to plat river to day.

May 11th   came about 18 miles to one branch of plat river.   drove our cattle over on the island and found grass better than we ever have before, but wood very scarce. found the man camp't near us that killd an indian on big blue for driving of his cow.   while he was shooting him, other indians drove of the cow and he got her no more.   they came back and demanded the man but he was among the missing.   they took the dead indian up on A poney and carried him away.

May 12th   we have staid here all day and it is one long to be remembered   it has been a windy cold rainy day, and cant get wood enough to make a good fire

    Mr Cook joind us here with 5 wagons   there is about 10 thousand head of cattle campt near us, and 100 wagons mostly bound for California   our cattle mix together, and makes a great deal of trouble,   we hear more noise than if we were in the bustle of town,   the men hoy hoy hoying, and the cattle bawling, and the bells rattling   oh what A time.

May 13th   come 8 miles this morn and arived at fort kerney.   come on about a mile past and campt for the night   had to make out without any wood.

May Sunday 14   came on 15 miles and stopt on plat river without any wood   are gethering up the chips, some have got on the horses and rode over the slough and fetched some little wood, which we made out with.

May 15   traveled about 18 miles to day, and campt again on plat river, but not a stick of timber nor brush on this shore, but an abundance on the other side.   our folks went over with the team, and hauled over an old tree which will supply our want for fire.   this is a very cool, winday, cloudy day.

May 16   have had a dreadful storm during the night of thunder wind and rain.   the wind blew the tents down in the night, and have had to lay by to day.   it is storming so this morn, that the womin cant come out and the men have had a great time getting breakfast, and was good enough to bring us some to the wagon.   we thought our wagons would blow away.   it has cleared of this afternoon in time to dry out things   Ben Miller killed an antelope, and W turnham killd two wild geese.   here it is flat prairie clear in too the river and not a stick on this side   there is very plenty on the other side, and it looks well pleased to think we cant get to it.   it stands close to the shore dressed in a brown petticoat, and green sack and vail with uplifted arms, and looks very pleasent, and is continualy noding to us but cant come over.   our men go up to the shore and pull of their hat, and scrach their head, and wish it was over here.   at last they mount their horses and find plenty down, so they fetch over all they can on the horses, and soon have a good fire to get supper, although it stands there still eternaly   yet fording the river we can always fetch over enough to do us

May 17th   come about 15 miles to day and stopt again on the barren plat river the 5th night we have campt on it.   this is a very cool winday day, after the storm   one of our horses has gave out and we have had to put oxen to the little wagon to day.

May 18th   come about 20 miles to day and stopt as usual on the bare plat river.   have gone over on horse   back after

wood and are thankful that we can get it that way, for trying
to make out on wet chips without any wood is the last
chance.   we met 8 cover'd wagons of fur traders going to St
Jo   their wagons were marked Buffalo skins, Bear Skins,
Tigar skins, Monkey skins, Wild Cat skins &c   and the
men looked like A wild cat themselves   some of them were
dress'd in greasy, raged leather coats and pants and looked as
though come from the wild cat nation.   we see antelope
every day, but have not got but two yet.   there is 4 or 5
small round islands close by us with a dozen or more pretty
trees on them.   we saw about 25 wagons at once going up on
the other side of the river.

May 19th   traveld about 18 miles to day, and campt on a
slough, a great deal worse than plat river   this is in sight of
the river probely a mile and a half from the river and not A
bush in sight or tree too meet us with their pleasent
looks.   we have to do the best we can with chips and have
plenty of saluratus[4] water.   have met 3 two horse wagons
going towards St. Joseph   we have not seen a live Buffalo
yet, but see 20 heads and carcases every day, but are scared of
out of sight by the passing croud along the road.   here is a
flat level barren river bottom 2 and 3 miles wide from the
river to the range of bluffs.   we saw some small cedar groves
in the bluffs to day for the first and the boys kill'd a young
kioto [coyote] wolf with the dogs.

May 20th   came about 13 miles to day and crosst plat
river.   it was about a mile wide, and very shallow with
gravel bottom   it is uncertain whether any person ever saw
the bottom. it is so muddy and runs swift   this is the 7th
night we have campt on it, but the trees we admired so much
on this side have all disappeared at our presence, and we are
again left out of sight of timber and nothing to burn but the
chips, and few wooden chips that we found over the river.

---

[4] Saleratus was water impregnated with either potassium or sodium bicarbonate.

May 21st   Sunday morn comes on very pleasant and serene,
and our home meadow lark, with the dew upon her breast has
come before sunup to charm us with her songs and seems to
be welcoming on the day of rest and says, yes my native land
I love thee, and I love to visit the stranger and welcome him
to our soil.   come about 18 miles to day, and campt again on
north plat, and not A stick of timber in sight on neither side
of the river, and chips rather scarce, but as the old saying is
misery loves company, we discover that we are far from being
alone for the other side of the river is stuck full of wagons and
stock, and they are in the same situation, but we all keep up
good cheer, and trust to provedence for plenty of wood
soon   we are yet in the pawnee and soo nation but have not
seen one and have not the least uneasyness.   our lives the
holy angels keep, From every hostile power, and un[con]-
cerned we sweetly sleep, as Adam in his bower.

May 22   a short time after starting this morn the river
bottom come to A point, and the bluffs come into the river,
and the road turn'd upon the high land until we come down
into the bottom   it is now about A mile and A half wide to
the river   we have drove about 18 miles to day, and stopt
again on plat river, and see 26 wagons on the other side of the
river   have not seen a tree to day.   it dont apear now as we
shall ever again, and we have nothing to burn but the rotten
manna that fell on the ground but we all take it patient
without a murmer, and are glad that we are all alive, and well
I suppose and dont have to murmer for water for this is the
9th night we have tented on platt river.

May 23 Tuesday   have come about 18 miles to day   after a
hard days travel up hill and down and through deep sand
passed by 3 or 4 springs and plenty of Cedar wood to burn
right under the bluff about A mile from the river.   we see a
great many going upon the other side of the river and look
like they were level with the river

May 24   have laid by to day and about 10 families of us
have washed out of the spring.   there has been about 50
Cedar trees, two and 3 foot over cut down here and burnt up
for the travelers fire, and only one tree standing.   we have
chip't plenty of the old stumps   we were highly honored to
day by 5 sious visitors   they come up and shook hands with
us, and lookd very innocent, we gave them some thing to eat
and they apeared well pleased.   there has 6 hundred
collected near here going to war with the pawnees.

May 25   there was 4 or 5 yoke of our oxen gone this
morning, and we thought the indians had got them, but was
mistaken, and found them 6 or 7 miles back.   have not
gaurded them one night yet   see about 40 wagons passing
up river on the other side and have not seen a stick of timber
over there for several days   the bluffs are close to the river
over there. Mr Cook wounded a wolf and the dogs caught
him.   we came on abot 10 oclock   came through ash
holler.   it has its proper name, on two accounts, the high
rocks and bluffs on each side of the road look very ashy, and
the ashy sand is very deep in the road, and there has been a
good many ash trees down in the hollow but are most all cut
down to burn.   on the mouth near here is a traders
tent.   they are buying up give up cattle for a trifle and sell
their things at 5 prices   whiskey was 4 dollars per gallon
and other things in proportion.   here is an island out in the
river with about 2 dozen cedar trees and another with two
large cedar trees   a curiosity to see them in the river, and
the craggy bluffs to day are a curiosity with hundreds of little
cedars over them.   we caught up with the 6 hundred indians
who moved this morning before us, and such another move
as it was   I have counted a hundred and 50 ponys that they
have moved on, and draged their wigwams with.   the road
is skrach'd all to pieces with their poles   we came on too
their city which they have built to day   they have about 50

wigwams made of poles set up tent fashion and are fastened together about the middle of the pole   the others put sticks up as below for an ornament, and the lower part are wraped round neat with buffalo skins, some come a good way to meet us and came right up and gave their hands with their paper, which recommended

[Added note:] still on platt Nathan B left to day

them to be a kind good sious indians, belonging to the osage band and would be glad to get bread and meat coffee or sugar or any thing to eat.   another went by the name of french grry [?] and they were beging for all   would be glad of a few eatables, and when we got against their town probably a 100 yards off the road, and big and little old and young come runing every direction, with their old blankets and taglocks a flying, some had painted faces and ornamented with rings and beeds.   some handed us beads and wanted something for them.   some of the children got a streing of beads for A biscuit, and got a pair of mockesons for an ox bow   they got a little something to eat among us, but we cant afford to feed them much   two squaws had their papooses and they ran along with us a good ways.   have met two too horse wagons to day   we are now within 125 miles of fort Larama   to day sold two head of give out cattle for 4 dollars   a drove of mules campt near us to night.   have come about 15 miles to day

May 25   Bitman left Mr Cook this morning   before we got ready to start the indians began to come and those that come before we cleard the table away we gave their breakfast, and here come the whole 6 hundred moving their tents. they lash their poles on each side of poney like shafts and carry their other plunder on the back end of them draging on the ground and we saw 29 dogs with shafts hauling a 6 galon keg and dressd buffalo skins, their tent covers.   their teams

went on a head of us and the men squaws and papoos and
children of all sizes were all among us and our children swapt
bread for a good many strings of beads. we struck in behind
them   it soon began to rain and first we knew they had built
their houses in twenty minutes and was the busyest people
you ever saw turning out their horses and gethering weeds to
burn, and we have been very much pestered with them all
day, and have passd about 50 other lodges, and have tried to
get beyond them to not be pesterd with them to night but as
soon as we stopt they have come a swarm of them.   we have
traveld about 15 miles to day and campt again on platt.   they
are an innocent harmles being, and wont touch a thing that
dont belong to them   all they want is something to eat

May 26.   have traveld about 18 miles to day and stopt again
on platt.   4 or 5 of them staid until after dark to get supper,
and took our frying pan, and to our surprise have not seen
one to day.   there is about 40 wagons in sight of us now,
with droves of cattle   we have stopt against the lone
tower.   it is a high clayey mound and square off around the
sides, and in immagination resembles and old anchaint castle
or fort and there is no other mound near it, and are in sight of
chimney rock   can see the chimney.   it looks like a pole
stuck in the ground

May 27   have laid by to day on acount of rain and nothing
particular has occured   we have pass the day very cheerfully
away. I have spent it in writing to our friends.   others have
spent it in the tents, and wagons, in social chit chat, and
never started to be scared by the Elephant.   we expected to
see him, and have not been disapointed.

May 28   came about 18 miles to day and pitch't our tent on
the river.   afternoon got against chimney rock.   it is a high
bare mound with a chimney on the middle   here is a french
traders tent, and an indian wigwam with a good looking
white man, and an ugly black squaw for a wife and two

children. she wore an old blue callico dress, and her old
blue blanket wrapt arround her like another indians and sat
on the ground bareheaded against her tent, and another
young squaw was with her fair skin'd   husband sat down
with her, and the yellow babes played on both of them.   the
indians and work are at perfect peace with each other.   they
do not know a thing more about work than the Buffalo wolf
and antelope that lives among them

May 30th   soon after starting this morn, we left the river,
to let the proud Scotts bluffs go between us and the
river   passt two french traders cabins and 8 indian Lodges
tented with them

May 29   have drove a mile and A half of off the road and
campt up in a wall'd in hollow, with the most curious bluffs
clay built and towers and peaks with their sides covered with
cedar.   here we had A severe hail storm, and here we found
a dead indian, reared up on a scaffold, as far towards heaven
as they could get him on a scaffold

May 30th   came on to platt river again and passt a traders
tent of french an[d] indians.   a good looking white man
with A black squaw for a bosom companion.

May 31   past three trading post to day, and the indians
more than A few.   stopt half way to the river and get water
out of a spring.   the half starved indians gethered around
us, and wanted to swap mocosons and beads for bread and we
got some   met to day 6 large covered wagons loaded with
fur

June 2nd   we laid by to day to get blacksmiths work
done.   it has been one of the windyest days ever bloud, and
A hail, and thunder storm at night.   4 indian graves were
put up near us, and the hungry indians has been with us all
day. I gave them a quart of gravy that was left and some
scraps of bread, and they scraped it into a sack. A leather one

I should suppose.   we threw the dogs some dirty crumbs,
and they drove them away, and picked them up, and they
went all around the camp and picked up the bacon rines we
threw away.

June 3 rd   come on to day about [blank] miles, and here was
7 or 8 log huts and a bakery and store, and whites and indians
all together   here was flour for sale for 20 dollars per sack,
not A 100 weight in them and bread for 29 cents per pound.
Mr Sutton said before he would give that he would live on
dumplins, and bread was 25 cents per pound   here was two
more dead Indians dress in red, and sent to heaven. We
call'd at Larama and left A number of letters, came 7 or 8
miles past, and stopt on plat river   good news and glad
tidings to us once more.   we have plenty of wood again.   we
paid 25 cents apiece for each wagon crossing on Larama fork
of plat.   a trading post at the bridge.

Sun[da]y June 4   have traveld about 15 miles to day   past
A traders post and about 20 indians wigwams with them.   have
commenced climbing the rocky mountains pine and Cedar
are thick on them   saw snow to day on Larama peak   have
campt among the hills near a spring

Mon June 5   came about 18 miles to day, and have arrived
again on plat river after forsakeing it two nights.   we have
got home again.   we met 7 mormon wagons to day and 20
mormons with them.   they have started to go out over the
world, to proclaim the new salvation to wretched fallen
man.   we have traveld over the black hills the last too days.
To look at them, they appear as thought they never could be
crossed, but we have Beautiful natural roads, and the pioneers
of these western mountains deserve great credit, for selecting
such good places for a road.   one of the company oxen got a
horn knocked of to day.   saw only A few indians to day.

Tuesday June 6   come about 12 miles to day.   have past a

good many indians   came past a train that was laying by, on account of one of their men being wounded by an indian the day before.   have stopt on creek where there is plenty of wood and water.

Wednesday June 7   came about 18 miles to day and campt on A creek where there is plenty of wood and water   past a town of indians and whites.   crosst plumb creek   saw quite a stir among indians moving and so forth.   are crossing red hills to day.

Thursday June 8   come about 16 miles to day and campt on a creek in the mountains   have crosst two or three creeks in the hills to day and passt a trading post, but have not seen any indians to day.   was about 40 wagons in sight to day.

Fryday June 9th   have traveld about 15 miles to day, and got home again at night on plat river.   the river is got to be quite small, and is much deeper than it was at first.   we see several large trains going up on the other side.   have past A trading post and an indian wigwam with them   here we sold two lame cows for 15 dollars a piece, and saw here at Deer creek about 50 indian ponys   two of our company bought one at 40 dollars piece.   saw snow to day on the mountains. after traveling about 80 miles over the rocky black hills, we have left them to day to travel again up the level plat river.   we have plenty of good neighbours, and friends all along this broad road, and good health and luck attend us this far on our pilgrimage, and heaven and the holy angels are interceding in our behalf we believe, and are saving us out the hands of the enemy, that are on every side of us

Saturday June 10   came about 14 miles to day and campt on a branch between the mountains and the river   have seen snow all day on the sides of the mountains.   have past a traders station to day and an indian Lodge with it   saw 23 freight wagons bound for salt lake and 40 men.   no dought but the most of them understand the mysteries of mormanism have past through the mill.   there is a great croud of emegration

Sunday June 11th   came about 12 miles to day and stopt again on the north side of platt river.   have cross't to day on the bridge and paid 5 dollars per wagon and 5 cents per head for stock   no doubt they have made 500 dollars to day.   there was a traders station, and 6 indian Lodges with them.   they had plenty of buffalo meat drying out in the sun.   have seen snow all day on the hills near us.   have no wood to night and are picking up the dry chips, and sage

Mon'y June 12th   come on about 8 miles and stopt to day for the last time we ever expect too on platt river   we was told that it was 18 miles to the next water and it was two hard A drive for us, and our cattle need rest, and the grass is very poor, and our undertaking requires patience.   the roads on both sides of the river have left it here, and we have to take over the hills, and wory along to this side of Jordon, and try to possess the good land which we believe is reserved for us and our children, for John the son of Nun has been there and James the son of John has searched out the land.[5]   they went upon the mountains, and came into the vallys, and they saw we must go up and possess the good land, for it is not like the land of Egypt, but it is A land of hills and vallys and watered with springs from the mountains, and flows with milk and butter, and an abundance of green grass for our cattle   so John, and James, the son of John returned to their own land and told the good news that they had found a good and pleasent land and had come for their families, and friends to go with them, to enjoy the health and mild climate

[5] This was a little play on words by one who knew her King James Bible well. There are many references to "Joshua the son of Nun" all the way from Exodus to Nehemiah. In the book of Joshua alone there are 30 such references. Here she refers to John, her husband, and to his son, James. They had been out west before to scout out the land.

of that far land that is set before us.   but it is away yonder
over the rocky mountains, and through the great wilderness,
and acrosst wide spread deserts, but come on never fear, be
not afraid of the face of man, for God says I will be with you,
and lead them that trust in me safe through!   and charge
John, and James his son.   encourage them and strengthen
them and speak comforting words to them, and they shall go
before to lead you on the right way.

Tuesday June 13th   have come about 18 miles to day.   bid
our lov'd friend platt river a final farewell this morning after
camping nearly every night on it for a month, and are again
left intirely out of sight of timber, and have to make out on
sage   past two traders tents and an indian Lodge with
them.   our company have to day killed the only buffalo we
have seen   came to the willow spring and filld our vessels
with water.   here was a thief shot in the back dead, while on
a stolen horse by the owner in pursuit of him   there was so
many on chase they shot 18 balls in him [the buffalo] so we
have plenty of fresh beef for supper all around the camp of a
remnent of isreal.   our Beards town friends W Dunbar and
Treadway caught up with us yesterday, and have pitched
their tents near us to night and there is about A 1000 head of
cattle herded near us to night and there has no plauge
[plague] come a near us, and we have not yet seen nothing
terrible on our journey

Wednesday June 14   came about 16 miles to day after two
days travel from platt river.   we have arrived at sweet water
river. Just after noon to day as we were traveling along the
road we had A severe thunder storm, and hard rain, and hail
with wind   here is independent Rock, a curiosity different
from all others we have seen, and standing out by itself
independent of all others. here is stationed a white trader as
usual with an indians wigwam with them   have passed three
traders to day   still see snow on the side of the mountains,

and it is as cold all along here as march in Illinois. paid 50 cents A wagon for crossing on A bridge   here a squatter told us, that being Mr Sutton belong'd to the same society he did, he would tell us where there was good grass just across't the bridge, and he would not charge anything for the horse wagon, and would furnish us wood to burn so acording to his kind directions we drove acrosst the bridge and pitched our tents, where there was much sweet water, and was all rejoicing at the kindness of the stranger and about a dosen of them went back after some wood and he charged them 25 cents apeice.   they paid him the money, and came back in A high gale of laughter at the trick that had been played on them.   some of the brethren of the I.O. of O F. went to visit him, and try his grit, and found out that he did not know the mystery, and I dont beleive any man of A good principle will live here with the indians, and their smoky Buffalo skin wigwams with a slick greasy hole to slip in at, like a wolf, built with them

Thursday June 15th   left the bridge soon this morn with the hospitable stranger, and his venomous looking Snake indians.   here are the very high rocky mountains on each side of us with now and then little cedars in the crevass's and on one side the tops nearly covered with snow which looks as though it fell yesterday. Yet the *Lord* of heaven and earth has made this part of the earth to be crossd, and has left a space for good roads, and sometime just room enough for A good road with the craggy cliffs on each side of us, and so many names inscribed in the rocks, as though all that crosst the plains had left their names on record behind them. within 3 or 4 miles of the bridge, we came to what is called the Devils gate.   the high mountains like the Red Sea, had fled back, not to let the Isrealites pass through, but to let sweet water river run through.   the high wall on each side were strait down as the side of a stone house and the river took

such a horse shoe turn that the visiter could not get within a
100 yards of it, without ascending the mountain and looking
down, or crossing the river, and looking through the
sides   there is more to be seen on this wide road, to remind
us of the mysteries of providenc than in all our lives before.
God moves in A mysterious way His wonders to perform.
He plants his footsteps in the sea. He rides upon the
storm.[6]   here was two indians Lodges, and 7 or 8 little
cabins of traders, and numbers of half indian children. have
came about 18 miles to day and campt for the night at the
foot of the rock mount, and have sweet water to make use
of.   we have for years past heard of the rocky mountains but
unexpectedly the time has arrived, when we can look at them
for ourselves and can see that they are made of soled rock,
and heaps upon heaps of rocks, and not earth as the
mountains were in our own land.   in some places the pines
and cedars grew large enough to build there little cabins that
these french and indians traders reside in.   these settlers do
not pretend to raise a thing, not even a garden.   one thing
the land seems too poor to support any growth. Another one
gentleman told us, it was useless to try, as there would be an
hundred red indians to every ear of corn, and they would sit
down by it until it got into roasting ears, and then fight who
should have it.   here they depend on the buffalo and bear,
and what is wagond here A 1000 miles or more.   this is a
very cold windy rainy evening but one blessing has attended
us this cold eve, we have plenty of Cedar wood to burn, from
the sides of the mountains of Lebenon.   these roads are
infested with theives and robers watching for good opper-
tunity to take Emegrant cattle and horses.   the indians are
far better than whites in any estimation.

---

[6] This was a famous hymn by William Cowper, still in use in many churches. He
entitled it "Light Shining out of Darkness." William Cowper, (1731-1800), *Poetical
Works* (London, 1967).

Friday June 16th   have traveld about 16 miles to day and campt on sweet water.   no wood here   we passt two traders tents to day.   one told us that 60 wagons had passt this forenoon.   grass is very poor short and dry

Satey June 17   were detained late this morning on account of Wm Turnham and Wm Marlet leaving us, and having to divide the cattle. Benjamin Miller left Marlet and came with us to day. The tops of wind river mountains are covered with snow and half way down the sides, and the weather is cold   we had to drive late and then stop without wood and water half a mile of and grass very poor.

Sunday June 18th   drove on about 5 miles to a ford on sweet water.   here met one of our neighbours on his way home from oregon and glad to hear of each others whereabouts.   we stopt with him two or three hours and sent a letter back to Illinois   came on about 6 miles and camp for the night on sweet water   no wood   have to make out with sage and chips.

Monday June 19   have laid by to day on sweet water to rest our stock and wash some   Mr Cook kill'd an antelope. there was as many as 60 wagons passd us   a great crowd passing all the time   it has been A cold windy showery day

Tuesday June 20th.   began to climb the mountains soon after we started, and they were the rockyest ones we have seen yet.   the road is crowded as far as we can see both ways   have met 10 or a dosen Morman wagons returning back with their families and told the Californians they were a going to the City of distruction   we have met 30 or 40 pack mules loaded with men women and children, and provisions returning back from Oregon.   they said the winters was so cold, and it was so sickly, and money so scarce that they wanted to be found getting away.   we have been nearly smother'd in dust to day, and it seems very good to get out of the croud. we have drove about a mile of off the road, and campt again on sweet water, and plenty of snow on the bank of the creek 4 feet deep and great peaks of mountains of snow just before us. the youngsters are threatening snow balling each other. no wonder we have been nearly freesing to day.

Wed'y June 21 have come about 15 miles to day and campt again on sweet water. the weather has moderated very much. it is quite pleasent this eve. we have passed a trader and blacksmith shop to day and are in sight of an indian town. they are begining to come, the snow mountains, like the cloud by day have followed us 4 or 5 days and rest before us at night they are much nearer than they were last night this is the 7th night we have tented on sweet water saw two new graves to day for the first Mr. Ebbs died on the 16th of June aged 52 are in sight of a large indian village. they have gethered around us as thick as musquetoes have fetched antelope dress skins mockesons and beads to swap for something to eat

June 22nd have traveld about 15 miles to day and stoped without wood and water. passt two traders and a black-smiths shop to day

June 23 one of Jo Carter oxen died of murrin [murrain: anthrax] this morn left him on dry sandy the boys have killed several sage hens and mountain rabits and ground squirils to day. have campt to night on big sandy

June 24 one of Missouri Cooks horses was dead this morn kill'd itself with the rope that was around its neck Newmyer left us this morn for california came on and camped again on sandy in a very pretty place

Sunday June 25th came from big sandy to green river 16 miles and have found a pretty place of wood and water. we have had as dusty a time as any person ever saw thought we should smother, and were obliged to stop in the road, untill the gale passed away some, that we could see the road.

Monday June 26   came on about A half mile this morning to the ferrey.   here is quite A town 5 or 6 cabins, and 4 or 5 stores and one indian wigwam[7]   we have to pay 4 dollars per wagon, and 50 cents a head for horses crossing.   the river is high   whiskey is cheap enough here to get drunk on.   have heard of several in that kind of A fix   the stuff is only A dollar A pint.   here we have sold a yoke of oxen for 55 dollars.   have come 4 or 5 miles past and campt on again on green river.

Tuesday June 27   have traveled about 20 miles to day through wind and dust.   to have grass for our stock we have stopt A mile from water.   the boys have carried it in kegs   we are on the bear river mountains.   their sides are covered with snow

Wednesday June 28   have come about 12 miles to day and campt in the valey of the bear river mountains, with plenty of wood and water and our situation is not deplorable   have passed a blacksmiths shop to day.   the mountains are a hard road to travel

Thursday June 29   have traveld about 12 miles to day over the highest mountains, and the roughest ones we have passt yet, and have stopt for the night in the valey on the hams fork of green river.   the indians and their little ones have honored us with A visit   they are Shawnee [Shoshones?] are poorer and meaner dressed than the soos and are not ornamental with beads as they

Friday June 30   soon after starting this morning began to ascend the mountain and after reaching the top, we stopt and took a saw Mrs Lucinda Jacksons grave on the 29   view

---

[7] Here the modern city of Green River, Wyoming, was aborning.

down into the valey below.   saw plenty of fir trees, and
snow on the sides.   this was not mount Pisgah, for we did
not see that delightful land that flows with milk honey   so
we have to go on untill we come to that good land if not like
Moses are not permited to go there, but like him have to stop
and lay down our lives on the side of Jordon, as hundreds
have   but probely some of us like Caleb and Joshua will live
to get to the end of the race, and see what we are at all this
trouble for, and whether it is worth all the vexation and
difficulties and suffering of man and beast, cold and storms
of dust rian and hail that we have to worry through.   here is
a good spring on top of the mountain, and here is a grave,
and A great many camp upon the mountain   we have come
about 13 miles to day and campt on bear river mountain near
a grove of thick fir timber, and A great spring not far distant
Sat July 1th   soon after we started we passed through A fir
grove of 80 acres and came down the worst mountains that
was ever seen or read of by any one that never crossed
them   here man and beast meet with the same fate.   yonder
is a grave, of one who spent their last days, in Jolting over the
rock, and Jumping off places through the mountains.   there
lies a dead ox who have lost their lives in trying to drag
people across the plains.   they are now seen on top of the
mountain, and down in the valey every day   we came on 10
or 12 miles, and campt on a branch of Bear river.   the
mountains on each side of us they say were A mile high, and
to steep to ascend on the other side next to us.   here we had
to pay 1 dollar a piece for wagons for crossing on a bridge
where it has always been forded.   here was indians and A
white man living with A squaw for a wife
Sunday July 2nd   at the start this morning we had to pay A
dollar per wagon for crossing, on a bridge across a slough of
bear river, and in 5 or 6 miles travel we came to a little bridge

across a mud hole, and an indian standing by, wanting a dime per wagon. he got it without a word, and we come on 5 or 6 miles more, and campt for the night on a fork of bear river. have caught some fish in this river. as soon as we stoped were were attack'd with the most savage warlike enemy and they gave us the alarm by the sound of their horn, and they had prepared themselves, and were well armed with a long sharp spear to meet us for war, and as soon as we met there was heavey battles fought, but on our side there was some blood shed it is true, but no lives taken, but on the enemys side hundreds kill'd and wounded but none missed. they were of the Musqueto tribe, and well known the world over.

July 3 came about 20 miles to day over the longest and roughest mountain we have passed yet and came down to bear river again campt on A small branch that runs swift from the mountain have good grass but no wood of consequence. paid 2 dollars per wagon for crossing on bridge across a fork of bear river. see snow all the time on the mountains. have warm days and cold nights. here comes on the Glorious 4th of July and a beautiful still, clear, serene and peaceable morning it is, and all nature apears to smile freedom. With every benevelent reason... *God* spreads out the bright summer sky. And just in the midst of the season, He sends us the fourth of July, Then up with the voice of Thanksgiving, To *God*, the great giver on high, And while in the land of the living, Still honor the forth of July. although we are 1500 miles from our native land, and it has been A very comfortable day with us, good health and luck attend us. we have crossed several fine gravel bottom branches, that come from the mountains and came about 14 miles, and campt near the creek with very good grass, and scarcely any wood. some little bunches of green willow along the creek.

Hail the day that bought our freedom,
Bought with our forefathers blood
Lo! their happy sons and daughters,
On this glad and welcome day
By the springs of mountain waters,
O'er the hills and valleys stray
Independence then shall clear,
Our path to heaven

July 5th   this morn the weeds and bushes were frose stiff,
and plenty of snow in sight on the mountains   the days are
very warm, and the night cold enough for 4 blankets.   have
come about 14 miles to day and campt near Soda springs on
A creek and about half mile from plenty of Cedar   the boys
have all gone for some to get their supper.   we left one of
our calves to day nearly dead of murren [murrain]
July thursday 6   came on to the springs calld and took a
look at them.   there was some of the mistery about
them.   here was a blacksmiths shop, and two or 3 traders.
we enquired about flour.   they had none to sell, but when
they had they sold for 26 dollars per 100.   whiskey was 2
dollar and A half A pint, cheese 50 cents A pound.   we did
not spend a dime with them, nor hardly ever do.   good
looking whites, living with the indians, should not be
noticed   here we left bear river after camping on it 4 or 5
nights   went down it all the time   we came about 3 miles
from the springs and here the road turned of for Callifornia,
and we were happyly released from a great croud that have
hindered us from many a mile, crowding along before and
behind   here we had to part with two good hands, that
started for Calefornia.   we were all loth to part with each
other but the best of friends must part, such is life.   what a
great change in roads.   now the gras is near two feet high on
each side of the road and not trampt down with stock.   there
is but few going to oregon   we came on about 16 miles and

campt on a small creek.   no wood but grass like a timothy patch   it has been a cold day.

July Friday 7   this morn ice was an inch thick around.   the roamingites[8] and 5 quilts was none to much cover, and it has not got warm yet at noon.   came to a little bridge at noon and paid a dollar for crossing, and came up and down mountains all this afternoon, and have campt on a spring branch, with pretty fir trees near us, dry and green

July 8th   had a late start this morning, as it was to cold to leave our warm beds.   the further we go the colder it is.   plenty of ice in our buckets   one of our cows gave out last eve, and we had to leave it a mile behind.   went back after it, and it was dead.   we have now 11 less than we started with.   nothing particular has occured to day   we have got into snake river valey and have traveld about 14 miles through dust and campt on a branch of water without wood

Sunday July 9th   come on 8 miles to a bridge across Port Neff   paid 50 cents a wagon for crossing and noond just across.   here is a store, and plenty of french and indians. Just as we were ready to start, Mr Cook got the axeltree of his wagon broke, and we have to stop.   he has gone 7 miles to fort hall to get one

July 11th [10th?] got a new axeltree against noon and started, and left Port Neff [Portneuf] with the indians and their set of whites and came about 12 miles, through a thick dust, and campt on a dusty hill with a creek at the foot of it, and was nearly devoured with the most uncivilised tribe of Musquetoes we ever met with

July 11th   we have traveld about 15 miles to day down

---

[8] This is a puzzling invented word. She evidently meant the overlanders themselves. She combined the word "roaming" with the biblical endings such as in Amalekites, Israelites.

snake river   stopt at a spring and noon'd.   here two indians met us with some fish.   we gave them some bread and got them.   come on to the falls and campt for the night, among the sage.   grass scarce, caught some fish here

July 12th   this is calld the american falls deriving its name from 4 unfortunate americans being sucked in to them in a boat and went over, and only one escaped alive to tell the dreadful tale.   it is a cliff't of rocks across the river.   this is a rough road to travel, some very steep ravines. Mr. Chapman caught up with us to day moving to Salem Oregon.   the mountains here are covered with Cedar, which look beautiful to us after spending weeks with out seeing trees of any kind   our fire is made of sage.   caught fish enough at noon for our supper to night   [in margin:] one of T Cooks oxen died this morning of murren [murrain]

Thursday July 13th   soon after we started this morn crossed fall creek and come through some deep hollows, with Juniper trees on each side of the road and came down to Raft River at noon.   crossed it and carell'd for the night on this side.   as it is 15 miles to water, it is two long A drive for the afternoon   here is nothing to burn but sage, and that scarce   here come A great company of indian packers and campt near us going to fort hall   3 fine dresst squaws with their pappooses come to take a look at us.   the boys kill'd 5 mountain rabits and some fish this evening.   the weather is fine, and our healths are comfortable and our case is not as bad near as it might be

July 4th   came the 15 miles stretch about the middle of the afternoon   found it to be a rough road, very rockey, and dusty.   kill'd several rabits along the road to day.   have stopt at the march springs and campt for the night in A pretty place with good water and grass.   the boys have killd 11 rabits one duck and a snipe this eve

July 15th   starting soon this morning   came on about 6 miles, and found Frances Kimballs grave, close by the road.   on a high raise of ground, and about one 100 years [yards?] from it at the foot of the hill is a neat little branch of water.   we could not help feeling a sympathy for our Neighbours, that were in distress here at the loss of their youngest child, while we were in health and prosperity. the troubles are great enough on this road, and have all the good luck we possibly could,   Mary Spencer was buryed with her in 1853.   we have crosst two creeks to day.   one is goose creek   came about 20 miles across a baron country. scarcely any thing but sage on it   have come to snake river and campt for the night, with plenty of drift wood to burn, and pretty good grass.   the boys have kill'd some rabits 8 sage hens, and fish this evening. Saturday after sun down

Sunday July 16th   came abut 12 miles and noon'd on pool creek.   here has been a great place for camping and here are two graves buryed in 52   come to snake river two or 3 miles back, and the banks were so steep we could not water our stock, and were obliged to come on further.   traveld about 20 miles to day and campt on rock creek   good water and pretty good grass

Mon'y July 17   this rock creek was named right as its natural production is rock, and sage.   it will produce 200,000 bushels of rocks to the acre   some say they cant think what this part of the world was ever made for, but thank the Lord it is no mystery to me, for I can see God in all around us.   he had made this foundation, for the inhabitants of earth to pass from one part of the world, to the other, and he has put on it fine creeks of water, that they can drink every day whenever they feel like it   we have never missed A day yet but we have come to a river branch or spring.   it is call'd the plains or desert, but we have never failed of having

fire enough, to cook our meal   the sage was put there to
make our fire, and we are thankful it is there, for many A
time we should have to go hungry without it.   we came
about 8 miles this morning and noon'd at rock creek.   here
is 8 wagons of emegrants, the first we have seen for four days.
this country for a few days travel has formerly been famous
for indians robing and killing people, but good luck to us we
have not seen one for several days.   we came on about 7
miles, and campt for the night on rock creek.   some little
grass close to the creek, and plenty of dry willow to burn, but
the highest bank we ever saw to any creek, and on the opesite
side, a high rock wall strait down. Mr Chamberlain caught
up with us this morning with his drove of sheep   about 4
days ago some indians in ambush shot 3 arrows in one
sheep   he saw the sheep jump but did not understand the
cause at first, and did not stop to search as he was behind and
not around but they stole about 40 head that night and kept
them

Tuesy July 18th   left rock creek soon this morning but did
not leave all the rocks with it.   wish we had traveld nearly
all day in sight of snake river   we drove on to the bank
about 11 oclock took of our teams to take down to water and
were obliged to give it out as the bank was two steep and
rocky to go down.   some said it was more than a mile from
the bank down to the water, so we came on nearly smothered
in dust untill the middle of the afternoon, and found A place
where we could water our cattle.   it was about a half mile
down to the water here   J Cook left one of his calves.   it
went down to drink, and was too weak to return.   we then
drove on 3 or 4 miles and campt for the night on snake
river.   grass scarce, but we are glad to get any.   the banks
of the river are low here,   unexpectedly two indians come to
visit us.   we got some small fish of them, and gave them

supper.   they clasp't their hands and looked up toward heaven, as if to thank the great Spirit for their supper.   they said good bye and started.

Wed. July 19th.   came about 7 or 8 miles this morning and crossed Clark river   the bank on the oposite side was very miry.   had to double teams to most of the ox wagons, and our horses to the little wagon mired down, and wallow'd in the mud   onhitched them, and had some trouble to get them out.   hich't 3 yoke of cattle to it and it run out easy   all got over, and noon'd on a spot of pretty good grass   here is a high precipice with torronts of water runing out of the top, resembling the rock that Moses split, but it is not the same, for Snake river runs at the foot of it.   it is on the oposite side from us, and the water runs into the bank about half way down.   we cant comprehend the amazing sights that we see.   we can only look and medetate that mysterious are the ways of providence, past finding out. who can know them.   we have concluded to stay here until morn as it will take so long to fery over and get to grass   and old indian has fetched us 4 or 5 dozen fish   we gave him his supper, a shirt and some old clothes and got them   Mr Lockwood came to go with Jo Carter to day

Thursday July 20th   came on 5 miles to the ferry   have to pay 4 dollars per wagon, and swim over the cattle   we can go down on either side, but on acount of having grass and water for our cattle while there is scarcely any on this side.   some of our neighbours and acquaintences have left us, and gone on this side, rather than to pay the ferriage. I must not forget to mention about the springs we saw, running out of the rocks, soon after starting this morning.   they pour'd out of the cliff about half way down and run into the river.   it looked to me as it was place'd there to shew us that water can run out of A rock.   the indians swam the river several times, taking with them horses and cattle   we all got safe over about 2 o'Clock and came on about 5 miles and stopt for the night   grass is X.L.NT and our stock is well pleased.   they have a change of diet, while we have not   Thomas Cook bought a yoke of fine large oxen to day for A 100 dollars.   several indians have followed us to our camp ground and help't drive the cattle.   those that swum our cattle over we give them a shirt apiece, and some thing to eat.   Just at dark there was 6 come, and one squaw and unsaddled their horses, and turned them out on the grass, and staid all night with us.   we did not wish to insult them, and we got along fine. I suppose it was A visit of friendship as the[y] never fail of visiting the emegrants and are a great deal more enlighten'd & civilised than they formerly have been by seeing so many whites and the most of them have a shirt on or some thing the emegrant has give them, and they are not as dangerous, but think more of the whites than in times past

Fri July 21th   several more indians come to see us before breakfast this morn.   we could not feed them all much.   we started early and left them all on the ground.   come up a long rough rocky mountain and very sandy road about 5 miles   come to one of the worst creeks we have ever crosst yet.   one of Mr Chapmans wagons turned over in the creek and the bed came off and wet all that was in it.   we call it Canyon creek.   the men waded nearly to their arms to roll the large rocks out of the road, and had to put their heads under to do it.   about a dosen of them waded each side of wagon escorting it across and all got safe over   the water ran into the wagon beds some.   we were detain'd about two hours getting over.   we then noon'd on the other bank and had to drive 12 miles to water the afternoon, and did not make it untill after dark.   we were all so tired, and saw no sage near to make a fire.   we concluded to go to bed without any supper and did so for the first time since on our journey.   we come to a creek we call flag creek and good grass

Saturday July 22nd   we all eat about as much again this morn for going without supper   we come to a cold spring soon after starting this morning, and fill'd our vessel with water.   have been going up hill and down, over rocks, and acros't the baren desert and noon where we can   water our stock on dry rocky creek with now and then a pond of water   we name the creeks ourselves as we go, as there is no one in the company has went this way before, or knows the name of them.   have come about 16 miles to day and campt on skin flint.   some grass here.   it has been very hot and sultry to day.   one of our cows gave out & others are very near it   hear is a killing time on wagons and team.   the wagons are broke down banging over the rocks and mountains, and the cattle give out worying over the mountains, and are left to die.

Sunday July 23   started soon this morn and came up a hill about two miles long and A good part of the way very rocky   cross'd one creek come on to another spring creek about noon, and will stop for the night   our cow that give out yesterday could not be found dead nor alive this morning.   we refited our wagons and left a good many things to lighten our load we would be hapy to have at home. Mr Chapmans train campt near us to night.   misery loves company   have good water, wood, and grass.   all but the scent from dead cattle, is very pleasent

Mony July 24   came up on a very rocky hill this morning at the start and a good part of the way is very Rocky.   come on about 8 miles to grass and water and noon'd at a grave yard where there is 10 died August 1852   here is the grave of Mary Elen Orchard, great has been the suffering of man, and beast, at this place.   we cant tell where it is, as there is no one in company has ever been here before.   we cross'd

snake river at A new ferry, and came a new cut off, with one
of the most wretched roads any person ever traveld and we
dont know where we will come to, but expect to strike the
river soon.   we are now on Grasshoper creek, on the desert
of death, and dispair.   the grasshopers are as thick here on
the grass and in the air as a snow storm.   one of our
yearlings has died here in sight since we stopt.   we come on
to willow creek and stopt for the night.   one of our largest
and best oxen died to day, and just before he stopt he ran into
the team, as it was going, at the place where he has worked 4
months.   it was hard work to get him out just to have it said
that he died at his post, making 3 that has died in two
days.   one of Mr Chapman died at the same time.   they
make it 14 we have lost since we started.   the country is so
poor the indians are ashamed to show themselves on
it.   have not seen one for 5 days, and the only game are
snakes, Lizards & the big crickets, and grass hopers   here
are two graves   Mr Chapmans said they would not come
until the cool of the eve, and one of their wagons turnd
over.   it broke the coupling pole   it detaind them until
morning

Tuesday July 25   laid by here until afternoon and done a
big washing, a beautiful spring branch and soft water to
wash.   come on about 8 miles and tented for the night.
here is a good spring and good grass   we were nearly
smotherd in dust.   could not see the next wagon to us.   the
soil is a kind of ashy sand, and bunches of sage thick on it,
and as clean as though it was hoe'd

Wed July 26   come on about 5 miles, and call'd, and
looked, and felt of the hot springs here   was 15 or 16
springs, smokeing and boiling up out of the ground, and
nearly boiling hot. A good deal to hot to go to washing
clothes in, and little branches of hot water, runing from
them.   we have nothing to say, as we cant understand the

cause, and dont know from whence they come nor what fire
is heating the water.   saw 5 graves altogether this morning,
2 or 3 miles this side of the hot springs was a grave by the side
of the road   had been dug out by the wild animals.   saw
the bones and clothing.   he died in August 52   could not
make out the name   here many a one in the bloom of youth
has met with an untimely death, by leaving friends and
home, to die on the plains, and spend their last hours in
jolting over a rocky road as we have to day   we noon'd on a
spring branch, and here are 7 graves all in roe, and close by
them lays a dead ox looks as though it died last night.   came
on about 10 miles afternoon and campt on rock river   a
pretty gravel bottom creek with good grass   here was two
clever looking indians with some little fish to sell.   we gave
them some bread and got them so we had fish for supper, and
sage hens for breakfast this morning

Thursday July 27th   one of the good indians come soon
this morn and was in A great way to tell us something.   the
way we understood him was by his signs and motions that
some of the indians had stole a horse from the train that had
gone on, and the indian had gone on with the horse   we
came on 3 or 4 miles, and met Mr Chapman coming back,
and said the indians had stole one of his horses   two of our
men saw the indian on him going off, and James Sutton has
gone on with him to try to get the horse.   we are noon'd at a
spring among the hills.   had to leave another of our oxen to
die this morning, and our team part of it is about to give out,
as it is half cows   come on about 6 miles, and caught up with
Mr Chapmans chain of 8 wagons, and we all campt close
together in A deep narrow vally, with a spring branch and
pretty good grass.   passed about 5 dead carcases of work
cattle to every mile.   the men returned from pursuit of the
stolen horse, without him   they got on track of him, and
followd the track in different directions, until they gave it

up, come back and saw the old indian that inform'd on him and told them that he would steal him from the indian and bring him to them, and they promised to give him A shirt, and the other presents if he would do so.

Friday July 28th   We have concluded to lay by here to day to rest our worn out teams, and some of Mr Chapmns have gone to see more about the stolen horse.   it is about 18 miles back.   the boys have kill'd about 18 rabets and 4 sage hens this fore noon.   the girls are washing, and baking aple and peach pies, stewing beans, and rabits and apear very happy.   are all in good health and know no trouble.   we have only 8 girls to do all the work   this trip is fun for them, although the roads are very rocky, and mountaineous, and the creeks banks are awful frequently.   yet if our teams would only hold out to get through, we have not much against it. we have lost 4 yoke of our team, and are now working 8 or 9 cows.   our case is some what discourageing at present but we must only trust to providence, and hope for his blessings to rest upon us   Mr Chapman has not got back to night.

Sat July 29th   yoked up our teams this morning to start, and discovered one of our cows was sick   turned her out, put in another and started.   we had not got far until we saw one of Mr Cooks oxen was sick and could not work.   turned him out, and gave them both a dose of lard and pepper, and they both died in two hours after, and one of Mr Chapmans oxen died at the same place yesterday very sudden. Mr. Cook had paid 100 dollars on snake river a few days ago for his oxen   only worked him two days   the *Lord* only knows what we are to do, if we lose any more   it is all we can do now to get along, but we have the promise if we will but trust in him, he will help us out of all of our troubles.   we have crossed two creeks to day, and came about 12 miles, and campt on chicken springs and have made them some scarcer

since we stopt by a dosen, and have thin'd the rabits like
wine.   Mr Chapmans returned this evening with their
horse, after spending 3 days trying to get him.   they took
the indians with them, and slept near the indians had the
horse, and their indians got him while they were asleep.
they have passed since we stopt here   had the indian with
them to give him some presents   gave him a gun, and some
cloaths.   it was two days travel back   here is 3 graves   one
is Adam C Cain aged 20 years kill'd by the indians 7 of
september 1843 from adams Cy Ill.   our horses have gave
out to the little wagon to day, and we have hitch'd it to
another wagon.

Sunday July 30   3 shawnee [Shoshone] indians come to see
us before breakfast this morning.   we gave them their breakfast,
and they staid to see us start, as their custom is to look over a
camp ground, to pick up the bacon rines, and crumbs and
any thing we leave.   we apeared to come 4 or 5 miles up hill
this morning, and about the same distance down and noon'd
on Bois river.   it is a pretty gravel bottom'd river, good
grass, and plenty of Balm Gilliad [poplar] trees, about the
first trees we have seen in two months   come on about 4
miles this afternoon, and stopt for the night on the bank of
the Boise river.   have very good grass, and plenty of wood
once more.   we have balm of Gilead here, but have no need
of A physican for our bodyly health, but the physician that
cure the sin sick is greatly needed, to give us a quantity of
fortitude and patience, and teach us to trust in him and know
that behind A frowning providence, he hides A smiling face.

Monday July 31th   one of our best wheel oxen died before
we started this morning, that worked all day yesterday.   we
did not know that he was sick until this morn.   they had
miss'd one day without any dieing, and we were in great
hopes that they would not any more, but we were not so
fortunate.   we are to noon on the beautiful Boise River,

under the balm gilead trees.   this river would be call'd A
creek in the states, but on this trip all the large creeks are
call'd rivers. this river has rocky shores and bottom, and the
prettyest banks of white coarse sand we ever saw.   we think
the 500 miles that we have to go, will be worse than all the
way we have come.   what team we have left are wore out
with fatigue, and time will determine what we can do   our
prospect is gloomy at present.   an indian has come to us on
a pony with a salmon fish   he gave us to understand he
wanted A shirt for it.   they told him, to much.   he then
wanted some bread.   they gave him some & got the fish   we
dont know where he came from as we see no apearance of
their residence.   have come about 6 miles, and camp't about
a half mile from Boise on a branch that runs into it   have
most X Lent grass, which is the most pleasing object with us
at present, and have plenty of small wood to burn, and plenty
to cook yet such as people generaly have on the plains paid
12 dollars for the last sack of flour, and 20 Cts per pound for
bacon.   have not see a vegetable growing this year   we
have not seen any rain for two months nor do we expect to see
any soon, and we are nearly smother'd and covered with ashy
dust and the sage among it looks as though it would set on
fire without help.
Tuesday August 1   one of T Cooks oxen was dead this
morning, and one of Jo Carters sick   we started and drove
him a mile or two and could not get him along any further,
and let him alone to die.   they die very soon after we notice
they are sick and we never heard of one getting well.   we
have not determind on the cause.   it is probely partly being
suffocated in the hot alkily dust, and drinking bad water and
exausted with the long trip.   we are stopt for the night on
the clear stream of Boise.   4 indians has come on ponys, to
sell us some dried salmon   we got them for a shirt and some
powder, and caps   saw some emegrants to day who had

come back on the hunt of 4 horses the Indians stole from
them last night   they found one to day.   they had sold to
A white man

Wedn August 2.   the indians come soon this morning with
some fresh salmon.   they got another shirt.   if they will
keep on so they need not go without as they nearly all
do.   we were suspicious about our horses being taken last
night and tied up some of them to the wagon   have noond
again on Boise river, under a balm of Gilead tree 2 feet
through. there is enough of such timber here to fence fields if
necesary, and this bottom we think would yeild comon
produce well, but it is not probeble it ever will be
cultivated.   it is to far away in an uncivilised land among
the savage indians who know no more about work than the
grasshopers and never saw such a thing as a garden vegetable
growing   here we leave boise to see it no more   the men
that were on hunt of the stolen horses pass us this eve with all
their horses.   found the indians on them running down
rabbits.   one would not give up the horse without a shirt,
and they gave him one.   have travel'd about 15 miles to day
and campt again on Boise

Thursday aug 3   have come about 12 miles to day and
ariv'd at the second crossing of snake river   it is two weeks
to day since we crossed it first and a sorrowful time it has
been to us.   we have lost 8 head of our work cattle, and one
yearling   it is about 140 miles and we have seen more graves
and dead cattle all along the road, than all the balance of the
way and we cannot get along as we are much further.   we are
working the last old cow to make out & get along at all, but
we trust to providence, and hope for his promise.   at this
ferry fort Boise we have paid 6 dollars apeice for 5
wagons.   have pull'd them out of the boat by hand, and
camp't for the night close to the water, and some went back
and slept with the cattle.   will swim them over in the

morning.   here is a low sod establishment they call the
fort.   that is all the building there is, with 1 covered wagon
and 3 cloth tents, and 7 or 8 indian willow wigwams and the
poorest dirtyest looking tribe we have yet seen.   several are
entirely naked.   they do steal cattle from these traders they
stay with and drive them to the mountains, and kill and eat
them, and there is no way to punish them but to kill them,
and they will not do that   they have a garden enclosed here
with poles but the grasshopers have eaten it up.   it is now
one hundred miles to the grand rounds and 500. & 50. to
Salem Oregon.   snake river is about half as wide as Illinois
river, & runs into Columbia. Boise runs into snake river and
is about half as wide, and a much pleasenter river, with its
beautiful trees, pretty enough to stand in a Horlecultureal
garden, while Snake river has nothing but bunches of small
willow.   can hardly make out to get a bite to eat here

Friday August 4   our folks went over soon this morning
after the cattle and got them started to swim several times but
with all their hardest exertions they would go back.   they
concluded about 10 O'clock to all come over and get their
breakfast, and try it again.   we had calculated we bought
some salt for 60 cents per pound.   sold dried peaches for the
same.   sold a peck of beans for two dollars to go 10 miles to
day to Maleher [Malheur], and some familys are waiting
there for us, but we frequently are disappointed in the same
way.   there was 3 or 4 indians here, & the men told them
they would give them a good rifle gun if they would swim
over our cattle.   they said they would, and before noon got
them all over but two, and we have paid an indian one dollar
to fetch them over, so we gave them a gun powder & shot,
and shirts, pants, coats, not a few, and some for pappoos.   we
are at the same spot to night as we were last night   spread
our table on the gravel close to the water.   we have had a
croud of naked indians around us all day, but as Adam and

Eve in the garden, have discoverd their nakedness and have
made themselves an apron, about a half yard square   is
every thing the most of them wear and that is often made of
red flannel.   here was two indians had on pants, some
emegrant had give them, with their knees all out.   they
stood by me looking at me sew, and they haul'd of their pants
and threw them down to me, and shewed me how they
wanted them mended.   acording to orders I pached both
pair, and they come up close to me and put them on well
pleased.   they here all wear their hair long.   some look as
though they comb it and plait the sides.   others hang long
all over the face and eyes, and looks as though it never was
comb'd & I dont suppose it ever was, as they had no
comb   we had one squaw with us nearly all day, with her
pappoos on board, with leather fastened on it griter [garter]
fashion to slip it in.   she took it of and put it in the river,
and wet it all over and it squalled manfuly.   the next cattle
they swam over had the same trouble and drownded one
weak gave out one.   the indians went to skinning it before it
was hardly dead, and soon had the meat carried away to their
wigwams   friday eve after sundown here is too wagons just
landed with us and two more too ferry over. I am tired of this
place.   here is more noise and confusion, than in the midst
of A city, the innumerable indians, and the noise of swimming
cattle, and so forth

Saturday August 5   left fort Boise and snake river soon this
morn with the snakes and a few white skin flints, and come
15 miles without water across the most dust dry and hot bare
desert that any person ever travers'd and campt for the night
on the creek Maleher.   here is a hut and tent ocupi'd by A
Mr. Turner of Oregon a trader.   we left 4 wagons of
Missourians at the river who had the 4 horses by the indians.
A Mr. Tipton   they have been very unfortunate in loosing

50 head of cattle and one of their horses died last night that they rode to death in hunting the stole ones, and the indians rode them they had nearly to death, besides they paid another indian 70 dollars to find them and go with them.   after we paid the indians one dollar, for bringing our calves he would not fetche them.   said he would for a shirt, so they were swam over with some other emegrant cattle, and he kept the money.   we have seen they lost another horse this morning   one staid back all day looking for it and did not find it.   think the indians got it   several dead cattle to day, and here is 3 near our camp.   here is a good cold spring, which we seldom see of late.   saw some hot springs to day   it has been death and distruction on cattle this year but healthy for people

Sunday Aug 6   did not start until nearly noon.   have been putting oxen to the horse wagon and lighting our load by throwing away the false floor, and such as we can do without.   the wife of Mr Turner came to see us this morning.   this is the 2nd season she has came out from oregon with her husband to spend the summer in this savage land, far from any society but her husband and two children.   she is a very lively pleasent interesting intelegent woman.   they are a going to oregon this week, the new rout.   we came from Maleher to sulpher spring, and campt for the night

Mon Aug 7th   came about ten miles this forenoon to birch creek.   here Mr Tiptons family had to stop for the night, as Mr Tipton has gone back to look for some cattle that he could not find yesterday morning, and they have to wait for him, and they were unwilling for us to go on and leave them along, and we have concluded to stop with them.   we are now among they most theivish indians we have had all the way   they are still the snakes and will steal all they can.   we are campt for the night on birch creek in sight of snake river   grass not very good.   surrounded close to us with mountains

Tuesday Augt 8th   we left snake river for the last time soon this morning and came to burnt river in 6 miles travel and crossd it 3 times.   the road has been very mountainous and rocky to day.   we have come about 12 miles to day and campt for the night on burnt river.   the road is strung with dead cattle old and new.   grass is pretty good   the mountains are very high over our heads   Mr Tipners 4 wagons are campt with us to night, and the widow Waldo with 7 negroes

Aug 9   one of Mr Greys cows and one yearling died last night, and one of Jo Carters and one of our own making it 4 to day   to day we have about 15 miles to day and campt on a branch of burnt river   it runs in a narrow valey with very high mountains on each side   we have crossd the river 5 times to day.   here is considerable small timber on this creek such as Quaken asp, balm of Gilead, Alder, Haws, Larches, birch &.c.   saw a great many piles of bones and some graves, no graves yet that have died this year.   it is cheering to us to have such beautiful branches of swift runing cool water several times every day, and pretty good grass.

Aug 10   came about 8 miles and noon'd on burnt river.   met 3 men with about 20 pack horses and mules packed with flour and other eatables, and materials for gold diging on burnt river.   they had been out here prospecting and we heard they found as much as 10 dollars per day and had gone back for provisions   our boys have prospected some, and found gold.   came on this afternoon, and passd a wagon and yoke of oxen dead by it.   one wagon and family and 2 yoke of oxen to it, campt with us night before last.   they went of and left us very lively, and it is their oxen dead, and they had fixed a cart of the 4 wheels, and gone on   one of thomas cook oxen died this morning and 3 of our cows are sick this eve   we are tented to night on a branch of burnt river, and pretty good many dead cattle to day that have died the last day or too, and wagons and cloathing of all kinds threw away.   we are trying to get to grand rounds before we leave any.   our case looks desperate but some of us have faith strong enough to beleive we shall get to Oregon.   we know in whom we trust and are waiting patient for the promise

Friday Aug 11   are at the same place this forenoon   one of our cows has died here to day & one of T Cooks yearlings. another train of miners has passd us to day   will stop in a half days travel from here   two kiouse indians have come to see us to day.   they wanted some matches for salmon fish   we gave them some and got it   we come on about 4 miles this afternoon and campt near a spring   pretty good grass, and no wood

Saty Aug 12   come about 14 miles to day   have campt by a spring and some ponds   pretty good grass but no wood, but little brush and chips.   left one more of our cows this forenoon to die, and have two more sick   we are in powder river valey.   it is 3 or 4 miles wide, and on our left the mountains are coverd with tall pine trees down to the foot of them, and very rich perraries [prairies] joining and it begins to look a good deal more like getting to some place than we have seen all the way

Sabbath eve, Aug 13th   When will our pilgrimage be done the worlds long week be over. The sabbath dawn that needs no sun. That day that fades no more   we have travel'd about 12 miles to day and campt on powder river   3 of Mr Tiptons cattle were dead this morn all close together.   we have miss'd one day without losing any.   we hope and pray that providence will give us the remnent of our cattle   we can barely get along with two yoke of oxen and cows to 4 wagons, and they weak and wore out.   one wagon and some men pass't us before we got started this morn   said they saw the miners diging a ditch to drain a branch, and they told them they were finding as much as 8 dollars per day in the ditch.   this valey is much prettyer than it was yesterday, and 7 or 8 miles wide.   the mountains are high on the left and covered with timber and plenty of snow on the top of them, the river runing through it, and plenty of springs runing down the mountains.   must be very cold in winter but if there Gold digings prove good, it will soon be settled   here we found Governer Gaines of Oregon waiting here for his sons.   here are some traders come out from Oregon with provisn to meet the sufering emegrants who have lost nearly all their cattle, and some we know have spent all their money, and others nearly all, and they only ask 35 dollars per hundred for flour and sugar 40 cents per pound, and cheese 75   we expect to get to the Grand round tomorrow, and hope to meet with a more pleasing prospect we have very good grass here good water and wood and all well, and have some thing to eat yet, but nearly out

Monday A 14th   3 more of Mr Tiptons cattle died last night and this morn   we came about noon 8 miles and stopt at a cold spring   saw some handsomer situations for farms than I saw in Ill.   the land very rich and the side of the mountains coverd with pine and fur and beautiful place to build by scatering fur trees and springs.   we have stopt for the night within 3 miles of G round on a good spring, grass good fur timber very pretty near us the hills low, but we beleive it too cold to live here as there is now frost every night.

Tuesday Aug 15   the axeltree of the wagon broke to day

and we had to leave it   came up a very long hill and down the longest and rockyest one we have all the way   all the foot of it is the round [Grande Ronde]   it resembles our large prairies in Illinois with low mountains all around it covered with pine timber.   the land rich and dry with a great many cold springs and the land is flat clear up to the mountains we drove for 8 miles across the edge of it and stopt and

[Here the diary ends. See introduction to the Sarah Sutton diary to read about her death several weeks later in the Tygh Valley just east of Mount Hood.]

ELIZABETH [AUSTIN] ROEDER
Courtesy, Whatcom County Museum of History
and Art, Bellingham, Washington.

Vermillion Wagon Train Diaries, 1854
❦ Anna Maria Goddell
& Elizabeth Austin

INTRODUCTION

The diaries that follow were written by two young women who traveled from Vermilion,[1] Ohio, to Grand Mound, Washington Territory, in 1854. Elizabeth Austin and Anna Marie Goodell[2] were close personal friends and members of what might be called the "Vermilion Wagon Train." What is new about these records is that these overlanders were traveling to the brand new Washington Territory by the Naches Pass route north of Mt. Rainier, an incredible journey. The Austin diary is in the University of Washington Library in Seattle; the Goodell diary is in the Washington Historical Society's collection in Tacoma. They are both typescripts. They are printed here with permission of the respective libraries.

We will take up the writers one at a time:

ELIZABETH AUSTIN

She was a single woman, 27 years old, who was betrothed to Henry Roeder (pronounced Roder) who had already crossed the Plains and awaited her in Whatcom County, Washington Territory.

Henry and other founders of Bellingham lived right on the shore of Puget Sound. He had been born in Germany on July 4,

---

[1] The women inevitably spell the name of their town in Ohio "Vermillion." The established spelling today is "Vermilion."

[2] Mrs. Goodell's names call for explanation: Goodell is spelled that way by some members of the family. Others have changed it to Goodale. Her first and second names appear as Ann and Anna and Marie and Maria, or Mariah.

1824, and was brought to Vermilion by his parents in 1830. Henry and Elizabeth seem to have become childhood friends and now had serious marriage plans which would be consummated when Elizabeth arrived at Grand Mound with the Goodells. He had been a sailor in the Great Lakes trade and knew those inland seas intimately. He transferred his nautical abilities to that other inland sea, Puget Sound. After his arrival at the new port of Bellingham on December 15, 1852, he became active in numerous pursuits. He built a lumber mill; he constructed a sailing sloop, the *H.C. Page;* and he built a log cabin and later a frame house for himself and his bridge-to-be when she would come from the east.

Her arrival overland took place at Grand Mound, south of Olympia, on October 8, 1854. Word finally got to Captain Roeder at the other end of the Sound at Bellingham, and he sailed his newly constructed sloop the full length of that body of water to meet her. The marriage took place at the territorial capital on February 10, 1855. It was performed at the Hotel Olympia by Chief Justice Edward Lander of the Territorial Supreme Court, with George Corliss and Melancthon Goodell, William's brother, as witnesses. The newly married couple then boarded the sloop and set sail for Bellingham where they spent the rest of their lives.

Elizabeth was described by a friend as "beloved by all who knew her." Her nickname "Lib" or "Libbie" became "Aunt Libbie" in her later years. There are two features of the city of Bellingham that are named for her: Elizabeth Street and Elizabeth Park.

There were four children born to the Roeders: John Nicholas, b. August 11, 1856; Henry Austin, b. February 23, 1859; Victor Augustin, b. August 13, 1861, and Charlotte Tuttle, b. October 25, 1864.

Elizabeth lived until February 12, 1897, when she died in her seventy-first year. Henry Sr. lived until September 25, 1902.

ANNA MARIE GOODELL

It was on August 22, 1854, that this young woman wrote in her overland diary, "I am 23 yers old today." She had already noted on July 18, "The baby is five months old today." This means that she was born on August 22, 1831, and her baby boy, "Freddie" (Frederick Augustus) had been born on February 18, 1854.[3] She and William Bird Goodell, a Canadian from Ontario, had been married on March 16, 1853, in Vermilion. She was the daughter of Sylvester and Eunice (Sturges) Pelton. They would have three more children: Walter Gates and Charlotte Eunice, both born in Washington Territory. There was also an unnamed stillborn child between these two.

Like his friend, Henry Roeder, William Bird Goodell was a sailor on Lake Erie, tking part in the interstate trade and in trade with Canada. On Puget Sound he again took up sailoring on that body of water in the coastal trade to Oregon and California and with Canada to the north. This culminated in the 1860s in a position as United States Customs Inspector at the harbor of Port Angeles on the Strait of Juan de Fuca. It was through this port that trade with Victoria, British Columbia, was channeled. Today it is still a ferrying port for those visiting Victoria, B.C.

On Saturday, January 4, 1884, the Salem *Oregon Statesman* quoted a story from the Victoria *Chronicle* to the effect that a "dreadful calamity" had taken place on the previous Wednesday in the American town of Port Angeles. A flood of water came rushing down a ravine back of the city wiping out many buldings in its course. Among those destroyed was the customs house, and among those drowned was "Captain Goodell."

After the death of her husband Anna Marie decided to return to Vermilion, Ohio. She, with her three children sailed away for New York City. The last two entries in her diary, long out of sequence with the overland record, were written telling of her arrival in New York on September 15, and in Vermilion on September 17, 1864.

There Anna lived out her life. She gave her time to raising her children. Her death took place on October 30, 1902, in Lorain, Ohio, eleven miles from Vermilion.

---

[3] Frederick Augustus Goodell became a well-known sailor in the Great Lakes trade out of Vermilion., He went from deck hand to watchman to wheelman and eventually to Captain. He and Amelia Hinton of Vermilion were married on November 20, 1880. They had five children. John Brandt Mansfield, *History of the Great Lakes*, 2 vol., (Chicago, 1892), I, 544-45.

NOTE: We have had special help from the following persons and organizations: B. Naydinc Ziegler, Research Aide, Whatcom Genealogy Society, Bellingham, WA; Martha Long, Great Lakes Historical Society, Vermilion, OH; and Keith L. Miller, Beaverton, OR, historian of the Goodale (Goodell) family. Neill D. Mullen, past president of the Whatcom County Historical Society, Bellingham, WA, has been especially helpful. James F. Bolster of Bellingham, lineal descendant of Henry and Elizabeth Roeder, has given enthusiastic support, as well as the family's approval of the Austin diary.

Members of the Goodell family mentioned
in the Austin/Goodell Diaries:

Jotham Weeks Goodell and Ann Glenning Bacheler Goodell, the parents, had been married in Hamilton, Ontario, Canada, on April 20, 1828. They had crossed over the plains in 1850 with a winter stopover in Salt Lake City. They reached Oregon in 1851. There they lived in Polk county, then moved to Grand Mound, Thurston county, Washington Territory in 1853, where they settled on a 640-acre claim. *History of the Pacific Northwest — Oregon and Washington,* II (Portland 1889), pp. 346-47. Jotham met the Vermilion Company just east of the Washington Cascades and guided them over Naches Pass to Grand Mound.

William Bird Goodell, b. July 27, 1829, Ancaster, Ontario, was their oldest child. He and Anna Marie Pelton, b. Aug. 22, 1831, were married on March 16, 1853, in Vermilion, Erie Co., Ohio. On the journey west they had with them their first child, Frederick Augustus, b. February 18, 1854. A second child, unnamed, was born and died a year later. A third, Walter Gates, was born March 22, 1856, in Washington. A daughter, Charlotte Eunice ("Lottie"), was also born in Grand Mound, in 1862.

Mary Weeks and Phoebe Newton Goodell were twins, b. October 25, 1831, in Canada. Mary married Nathan Meloy on August 6, 1851. They traveled over the trail to Oreon in 1851, and, after taking the oath of allegiance, settled in Multnomah County, Oregon. Phoebe married Holden A. Judson on June 20, 1849. They arrived in Washington October 1, 1853, and settled on a claim in Lewis County on April 1, 1855. They later moved to Whatcom County. Phoebe in late life wrote her biography, *A Pioneer's Search for an Ideal Home* (Bellingham, Wash., 1925). A selection of quotes from her book are to be found in this series Vol. VI, pp. 130-34.

Melancthon Zwingle Goodell, b. Ancaster, Canada, November 6, 1835, traveled to Washington Territory with his parents in 1850. He married at Grand Mound, Washington, on June 7, 1858, Rebecca Euphimia Byles

Emeline Davis Goodale Gates, b. Ancaster, Canada, September 22, 1837. She was married to Levi Gates at Grand Mound on October 31, 1856. They later moved to Forest Grove, Oregon, where he operated a hardware store.

Other persons mentioned in the Austin/Goodell diaries.

We have been unable to identify some of those so-named. For instance, there were the Miller Train and the Andersons. There were many Millers and Andersons on the overland journeys. One needs more than the surnames to locate them. The two women mention one Dick Bradley. We have been unable to find him. Young men are particularly elusive. He could have gone south to California or Oregon.

George Wesley Beam was a 22-year-old young man from Illinois traveling with the Ebey Company. He settled on Whidbey Island in Puget Sound. His papers are in the University of Washington collection. *University of Washington Manuscripts* (Olympia, 1983), p. 376. He died in 1864 leaving a wife and three children. He was a cousin of the Ebeys. *Pacific Christian Advocate* (Methodist newspaper.), June 2, 1866.

The Ebey wagon train from Missouri traveled near the Vermilion overlanders and periodically exchanged visits with them. The leader was Jacob Ebey. Mrs. Goodell wrote in her diary on May 13, "There are six children and two grown persons,

father, mother, one son, two daughters, two grandchildren and
one nephew." The Ebeys became settlers on Whidbey Island
in Puget Sound. "Diary of Colonel and Mrs. I.N. Ebey,"
Washington Historical Quarterly, VII (July 1916), pp. 239-46.

"Captain" Richard Grant was an old-time Hudson's Bay
Company man, a Scot, born in Montreal. He had been in
charge of Fort Hall from 1842 to 1851, when he exercised an
option to retire. He moved to Cantonment Loring, an
abandoned United States military post, about four miles from
Fort Hall. This became the center of his activities from then on
as he supplied overland emigrants with all kinds of things and
plenty of advice. One writer described him as being like
Falstaff, "a fine looking portly old man and quite courteous for
an old mountaineer." Merle Wells, "Richard Grant," in
LeRoy R. Hafen, *The Mountain Men and the Fur Trade*, IX
(Glendale, Calif., 1972), pp. 164-86. John Grant was Richard
Grant's son.

Thomas and Sarah Ann Headley were with the Vermilion wagon
train. They settled in Pierce County near Steilacoom. He was a
farmer. The Headleys and the Whitsells settled on adjacent
claims according to territorial land records.

Ebenezer C. Hardy was a 21-year-old single man. He settled on a
claim in Skamania County soon after arrival in Washington.
He and his wife, Mary, were married on March 2, 1855. We
have not been able to learn her maiden name.

Lucretia Judson is named many times in both diaries. She later
married George W. Corliss from Vermont, a citizen of Olympia.
He is listed as a butcher in the 1860 census.

Charles P. and Louisa Judson were the older Judsons with the
Vermilion group. They settled near Olympia. They were the
parents of Emeline, Holden, and Lucretia Judson.

Emeline D. Judson married Levi L. Gates soon after arriving in
Washington Territory. They settled on a claim in Lewis
County. She was 17 years old in 1854. She died ten years later
leaving two small children. *Pacific Christian Advocate*, Aug.
15, 1864.

Holden Judson came out from Mound Prairie over the Naches Pass to meet the Vermilion train. He was the husband of Phoebe (Goodell) Judson who wrote the book, *A Pioneer's Search for an Ideal Home* (Bellingham, Wash., 1925).

Walter King is listed in the 1860 census for Chehalis county as a single man, 40 years old, a farmer from Ohio.

Moses and Nancy (Piper) Kirkland were from Jackson County, Louisiana. The name is spelled Kirtland by Elizabeth Austin. According to Washington land records they settled in King County in Oct., 1854.

J.R. Meeker and his wife, Nancy, are listed in the 1860 census as living near Steilacoom, Pierce County. Husband and wife had been born on the east coast, had moved to Ohio after marriage. They traveled over the plains with three children. On the crossing in 1854 another child, Sarah, was born.

Charles and Mary Van Wormer were a young couple often referred to as "Charlie" and "Mary" in the diaries. They had three children with them. They settled in Lynden, Lewis County. Robert E. Hawley, *Skqee Mus, or Pioneer Days on the Nooksack* (Bellingham, 1945), p. 185.

Henry and Margaret Whitsell were from Wisconsin. He is listed in the 1860 census as a laundryman. They also farmed near Steilacoom in Pierce County. They had five children with them on the overland journey.

The Rev. George F. Whitworth, an Englishman, was a pioneer Presbyterian minister, the "Father of Presbyterianism" in Washington. He was a pioneer in education in that area. He had been commissioned by the Presbyterian Board of Home Missions as "Missionary to Puget Sound." Whitworth College in Spokane is named for him. W.F. Prosser, *History of the Puget Sound Country* (N.Y., 1903), pp. 574-78.

Mary (Ebey) Wright and her two children were with the Ebey party. Her husband, Thomas S. Wright, had stayed in Missouri. They were divorced on February 13, 1857. She later married Urban E. Bozarth. "Diary of Colonel Isaac N. and

Mrs. Emily Ebey, 1856-7," *Pacific Northwest Hist. Quart.*, XXXIII (1942), pp. 297-323, especially p. 301.

Alexander (Alec) S. and Sarah Green Yantis from Missouri settled in Thurston County, Washington. They traveled with a family of seven children, all born in Missouri. They were farmers.

SELECT BIBLIOGRAPHY

Although it is planned that the final volume of this series will contain a comprehensive bibliography, it was thought that it would be helpful to include here a list of references especially for western Washington.

Barrow, Susan H.L., *et al.*, *Whatcom Seascapes* (Bellingham, 1970).

Blankenship, Georgiana, *Early History of Thurston County, Washington* (Olympia, 1914).

Edson, Lelah Jackson, *The Fourth Corner: Highlights from the Early Northwest* (Bellingham, 1968).

Hawley, Robert Emmett, *Skqee Mus, Or Pioneer Days on the Nooksack* (Bellingham, 1945).

Prosser, W.F., *History of the Puget Sound Country* (N.Y., 1903).

Roth, Lottie Roeder, *History of Whatcom County*, 2 volumes (Chicago, 1926).

Seattle Genealogical Society, *Washington Territory Donation Land Claims* (Seattle, 1980).

THE GOODELL AND AUSTIN DIARIES

[*Goodell*] April 18, 1854.   Left Vermillion this morning at 20 minutes past nine for Oregon and arrived at Sandusky about 10:30. We went to Uncle Levi Parsons and staid until after dinner.

Then went down to the daguerreanis and had our daguerotypes taken, then came back and went over to Sarah Derr's and staid until after tea, then bid them good-bye and went on board the steamer Bay City for Detroit. Left Sandusky at 9 P.M. We had a very pleasant time. The lake was smooth and the weather pleasant.

Sarah gave me some embroidering. It is very broad and pretty.

[*Austin*] Left home April 18th for Sandusky. At night went to Detroit; got there in the morning of the 19th, at 10 o'c. the same morning started for Chicago; got there at night; stayed there till morning.

[*Goodell*] April 19, 1854. We arrived at Detroit about 4 A.M. and went to the Western Hotel for breakfast. There was a good deal of company at the house. We left the house at 8 A.M. and went on the Central R.R. cars for Chicago. Stopped at Marshal [Michigan] about one for dinner. We arrived at Chicago at 7 P.M. We were very tired. We went to the Bissell House and called for as good a room as they had, but if the rest of the rooms were like ours, I pity the house. The bed was straw, the pillows the same, and all the light there was came through four panes of glass in the door. The room was very dark and damp and I was out of patience when I saw what kind of room we had to sleep in, but we made out to stay there. We were glad to get away. When we first got there we were shown into the private parlor where the landlady and two of her daughters were. She was very angry because we went in there.

[*Goodell*] April 20, 1854. Left Chicago on the Chicago & Aurora R.R. at 10 A.M. arrived at La Salle at 2 P.M., 104 miles distance from Chicago. We staid at the Tremont House, had dinner and a little better bed than we did at Chicago. It was very warm. Elizabeth [Austin] washed out some things for the baby. There were some passengers stopped in this afternoon. They were going for a visit. Mary Van Wormer got her a pair of shoes here. It is not a very pretty place. There does not seem to be much business going on here.

[*Austin*] The 20th. We started for St. Louis; stopped at La

Salle and stayed over night; from there to Bloomington; from there to Alton; got to St. Louis April 21st; stopped at the Missouri Hotel and stayed till the 24th.; then went aboard of the steamboat Sam Cloon[1]; stayed aboard of the boat till Wednesday night, the 26th., when the boat left for Council Bluffs; got to the Bluffs May 6th; the 7th went into a barn to live.

[There are no more entries for Austin until May 9th.]

[*Goodell*] April 21st.   Left La Salle at 4 A.M. on the Ill. Central R.R. and arrived at Bloomington at 8 A.M., where we changed to Chicago & Mississippi R.R. at 12 N. We came to a freight train that had run over a cow and were thrown partly off the track, which detained us about 3 hours. A train of passengers came up behind the freight train and we got into them and went on. We arrived at Alton at 6 P.M., went on board the steamer Reindeer and had supper and arrived at St. Louis at 8. Stopped at the Missouri Hotel where we staid until Monday morning.

April 22.   Mr. Judson, Charlie and William have been looking around at wagons and provisions. Mr. Chamberlain would like to fix them out, but I guess they will not get all their stuff here.

I have been writing a letter to Ma but will not finish it until tomorrow. Lucretia and Libbie have gone down the street a little ways. We have got a nice room, much better than any we have had since we left home.

The streets are full of drays and mules. I never saw a mule but once before. I wish I could get out and see what kind of city we are in, but William is so busy that he has not got the time to go with me.

---

[1] The *Sam Cloon* was one of the most active steamboats on the Missouri River in 1854. It was often mentioned in the Missouri newspapers. Louis Barry, *The Beginning of the West* (Topeka, 1972), *passim.*

April 23rd.   Today I finished my letter. William wrote
some of it. Mary Van Woermer wrote to her father. William,
Elizabeth and Lucretia have gone to look at the city. If they
don't see any more than we see from here they won't see
much, for all that I can see is some brick warehouses and one
little bit of a lone tree half suffocated for want of air. It is very
warm. Had a thunderstorm this afternoon.

April 24th.   Today William got his provisions and wagons
and went on board the steamboat Sam Cloon Capt John
McCloy. Elizabeth and Lucretia went up town this
afternoon. Lib got a fine comb 25¢, a pair of side combs 25¢,
a pair of stockings 40¢. Things are higher here than in
Vermillion.

There are eight families on board this afternoon from
Oberlin, Ohio. They are going to Iowa to settle altogether.

We had just had dinner and had everything good, sweet
potatoes, greens, lettuce, radishes and apples. Had a
thunderstorm this evening.

April 25th.   Elizabeth, Lucretia and Mary went to the
store again today. Elizabeth got a pair of gloves 25¢, one
handkerchief 25¢ 3 papers pins 36¢, and two papers needles
20¢.

It has been very warm today. Looks very cloudy. I think
it will rain before night.

The city from the river does not look very inviting. The
houses are mostly brick and very smoky. The streets are very
narrow. I think I shall be glad when the boat leaves this
place. We think we shall leave tomorrow evening. Have had
another thunderstorm this evening.

April 26th.   Freddie took a hard cold last night and is quite
sick today. I have given him some Hive Syrup. I think he
will be better in a day or so if he does not get any more cold.
There were three more families came on board today going to

California, an old lady with her son and three small grand-children, an old man with a young wife and 4 children. There is a young girl with a little child about 1 year old. She says it is her sister's child and that its father and mother are both dead. She is going to California with her uncle who is up the river somewhere. She says that she is the only living relative of the child. Some believe her and some don't. Had a hard hail storm this evening.

April 27th.   We left St. Louis last evening about 6 P.M. Freddie is better this morning. It is raining this morning. There has been a thunder-storm every day since we got to St. Louis and one or two very hard ones. There is a fiddler on the boat. He is playing for Mr. Shannon's little girls to dance. They are very pretty. They are about of an age. One is his little girl and one is hers. His wife is the sister of his first wife. She was a widow. After Mr. Shannon's girls got through their dance the rest of the folks had a cotillion.

April 28th.   There are two women sick today. The baby is better. I have not taken him out of the stateroom since Tuesday night. It has been very cold this afternoon, but has been pleasanter this afternoon. Caroline Mason was taken sick this morning and is quite sick this afternoon.

April 29th.   Been very pleasant today. Have run over a good many snags and been on four sand bars. We have passed some very pretty places, not villages, but farms. It is generally very lonesome along the river. I do not think I should like to live in Missouri very well. The river is very muddy and the water is not fit to use till it has been settled with eggs.

April 30th.   Quite pleasant today, but we have not got along very fast. Have been on several sand bars. The baby has had a dreadful hard crying spell this afternoon. I gave him some peppermint and he stopped and went to sleep. It is quite still today. The children are all very quiet, as it is Sunday, but tomorrow I expect they will be as noisy as ever.

May 1st Was very pleasant this forenoon, but this afternoon it has rained quite hard. We stopped at Richfield [Missouri] this morning and saw some Indians. They were painted with feathers tied in their hair. They looked very savage. Stopped at Kansas [City] this afternoon. Mr. Shannon's family got off there and start from there to California.

We have been on the boat just one week, have left Kansas and have just got on a sand bar. Don't think we will get off til morning.

May 2nd. Have just got off the bar. It is a beautiful morning. We stoped at Ft. Leavenworth and about 40 Mormons left the boat. This afternoon stopped at Weston. Saw a great many wagons and oxen and horses ready to start to California and Oregon.

Two women had a quarrel last night, Caroline Mason and another lady. Freddie is not very well this evening. He has not got over his cold yet.

May 3rd. We had to stop this morning on account of fog sometime. We got to St. Joe about 10 A.M. Staid an hour. Lib and Lucretia went ashore and took a walk. William got some flannel to make Freddie some shirts at 37½¢ a yard. Some of the passengers left here. We have run over a great many snags this afternoon and don't get along very fast. Caroline is very sick this afternoon. It looks much like rain this evening. I think it will rain before morning.

May 4th. Very rainy this morning. Rained quite hard last night. Have just left Iowa Point [Doniphan Co., Kansas]. There are very high hills on both sides of the river along here. We have just passed several Indians and squaws. One Indian ran about a mile to pick up hard bread and tobacco and other stuff that the boys threw ashore for them just to see them run. William has been trying to make me out an Irish woman, but I guess he won't make it out.

May 5th   Have not seen any Indians today. We laid opposite Sonora [Missouri] farm from 9 o'clock till 12. The water here is very shallow and they dare not go any farther for fear of running aground, so the Captain has taken a small boat and gone to find a channel. They found it and we started on and went about 10 miles and stopped at Linden Landing [Missouri].

Two familes left the boat here and when we get thirty miles farther the rest of the Oberlin folks leave us. We shall not get there until morning. Have just run over a snag and it came near throwing us all from our chairs.

May 6th.   This morning the rest of our Ohio folks bid us good bye and left us. We feel very lonely. We had got quite well acquainted with them. They were very pleasant folks. The cabin maid is sick this morning. We have just stopped at an Indian station. There are a great many Indians here and they are all dressed in their own fashion. We have run over a great many tree tops and snags today. Have just passed another Indian Station. Saw 43 on the bank. Evening arrived at our destination for this time, Council Bluff.

May 7th   This is the pleasantist morning we have seen in a long time. We staid on the boat last night. This morning there was a carriage came down from the village for passengers. We got into the carriage and went to Mr. Gardner's where we are going to fit out. We have got an old stable to stay in. It is prairie land here. Just back of the town we can see high bluffs. The people where we are, are English. I have written to Phoebe and Frederick since we stopped. The wind blows quite hard from the south this evening.

May 8th.   Today Libbie is washing. It is the first washing we have done since we left home of any account. The cabin maid let me wash out some things for the baby while we were on the boat. Freddie is not very well today. He took cold yesterday. The doctor gave me two little pills to give him. Mrs. Gardner gave me some onions and told me how to make a syrup for him. It is quite cool today. The wind commenced blowing last evening and it has been blowing all day. The baby seems some better this evening. I hope he is not going to be sick again.

May 9th. Elizabeth and Lucretia have been to town today. They carried several letters to the post office. Freddie has been very sick today. I have stayed in Mrs. Gardner's with him ever since we stopped here. I am afraid he is not going to get over his cold very soon. I don't know what in the world I would do without Lib here. The wind has blown for three days here and it is very cold. I hope it will clear off tonight. It looks as though it might. It is a dreary place here. I do not think I should like to live in Iowa.

[*Austin*] Tuesday, May 9th, 1854 Lucretia and I went to the city afoot.

[There are no more entries for Austin until May 16th.]

[*Goodell*] May 10th. I am glad to see the baby a little better this morning. I think now he will get along if he does not get any more cold. The wind has commenced blowing again and blows harder than ever. William and Mr. Judson have gone to town. There was a steamboat come to the landing last night. The Dr. that came up the river with us was here today. He says they are going to leave Saturday. William has torn his coat today and I shall have to mend it tomorrow. It looks pleasant this evening but I don't know how long it will last.

May 11th. Very cloudy this morning and looks very much like rain. I have written a letter to Joel and sent it to town and William lost it. Lucretia wrote one to Mary Leonard. It is cloudy up in the west and thunders. I think we shall have a hard storm. William and Charlie have gone to town. I have been mending Williams coat. They saw a man in town that was going to Olympia.

May 13th.   It is no warmer today than it was yesterday. The men folks have all gone to town. I don't know but it will freeze up it is so cold. Lib, Lucretia and Mary have been trying to do a little washing. Mr. Judson and William have got two more yoke of oxen and Charlie a yoke of cows. Mr. Ebey's company came here last night and camped beside our log mansion. We would like to travel with them if we were ready. They are going to Washington Territory. They have a son there. There are six children and two grown persons, father, mother, one son, two daughters, two grandchildren and one nephew. There is one other family with them, a Mr. Leslie. They are going to California.

May 14th.   The sun shines this morning   I think it will be pleasant today. I have a very hard cold and so has the baby. Mrs. Gardner is quite sick this morning. We are baking and cooking beans and trying to get ready to start tomorrow but I am afraid we shall not be able to go till Tuesday. The company that camped here last night have gone to the ferry and will wait there for us.

May 15th.   It rained last night and this morning. It seems very pleasant but I am afraid it is not going to stay so long. William, Elizabeth, Lucretia and Mary went to town today and have just got back. It has begun to rain again and I am afraid it will tomorrow.

May 16th.   It does not rain this morning but the wind blows very hard. The men are trying to get things ready to start this afternoon. We are very anxious to leave here. Noon. It is raining now and I guess it will all night. They have got all the things on the wagons and we are going to try and sleep in them tonight but it will be very cold and I am afraid we shall all take cold.

[*Austin*] Tuesday, the 16th — Got our things in our wagons and slept there.

[*Goodell*] May 17th.   It rains yet and blows like a furry, but we are going to start in a little while and go as far as the ferry and camp. We went as far as four miles and camped and then we got supper. We had bacon, baked potatoes, stewed peaches, bread and gravy and tea. Lib has been after some water and has picked some goose berries.

[*Austin*] Wednesday, 17th — Left Mr. Gordon's [Gardner?] Went a short distance and camped.

[*Goodell*] May 18th. It is very pleasant this morning but cold. We are getting ready to start again. We have got to go about 1 mile farther before we can cross the ferry. It is one mile of the worst road I ever saw. We crossed the Missouri river. Went about ten miles and camped. We crossed one mud hole after dark. The wagon stood on one end almost. The wolves howl and the dogs bark.

May 19th.   Came to Elkhorn Creek and camped. We traveled about ten miles today. We are some afraid of the Indians. We can hear them whoop. We have not seen any since we left the Missouri River. I hope we will not see any or have any trouble with them

[*Austin*] May 19 — At night stoped at Elk Creek and stayed till the next morning; the 20th we left Elk Creek and stopped about 25 miles on the Platte River. We left our first stopping place and went about three miles farther on account of the Indians being very thick about there. We joined a large camp where we felt more safe.

[*Goodell*] May 20th.   Crossed Elkhorn Creek this morning. Four Indians crossed the ferry just after us. One of them

came on after us on horse back and wanted something to eat.
Mr. Judson gave him some bread. At noon six more passed
by us on horse back going as hard as they could go. We saw a
wolf across the prairie.

May 21st.   Crossed an Indian bridge, had to pay one dollar
a wagon. There were lots of Indians there. There were four
that staid in our camp. They gave up their bows and arrows
to the men and slept under the wagon. They can talk
English and seem very friendly. We camped on the prairie
tonight and no water very near.

[*Austin*] May 21st — Sabbath; we crossed the Indian toll
bridge and had a great deal of trouble, but through at last —
traveled about 20 miles.

[*Goodell*] May 22nd.   It is very warm today. We have not
seen any Indians. I hope that we shall not. They say that this
tribe is the worst tribe that we shall have to pass through.
They are the Pawnees. We have camped on a little side hill
where there is plenty of wood, water, and grass.

[*Austin*] May 22nd, Monday — We traveled about twenty-
three miles and stopped, and stayed all night near a little
pond of water; wood scarce. The next morning we washed
some.

[*Goodell*] May 23rd.   Stopped half a day to wash. Crossed
Loup Fork. Sent a few lines home. William thinks I shall
have lots to write about today. We have come about one
quarter of a mile from the ferry and camped where there is
lots of wood, water, and grass, by going a little ways after it.

[*Austin*] May 23rd, Tuesday — We crossed Loop Fork;
paid 3 dollars apiece for the wagons; fifty cents a yoke for
cattle — traveled about 10 miles.

[*Goodell*] May 24th.   Left Loup Fork this morning
Traveled about fifteen miles and camped by the side of a

river. Elizabeth is sick tonight. I have mixed up two loaves
of bread, the first light bread since we have left the Bluffs.

[*Austin*] May 24th, Wednesday — This morning Lucretia
and I visited two small graves — Catherine Gibson two years
old, John Crabb, 7 years old — died July 6th. 1853. This is a
beautiful place — 96 miles from the Missouri River; traveled
about 6 miles and saw three more graves — all grown people,
died Mar 22nd and 31st, 1852. Camped fifteen miles. One of
the company had 4 horses stolen.

[*Goodell*] May 25th.   Last night the Indians stole four
horses, William and another man were watching, and they
crawled along on the ground and cut the ropes and started off
with them before they knew any thing about it. The men
started after them in the afternoon, they came back after
horses and four or five from another company went on after
them. They would track them to the river and six miles after
they had crossed.

[*Austin*] May 25th, Thursday.   This morning we are left
nearly alone. The men have gone to look for the horses. Very
warm today. Came back about 11 o'c. and started back about
1:00 with more horses & men.

[*Goodell*] May 26th.   The men have not got back yet. We
are going on and they will come on after us. I am afraid they
will not find their horses. We have camped out on the
prairie. The river is about one-half mile from here. There has
been some fuss with the Indians, one horse killed, one cow
and one man wounded. They robbed two wagons. Mr.
Meekers company camped just behind us. They are an
Oregon company and we are going in company with them.

[*Austin*] May 26th. Friday — We are about starting this
morning. The horse is not found yet, nor have the men
returned. We have traveled 13 miles — passed 7 graves. One

company had trouble with Indians; one man wounded; one horse and one cow killed & all their provisions stolen.

[*Goodell*] May 27th.   We joined the Meeker company this morning.   camped on the prairie where there is neither water or grass. It rains very hard. It has thundered very hard. The Andersons have camped about one-half mile behind us. There is a darkey in the company. He got his cattle in a mud hole and he had a fine time getting them out.

[*Austin*] Saturday, 27th, 1854 — Today we traveled over sand hills 15 or 20 miles, passed 3 more graves. The men overtook us this afternoon that went in pursuit of the stolen horses but found nothing of the horses or Indians; rained all afternoon.

[*Goodell*] May 28th.   It is a very lonesome and dreary day. It rains very hard by spells. We have crossed Prairie Creek and two or three other small ones. The mud was very deep. Part of our company are behind us some ways. My foot pained me some last night. I am afraid it is going to swell again. We have camped on Wood River. There is plenty of wood and water.

[*Austin*] Sunday, May 28th — It is very rainy today; have just passed Prairie creek — a very bad place; afternoon & still rains very hard; passed one grave this forenoon.

[*Goodell*] May 29th.   Today most every thing is going on. Most of them are washing and baking. Mary is washing and Lib and Lucretia are baking. Some of the men in the camp are shooting, some swearing, some playing on the fiddle and some on the accordion and flute. There is a little of every thing. The Andersons have just come up and camped here. They are going to form a company for Oregon tonight.

[*Austin*] Monday, the 29th.   Today we spent at Wood River and washed and baked; very rainy and wet. Thundered and lightened in the night.

[*Goodell*] May 30th.   We crossed Wood river today. Paid half a dollar. The bridge was made of logs. There was a store there. Mr. Judson got some drilling for a tent 25¢ a yard, a pair of shoes $2.00, some tar $6.00. Camped on the bank about one-half mile from the bridge. There was a very hard thunder storm last night. I sent a letter from here to Diantha and Elizabeth one to Phoebe.

[*Austin*] Tuesday, 30th, 1854 — Today we crossed Wood River, and camped a few rods this side. Meria and I sent each one of us a letter home. Meria wrote to Diantha and I to Phoebe.

[*Goodell*] May 31st.   We have crossed a good many bad places today. The roads are very muddy. There was another hard thunder storm last night. We have camped near the Platte River with plenty of wood and water, grass not very good.

[*Austin*] Wednesday, 31st, 1854 — Today we crossed a great many bad places today. At night we camped near Platte River; plenty of wood and water.

[*Goodell*] June 1st.   We passed one grave this morning. That makes seventeen we have passed since we left Missouri River. We went ninety-six miles before we saw any, then we saw two. We have crossed some pretty bad places. Crossed Elk Creek, I road across. We went very well, but the next wagon went partly off the bridge and lost out some things. It was a good camping place after we got over, plenty of wood and water and grass.

[*Austin*] Thursday, June 1st 1854 — Passed one grave this morning; saw one wolf. Just crossed Elm Creek; one yoke of cattle went off the bridge, and the wagon lost out several things. We were obliged to attach ropes to the wagons to guide them right. We have a good camp ground — plenty of wood and water. The darkies had a dance.

[*Goodell*] June 2nd.   It is very unpleasant this morning. We have passed a good many Buffalo bones and one grave. A Mr. John Chambers. The Ebey company passed it yesterday.

[*Austin*] Friday, June 2nd, 1854 — We have passed a great many buffalo bones and one grave — A Mr. John Chambers — died 1853, age 53.

[*Goodell*] June 3rd.   It was very cold and cloudy this morning. Thundered and lightened about noon and again about three or four in the afternoon. The wind blew and it rained harder than I ever saw it before. It rained most all night. We camped on the Platte River.

[*Austin*] Saturday, June 3d — This morning I wish I was at home. We passed two buffaloes this forenoon. It thundered and lightened very hard. In the afternoon the hardest storm I ever saw; stopped on the Platte River. Had to cross a stream of water to get wood.

[*Goodell*] June 4th.   This morning we have passed one grave a new one. Mrs. Susannah Wilson aged 55, died May 21st., 1854. We are going to stop some where soon to dry our things. We have stopped out on the prairie and have emptied everything out of our wagon. Things are very damp.

[*Austin*] Sunday, June 4th — This morning we passed a grave of a lady — Mrs. Susanne Wilson, died May 21st, 1854, age 55.

[*Goodell*] June 5th. We have traveled about twenty miles and some of the way was very bad going. Have camped by the side of a little pond of water but no wood. Have passed three graves.

[*Austin*] Monday, June 5th — Today we had very bad roads; passed 3 graves. Wm and Lucretia got mad.

[*Goodell*] June 6th.   The wind blows some this morning. Last night the cattle were frightened by the wolves. Crossed

a creek and camped about a mile west of it. The United
States mail have camped here with us. I have written a letter
to Jane Pelton.

[*Austin*] Tuesday, June 6th.   Today we have passed four
graves; very sandy road. Wind blew hard. Buffalo chips is all
the wood we have. Today I set up my stocking.

[*Goodell*] June 7th.   Very pleasant this morning. The baby
is not very well. He has taken a very hard cold. Mrs.
Anderson has lost three head of cattle and her son has lost
one. They have most all gone after them.

[*Austin*] Wednesday, June 7th — Was obliged to stop on
account of Mr. Anderson loosing his cattle, 4 head. Mr.
Hammond went to look for them, and has not got back at
night. I found A.B. writing his likeness.

[*Goodell*] June 8th.   Mr. Hammond has not come yet. We
are almost afraid he has got lost among the bluffs. We shall
not go far today. Mr. Anderson and Mr. Wright have gone
to look for him. It is almost dark and they have not got back
yet. We are afraid they have not found him.

[*Austin*] Thursday, the 8th — Mr. H. has not got back yet.
Mr. Anderson and Mr. Write went after Mr. H — has not
found him yet.

[*Goodell*] June 9th.   We have caught up with the Ebey
company, they have laid over on account of one of their
company being sick. He died today and was burried about an
hour after. We have just heard from Mr. Anderson and Mr.
Wright. They have not found Mr. Hammond yet. They
think the Indians have taken him. Mrs. Anderson found her
cattle in Mr. Ebey's company, they had strayed away at
night.

[*Austin*] Friday, June 9th — Mr. H is not found yet.
Overtook Mr. Ebey and Company. One of his men died and

we saw him buried. His name was James Wood. He died with no relation near him. Was buried in about one hour after he died, without a coffin.

[*Goodell*] June 10th.   We have traveled about twenty miles. It is very cold this morning. The baby is almost froze. Mr. Anderson and Mr. Wright came back this evening. They did not find Mr. Hammond, but they found horse tracks and three pony tracks, two each side of them and one behind and it is thought he has been taken by the Indians.

[*Austin*] Saturday, June 10th — Mr. A. has not got back yet. We camped near the river. At night Mr. A. has got back but has not found Mr. H.

[*Goodell*] June 11th.   And today is Sunday again. O what Sundays. There is nothing that seems like the Sabbath. I have been washing a little. O how glad I shall be if we can ever see any thing but the plains. Today we have ascended a high sandy bluff, the roads are very sandy along here.

[*Austin*] Sunday, June 11th — We have traveled all day today; camped near some traders — 2 white men and 2 Indians near the river.

[*Goodell*] June 12th.   We crossed Castle River this morning. William killed a rattlesnake. It was the first one I ever saw. We have camped beside Platte River tonight. The mosquitoes are thick enough to eat a person up and not know where you have gone to. Have passed two graves today.

[*Austin*] Monday, June 12th.   Today we passed two graves.

[*Goodell*] June 13th.   Crossed Crab Creek this morning. There was an Indian Wigwam and a tent and a white man with a squaw for a wife. Elizabeth has a very hard pain in her right shoulder. We have passed two graves, one of them a new one, died the seventh of June. He was a brother of one of the women in our company she feels very bad about it. We have camped opposite the Bluffs ruins. One of the oxens feet is lame tonight.

[*Austin*] Tuesday, 13th — We crossed Crab Creek this morning; saw an Indian wigwam; passed two graves where there was a man and woman buried — a brother of Mrs. Tell. Passed two graves that were dug but no one in them

[*Goodell*] June 14th. When we left our camping place this morning I thought we would get to Chimney Rock by night, but we have not. We do not get along very fast. Mrs. Meeker who has been sick is some better today, but not able to be up. We passed two graves today, one new one, died the 18th of May, the same day we crossed the Missouri River. The other one was 1850. We camped about one-half mile from an Indian Wigwam east of us and a mile from one west of us.

[*Austin*] Wednesday, June 14th — Today we started from Ancient Bluff ruins — have been in sight of Castle Rock; all day today and yesterday; have passed old Castle Rock; camped near a trading station kept by white men and Indians. It storms very hard tonight; have passed 2 graves; are in sight of another Indian wigwam. I was taken with the reumatism yesterday, and is not much better today.

[*Goodell*] June 15th. We had a very hard storm last night and it is very warm this morning. I guess there will be another before night. Stopped at a wigwam this morning. William bought a pair of mocassins. We have stopped opposite Chimney Rock to feed. It looks very much like another storm. It has been storming and is getting colder. Camped beside the Platte River.

[*Austin*] Thursday, June 15th — This morning we passed another trading station. Wm. bought him a pair of moccains; stopped at noon opposite Chimney Rock; camped near the river; Chimney Rock is still in sight. My Shoulder is still very lame; passed one grave today.

[*Goodell*] June 16th. This morning there is a man here going to California on horse back. He crossed Missouri River the 4th of June. He has stopped at the camp this morning to get his breakfast.

[*Austin*] Friday, 16th — Passed two graves today; passed Hatt's [Scotts?] Bluffs; camped near the river. My Rheumatism is some better today.

[*Goodell*] June 17th. Mrs. Meeker was taken sick this morning and we have stopped early tonight on her account. Mary is doing her washing and I am going to wash out a few things. Lib is not very well this morning. William bought her a pair of mocassins.

[*Austin*] Saturday, June 17th — I have laid abed all day today; my shoulder is worse. Wm. bought me a pair of moccasins today.

[*Goodell*] June 18th. This morning we left the Meeker company. Mrs. Meeker is no better they do not think she will live. It does not seem right to leave this morning. I think we ought to stay until tomorrow morning, but some of them think we ought to go so we started and went about 7 miles. Mr. Judsons oxen got frightened at some Indians and ran off side ways and came near upsetting the wagon. We drove down to the river where there was a camp and staid there. It stormed quite hard. Elizabeth has been washing. We have not had a chance to wash all before since we left home. William has been writing to his father and I have been writing some in my letters. We will send them tomorrow from the fort.

[*Austin*] Sunday, June 18th — We left Mr. Meeker's camp this morning. Mrs. M. is not expected to live. We traveled 7 miles and stopped with a California company. I did all our washing — the first good chance we have had to wash. We have plenty good wood and water.

[*Goodell*] June 19th.   This morning we have got ready for another start. We are fifteen miles from the fort. We got to the fort a little after noon and camped about two miles west of it. We heard from the company we left and Mrs. Meeker died last night. William and Charley have gone on ahead to see if they can see anything of the Ebey company. They have just got back and the Ebey's are about a mile from here.

[*Austin*] Monday, 19th of June — We have just got to the Fort about noon. Wm. went over and took our letters. We traveled a few miles and camped with a California Company. Wm. and Charlie went over the hills to find Ebey's Company. They found them about three-quarters of a mile off. We expect to overtake them in the morning. Mrs. M. [Meeker] died this morning.

[*Goodell*] June 20th.   We have come up to the Ebey camp. They are stopping on account of a sick man. He was taken this morning cramping. They do not think he will live. That man is dead, he died about 5 o'clock. He leaves a wife and four children. There are two or three in the camp that are not very well. There is another man just taken cramping but I guess he will get over it.

[*Austin*] Tuesday, 20th of June — This morning early there were four Indians with their wigwams on their ponies. Went by our camp. After breakfast we started to catch up with Ebey's folks. They have a sick man in their company, so can't travel this forenoon. The man died this afternoon. He was well last night but now is dead.

[*Goodell*] June 21st.   The morning we got a very early start. We have had very hard roads to travel over and some bad hills to go up and down. It is nothing but up and down hill as far as we can see.

[*Austin*] Wednesday, the 21st of June — This morning Mr. Ebey & Company and we started together from the place where they buried Mr. Burr. We traveled about 20 miles over the Black Hills; camped where there is no water; passed 4 graves.

[*Goodell*] June 22.   We stopped at a place today where there are four or five springs and a trading post. A Frenchman and a squaw wife she had a little baby five weeks old. We have camped by a little stream of water and it is twelve miles before we come to any more water.

[*Austin*] Thursday, the 22nd — We got water today at noon where there are a great many springs of clear water; camped early near a stream of water; passed 4 graves; better roads than yesterday.

[*Goodell*] June 23rd.   Today we have passed some more trading posts, and came down one pretty bad hill. The baby is very cross today. We have camped on the bank of the Platte.

[*Austin*] Friday, 23rd of June — We stopped on the Platte River and water the cattle at noon; no feed; at night stopped near the river — found good grass.

[*Goodell*] June 24th.   The roads are very bad. We have passed over some high hills. The road is good where it is level. We have camped by a river not more than three miles where we were at noon. It was very late when we stopped tonight.

[*Austin*] Saturday, 24th — We traveled over very bad roads — dreadfully bad roads — camped after dark near the river.

[*Goodell*] June 25th.   Traveled about three miles this morning and have camped by the side of the river. They have swum the oxen across the river to feed. We shall stay until Tuesday morning.

[*Austin*] Sunday 25 — We came 4 miles and stopped near the river and spent the day.

[*Goodell*] June 26th. Elizabeth is washing this morning and Mary is going to wash this afternoon. Mr. King has been hunting and has killed a deer. He has divided it in the camp so we shall all have a taste of it.

[*Austin*] Monday, the 26th — We have laid by all day today. I washed and baked — had pot pie for supper.

[*Goodell*] June 27th. Mary Wright is sick this morning. It is very warm. W. Ebey came very near drowning. They had been swimming the cattle across to yoke up and he swam across after and the current was so strong that it tired him almost out. His father waded in and got a hold of his hand and helped him out. We have camped on the bank of the river the feed is very poor. The Meekers are fourteen miles behind us. Some of the company have lost a child.

[*Austin*] Tuesday, the 27th — We started this morning on our way. Passed one grave.

[*Goodell*] June 28th. I have had a very hard head ache all day. Old Mrs. Ebey was taken with Cholera about noon, and one of Mr. Leslies boys is sick. There was a Dr. here to see them. He gave them Calomel.

[*Austin*] Wednesday, the 28th — I have not walked any today. I have not been well. Mrs. Ebey was taken sick about an hour before we stopped at noon. Mr. Less' [Leslie's] boy was taken sick today. They called the doctor.

[*Goodell*] June 29th. Mrs. Ebey is better this morning. The cattle got frightened at a horse running right out of the woods towards them. They run some ways, broke the tongue and one yoke for Mr. Judson and broke a bow for us. Camped at noon and put the cattle across the river.

[*Austin*] Thursday, 29th June — We stopped at noon and drove the cattle across the river, and stayed all night to prepare for a long journey the next day. The oxen ran away and Charley got hurt.

[*Goodell*] June 30th.   The men went and tried to swim the cattle back this morning but the current was so strong that they could not get them in. They are going to wait till the river goes down and then try again. The wind has blown very hard today.

[*Austin*] Friday, the 30th — The men could not get the cattle over the river. We were obliged to stay all today.

[*Goodell*] July 1st.   The men have had to drive the cattle down to the bridge this morning. We started about noon and come about ten miles. The wind and dust has blown like fury. Mr. Anderson and Wright passed us yesterday. They have left the Meeker company.

[*Austin*] Saturday, July 1st — They drove the cattle up to the bridge to get them across. We got started about noon and traveled 10 miles.

[*Goodell*] July 2nd.   We have started again. Last night we camped beside a little stream. Alkali in it. The horses got away last night so we did not get a very early start. We crossed Prospect Hill. We could see a great ways. Stopped at Willow spring and watered the cattle. Camped at night by the side of a little creek of clear cool water. The feed was not very good for the cattle. We did not have any wood but sage brush.

[*Austin*] Sunday, July 2nd — We started this morning and traveled abut 15 miles and camped near a creek.

[*Goodell*] July 3rd.   We have got to Independence Rock about noon. William and I went around it. Lib and Lucretia and the rest of the girls went over it. There is a wagon and tent on top of it. I do not see any names on it that I know.

[*Austin*] Monday, the third — We got to Independence Rock about noon and stopped. We went to the rock and around it.

[*Goodell*] July 4th.   I would like to be where I was last fourth at Vermillion. We left the Rock this morning and came about a mile and crossed the Sweet Water River. Five miles farther we passed Devils gate   we did not go very near it. We camped about six miles from it about two in the afternoon. William has gone back to a trading post to see about swopping some of his cattle, they are getting lame.

[*Austin*] Tuesday, July 4th — We left the rock this morning and camped 9 miles west. Mr. Anderson and Miller camped near by. Lucretia and I went to the camps at night.

[*Goodell*] July 5th.   Traveled about sixteen miles. Mr. Anderson and Miller are just ahead of us. Mr. Cameron joined our company today. William shod one of our steers.

[*Austin*] Wednesday, July 5th — We started this morning after Anderson and Miller and traveled in sight of them, but lost sight of them before night. Mr. Cannon Joined our company today. Wm. shod one steer today.

[*Goodell*] July 6th.   Crossed Sweet Water River three times. Stopped at two P.M. to shoe more cattle. William shod both steers and one of the old cattle. There was a child fell out of a wagon and hurt quite bad.

[*Austin*] Thursday, the 6th — Crossed over water three times today. Stopped about two to shoe some cattle.

[*Goodell*] July 7th.   Crossed Sweet Water once today and camped by the river. Mr. Judson shod one of his old cattle. Frank went hunting and killed an Antelope.

[*Austin*] Friday, the 7th — We traveled 3 miles, then crossed the Sweetwater and went three or four miles up the river and camped, to shoe some more cattle. We stopped the other side of the river.

[*Goodell*] July 8th.   This morning we met about one dozen men and two women on mules, and many more in wagons. They were from California. They started the second day of

June. We traveled about twenty miles without stopping. We crossed Sweet Water three times today. One of Mr. Millers men has just come to our camp. He has been hunting and will stay with us tonight.

[*Austin*] Saturday, July 8th — We traveled today about 20 miles without stopping; met a great many men and women on mules from California. They started the second day of June.

[*Goodell*] July 9th.   We have traveled over some very rough roads today. Camped on Strawberry creek. Strawberries are just in blossom. It is very cold tonight. Last night it froze water as thick as glass.

[*Austin*] Sunday, the 9th — We left John at the place we left this morning. He was going to wait for Miller's train. We traveled 15 miles and stopped by Strawberry Creek. We found bad roads.

[*Goodell*] July 10th.   We crossed a branch of Sweet Water this morning and about noon we crossed Sweet Water for the last time. We passed more packers at noon. It is ten miles from the river to the pass. We have camped down on the bottom of Sweet Water about five miles from the ford. First-rate grass.

[*Austin*] Monday, 10th July — We crossed Sweetwater today for the last time; met some more packers. Camped about five miles from the ford. Plenty of good grass and water.

[*Goodell*] July 11th.   Today we have passed through to the west side of the pass. Traveled about ten miles. Stopped about two at Pacific Creek. Not much grass and poor water.

[*Austin*] Tuesday, the 11th — Today we stopped about 2 miles west of the pass on Pacific Creek. Poor water & grass.

[*Goodell*] July 12th.   We traveled about twenty miles today without water. We camped at little Sandy Creek. The cattle were most choked. There is a girl in the company just behind us that wants to get in this company and go to Oregon and live with a brother.

[*Austin*] Wednesday, 12th July — Stopped and camped on Little Sandy River; a grave on each hill to be seen.

[*Goodell*] July 13th.   We traveled six miles then crossed Big Sandy then up the creek six miles farther and camped where there was good grass, water and wood.

[*Austin*] Thursday, the 13ths — We traveled about 15 miles today and camped by Big Sandy.

[*Goodell*] July 14th.   We did not start till nine or ten o'clock this morning. We drove about twelve miles then stopped and waited till about five P.M. Then we started and did not stop again until eleven P.M. We started again about three in the morning. We have come down some very long steep and stony hills. We reached Green River about ten and watered the cattle. We came on to the ferry and crossed about noon, then we drove down the river two or three miles and camped. Not very good grass.

[*Austin*] Friday, 14th — We started this morning on the way to Green River; traveled until noon and stopped till 3 and started. Traveled till about 12 at night, then stopped until three in the morning.

[*Goodell*   No entry for the 15th.]

[*Austin*] Saturday, 15th July — Today we have passed some very bad roads; had hard work to get the cattle along; had the wagons ferried over, but the cattle swam over. Mr Hadley [Headley] and three other wagons camped on the other side. We camped about two miles down the river.

[*Goodell*] July 16.   We started about ten this morning and came up a very steep hill. We have gone up and down hill most all the way from the ferry. We have camped on Lost River. William caught a trout for supper and a sucker. It looked some different from those we catch at the lake. Elizabeth set some salt rising emptins [yeast starter] and they are up and she is going to bake some light bread. It will be the first salt rising we have had.

[*Austin*] Sunday, 16th — We started from Green River this morning and came about 8 miles and stopped on Lost River and stayed all night; had some trout for supper. There is a man just came to go with Mr. Judson.

[*Goodell*] July 17th.   Today Mr. Judson and William traded off some of their oxen and got new ones. Mr. Judson got two yoke for three and William had to give $25. to boot between his cattle. We have laid over one day to rest the oxen. Lib is washing. Jessie was here this morning. Miller and company are two miles back. William and Mr. Judson are going to take a man together through to Oregon. I wrote a letter from here to Phoebe. Lib caught a fish.

[*Austin*] Monday, 17th July — We have all been washing today. Wm. traded oxen — paid 25 dollars to boot. Mr. Miller has camped two miles below us. Jessy came up where we were camped. L.R. and John and I went fishing. I caught three fish.

[*Goodell*] July 18th.   Today we have traveled twenty-one miles. Have climed some long steep hills. The baby is five months old today. We did not find any grass until night and it was poor.

[*Austin*] Tuesday, 18th — We traveled 21 miles today before we could find grass for the cattle, and then found very poor feed.

[*Goodell*] July 19th.   We did not travel but six miles today, but it is the roughest road we have seen yet. We camped near Hams fork. Lib went to a snow bank and got some snow and ice. Grass is good.

[*Austin*] Wednesday, 19th — We came six miles today —the

worst hills we have had; stopped where the grass was good. I got some snow to eat.

[*Goodell*] July 20th.   We have traveled sixteen miles over mountains and rough roads.

[*Austin*] Wednesday, July 20th — We have come 16 miles today over high hills or mountains.

[*Goodell*] July 21st.   Today we crossed Smith's fork. It was bad crossing. We came to a Mormon toll bridge but the company would not pay him anything. Then he started to steal our cattle. We camped on Bear River.

[*Austin*] Friday, 21st — Today we crossed Smith's Fork and crossed the Mormon bridge but did not pay; some very rocky roads and some very good roads; camped on Bear River.

[*Goodell*] July 22nd.   Today we crossed a mountain two miles going to the summit and three miles to foot on the west side. Camped on Bear River. Mosquitoes were very bad.

[*Austin*] Saturday, 22nd July — Today we have had some mountains to cross. We camped on Bear River.

[*Goodell*] July 23rd.   Have traveled about ten miles and camped by a stream of first-rate water. The roads have been good.

[*Austin*] Sunday, 23d — We traveled about 10 miles and camped near a beautiful creek.

[*Goodell*] July 24th.   Today we have traveled about ten miles and stopped by a little spring of cold water, but it is very hard. Have not had any very soft water since we came west of the mountains.

[*Austin*] Monday, July 24th — Today we have come about 10 miles and stopped by a spring; good grass and water. I baked pumpkin pies.

[*Goodell*] July 25th.   Today we have had a long drive twenty-one or twenty-two miles. We have camped beside a little stream where there are two beautiful water falls. Capt. Grant was here this morning.

[*Austin*] Tuesday, 25th July — We traveled about 20 miles today — camped near a waterfall in sight of Soda Springs.

[*Goodell*] July 26th. We came to the springs this morning. They are a great sight and there was a great many of them. We put some Lemon syrup in the water and it was very good. We passed a very large spring after we took the Oregon road.

[*Austin*] Wednesday, the 26th — Today we passed by the Soda Springs; camped near a stream of good water; good grass; willows to burn. Two Indians visited our camp.

[*Goodell*] July 27th. We traveled about twenty miles today and crossed a very bad creek. We stopped at noon. One of Mr. Judson's cattle and one of Charles is sick. Have passed three or four Indians.

[*Austin* No entry for the 27th.]

[*Goodell*] July 28th. Today some of the cattle are lame and some are sick so we have laid by. Elizabeth is sick this morning. Charlies ox is dead. We sold 15 # of sugar at 40¢ and 1 # of lard at 30¢.

[*Austin*] Friday, 28th — We have stopped all day here today on account of sick cattle — one of Mr. Judson's oxen died. The one that Charlie drove. Wm. sold 15 pounds of sugar to a French man.

[*Goodell*] July 29th. Have traveled all day. We stopped at a beautiful spring at noon and at night we camped by a small creek of good water. Grass very good. It has rained some today.

[*Austin*] Saturday, 29th July — Today we have traveled about 14 miles and camped; have crossed some bad hills and a great many beautiful springs.

[*Goodell*] July 30th. We have laid by for half a day on

account of the cattle, some are lame and some are sick. Have started on again. Have had some bad roads and some good ones. We have got out of the mountains.

[*Austin*] Sunday, 30th — Laid by a half day today, then started and traveled about 6 miles. I baked the last of the second sack of flour — made it into cake.

[NOTE: All that follows is written by Austin. Goodell does no writing until August 11th.]

[*Austin*] Monday 31st — Today we traveled 14 miles and camped by Snake River.

August 1st — Tuesday   We crossed Snake River today; got across about 2:00 in the afternoon — traveled about 3 miles, and camped by a spring; paid 5 dollars a wagon.

August 2nd — Wednesday   We traveled about 9 miles and stopped by a creek. I did our washing. I baked out of the 3rd sack of flour today.

Thursday, August 3d — We stayed in the same place until the sun rose about 2 hours high then started and traveled until 10:00, then stopped and started again early in the morning; got through about 5:00 in the afternoon.

Friday, August 4th — Today we started very early in the morning and traveled all day without stopping, and when we got through we found very little water; the cattle could not get enough to drink; had to go a mile after it, at the foot of a mountain.

Saturday, 5th — We traveled today about 9 miles and camped by a beautiful creek. Several Indians and squaws came to the camp a begging. I went in swimming.

Sunday, 6th — We traveled 5 miles today and stopped. I walked all the way by the bank of the river; started again about sundown & traveled 5 or 6 miles and stopped till morning, then started again.

Monday, the 7th — We started this morning early and

traveled until afternoon before we came to water. The creek was narrow and deep; good water and grass; no wood, but a little sage. I hope in six weeks we shall be to the place of our destination.

Tuesday, 8th — Today we traveled 12 miles and camped. George Beam killed a deer. Mr. Headley killed 4 sage hens.

Wednesday, — We had our breakfast out of some of the venison. We traveled over 10 miles of the worst road that ever was traveled. Camped near a creek. Wood very scarce.

Thursday, 10th — Today we traveled 15 miles and camped. I washed and used all our soap.

[*Goodell*] August 11th. We laid by today near a small branch. Mr. Judson cut off the back end of his wagon box. William took the sideboards off from ours and lowered the bows some. Lucretia gave away her trunk and packed her clothes in sacks. Threw away the trunk they carried their dishes in. Elizabeth washed this afternoon and after she got done she went and caught some fish. The water here is good and the grass too, but wood is hard to get. We have to keep a good lookout for Indians about this quarter.

[*Austin*] Friday, 11th — We laid by till noon. Mr. Judson cut off his wagon box. We camped near a river. Ursula and I waded the river. I caught 3 fish — one of them was the largest that had been caught in the company.

[Goodell makes no entries until the 16th.]

[*Austin*] Saturday, August 12th — We traveled 12 miles today and camped on the top of a hill; had to go to the river after water.

Sunday, 13th — We have traveled 16 miles and camped by a spring branch.

Monday, 14th — Today we traveled 8 miles and stopped at noon by a spring where we found a card with several names;

stopped at night by some mud holes where we had to use the water; 20 miles today.

Tuesday, 15th — We traveled 18 miles and camped where we had poor water. I have not walked any today nor yesterday.

[*Goodell*] August 16th.   Today we have had some very bad road along side hills which were very steep. Two Indians came to us on one of the side hills. They were very ugly looking fellows. They followed us to camp and staid there until after supper. Sarah Cannon gave them some bread and then they went off. We passed some very high rocks. They were as white as marble and stood separate from each other, some very tall and some very short. Some place there would be three or four piled together. They were quite a curiosity. It is called the Devil's Churchyard.

[*Austin*] Wednesday, 16th — We traveled today about 16 miles and camped by a spring branch. Two Indians came to camp and stayed till after supper, but they did not get much. Sarah C. gave them some bread; we passed over some very bad roads; saw a great many high rocks that were a great curiosity — white as marble — called by some the Devil's Church Yard.

[*Goodell*] August 17th.   We have had some very bad road today over the mountains and very stony and some pretty steep. They had to double teams up the last one. We camped where there was very little water. There were holes dug along in a branch where the water stood. Some packers overtook us just before we got to camp. One of them was John Grant. One of Mr. Hardy's oxen got out and Dick Bradley went back to stay with it until it was able to travel again. The Indians that were at the camp last night were here again this morning, but did not stay long. They went away across the mountains to Fort Boise.

[*Austin*] Thursday, 17th — The Indians came to the camp this morning. We traveled today until dark and then were obliged to stop where the men had to dig hole in the ditch to get water — a hard day's journey over rocks and mountains; one of Mt. H's oxen got tired out and they left him on the road; Dick went back to stay with him. A train of packers passed by us tonight and went on to find water.

[*Goodell*] August 18th. We left our camp ground and traveled about five or six miles and stopped by a little spring of water. One of our oxen is lame this morning and some of the rest of the company have lame cattle so we lay by today to wash and bake. Freddie is six months today and we have just been weighing him and he weighs 18½ pounds. Mr. Headley and Whitesall are taking the projections off their wagons. I swapped eight pounds of sugar with Mrs. Whitesall for four lbs. of soap. D. Bradley has just got back but he has not brought the ox. He is going back again in the morning.

[*Austin*] Friday, Aug. 18th — We started this morning and came about two miles and stopped by a small branch of water; willows to burn. I set in tins & baked light bread — two nice loaves, & then washed in the evening.

[*Goodell*] August 19th. Today we traveled about 12 miles in a canyon and came to the old road. We camped at night by an old pond and small spring a little ways off. Capt. Grant came up after dark with a lot of his men and camped a little ways from us. I wrote two letters to send in by him to Vermillon and one to Grand Mound. George Beam killed two or three sage hens and Frank Van Woermer killed one and some of the rest got some hens and rabbits. We have got a good long drive tomorrow to Boise River.

[*Austin*] Saturday, Aug. 19th — We have traveled about 12 miles today and stopped for Mr. H's ox. He is some better tonight. Capt. Grant's Company has caught up with us.

Maria has written a letter to Mr. G. and one home and she sent them on by him; got to the old road.

[*Goodell*] August 20th.   Today we have traveled about 20 miles but we did not intend to go more than ten or fifteen, but as we were mistaken about the distance, we had to travel a long time after dark. We started about the time Capt. Grant did and traveled 5 miles farther to White Horse Creek and stopped to wait a while for Headley's ox. We did not wait very long. We came in sight of Boise River just before dark, but we did not get to the river until long after dark. There were two or three hills to come down and rather steep. We were so tired when we got to camp that we went to sleep without our supper. There was no watch that night.

[*Austin*] Sunday, August 20th — We started this morning about the time Capt. Grant did; stopped 5 miles on a branch to let the cattle rest and drink; then started with the intention of reaching Boise River, 15 miles from where we camped last night. We got to Boise River about 2 hours after dark. We were so tired that we went to bed without supper, and were glad to get rest. So it was called 15 miles, but it seemed more like 30.

[*Goodell*] August 21st.   Today we have remained in camp. Two Indians came up before breakfast. One of them went away and came back after breakfast with two or three squaws and their young ones. Some of the company are washing, some are baking and cooking beans and other eatables for another long drive. William has swapped my shawl, an old coat, pants and shirt for a pony. Boise River is as pretty a stream as we have seen. The current is very swift and all along the bank are Balm of Gilead trees. Whitesall caught some fish.

[*Austin*] Monday, August 21st — Today we laid by all day; had a long, steep hill to go down to get to the river. There were several Indians came to the camp to trade their ponies. Wm. traded off Mariah's shawl, a shirt and coat and pants for a pony. Then the Indians started off, but came back again toward night.

[*Goodell*] August 22nd.   As we were leaving camp this morning we saw four wagons on the hill. We stopped and waited for a while for them to catch up with us as they seemed to be driving very fast. One man came on ahead and said that their train had been attacked by Indians the Saturday before and two men were shot from their horses and another very badly wounded. They shot two Indians and lost five horses. We traveled about twelve miles and camped on Boise River. The man that was wounded died about 12 o'clock. I am 23 years old today.

[*Austin*] Tuesday, August 22nd — This morning just as we were about ready to start we saw four wagons coming, and when they had caught up with us we found they had had trouble with the Indians. They had lost two men and one wounded. They killed two Indians and gave up 5 horses. traveled 12 or 15 miles and camped on Boise River. A man that was shot died about twelve o'c at night.

[*Goodell*] August 23rd.   Last night an Indian came to our camp and said he had a paper for Mr. Ebey. He read it. It was from Capt. Grant and said there had been four wagons attacked by Indians and all the people killed about four or six miles ahead, told him to keep out a good watch for them.[2] We all feel some frightened. They had partly finished burying the bodies and wanted us to finish burying them when we

---

[2] This was the famous or infamous, Ward massacre, which took place near the present Idaho town of Middleton on August 20, 1854. This was a wagon train from Missouri under Captain Alexander Ward. Eighteen of the party were killed in an attack by the Wihinast Indians, a band of the Shoshone Indian tribe. Two boys survived the attack, Newton and William Ward. The boys went on with other wagon trains to become citizens respectively of Washington and California. There is a monument at the scene of the battle. Cornelius J. Brosnan, *History of the State of Idaho* (N.Y., 1948), 120-21.

came along. The Indians had emptied the feather bed on the ground and taken the tick. The company had camped on the top of a little hill and they suppose the Indians had hid in the sage brush. We did not like to stay there very long. The Indian says one little boy came to the Fort with an arrow in his flesh.

[*Austin*] Wednesday, 23rd — We traveled 15 miles. There was an Indian who met us this afternoon and brought a letter from Capt. Grant, stating that the Indians had killed all of one train — 18 in all. One boy had made his escape; 10 men and 8 women and children killed. The Indian stayed with the packers but ate with the Ebey folks.

[*Austin*] Wednesday, 23rd [*Second entry.*] We started this morning and came about a mile and then stopped on a rise of ground, where they had dug a grave for the man who died last night. The man was buried and we came on, stopped at noon on the river bottom, as we had traveled along the bottom all the morning. We came as far as the road went, where the old ford was, but as it was not a good crossing, the wagons were taken back about one mile, where they could get up the hill. The women all climbed the hill where the wagons stopped. We traveled a few miles and descended the hill again, where an Indian met the company bringing a letter from Capt. Grant to Mr. Ebey, warning them of the danger there was of Indians, stating that there had been a company of 5 wagons, all killed but one boy.

[*Goodell*] August 24th.   We camped last night on the point of a hill not far from the river. The ground below us is covered with tall grass. Some of the men have mowed some of it down. We got to Ft. Boise today. Two Indians came to the camp last night all dressed up with little looking glasses on their necks. We kept a good watch on them and today after we had got within two or three miles of the fort there were as many as one hundred and fifty came out to meet us. We felt a good deal frightened when we saw them at first, but when the squaws came up they had peas and potatoes to sell or swap with us. They say they are the Nez Percies Indians.

[*Austin*] Thursday, Aug. 24th — We passed by the place today where the Indians killed the emigrants — crossed Boise River.

[*Austin*] Thursday, 24th — [*Second entry.*] We started this morning and traveled about 3 miles to the place where the battle was fought. It was a solemn scene. Some of the company stopped to finish burying the dead, which was partly buried; crossed Boise River about noon; are in hopes of reaching Fort Boise this afternoon. We traveled several miles and camped on the side hill; where in great fear of Indians. There were two Indians met us this afternoon, of the Pearcies [Nez Perces] and say there are a great many at the fort.

[*Goodell*] August 25th. We crossed the river last night and camped. Bought a lot of dried salmon and cooked some for supper. An old Indian came and begged something to eat. I gave him a piece of the salmon. The people at the fort say the Nez Pierce Indians are friendly to the whites. They want to travel with us until we get to the Grand Round [Grande Ronde]. They are going to camp with us tonight. They have got lots of horses packed with dried salmon. There are some good looking squaws, some real handsome ones. They say they are afraid of the Snake Indians and that is the reason they want to travel with us.

[*Austin*] Friday, 25th — This morning we started early for Fort Boise, and on our way about 100 Indians & Squaws met us on their ponies. We were somewhat frightened at first, but we soon found that they were friendly and had potatoes and peas at the fort to sell. We got to the fort about noon, and were ferried over this afternoon. I sold one of my dresses to an Indian for one dollar and we swapped some of the baby's clothes for some peas.

[Goodell makes no entries until October 6th.]

[*Austin*] Saturday, 26th — We traveled 15 miles today and camped on Mathews [Malheur?] River. Some of the Indians came up at night and camped with us. Garner and Gardner fell out, so Gardner went with the Indians. They had 300 horses.

Sunday, 27th — We traveled today 22 miles and camped near the Indians again. Lucretia bought her a pair of moccasins.

Monday, August 28th — Today we traveled twelve miles and camped near Burnt River. The Indians went on and left us. We burned a wagon for wood.

Tuesday, the 29th — This morning we had nothing but mountains to go over. We have crossed Burnt River 4 times this forenoon. I waded the first ford, which was wide but not deep. We crossed the river 5 times this afternoon.

Wednesday, 30th — We traveled twelve miles today and camped on the hill.

Thursday, 31st — We traveled 12 miles today & camped at the end of Burnt River; no water nor wood near. We had many mountains to cross. This afternoon, chips to burn.

Friday, Sept. 1st — We traveled 13 miles today & camped at Powder River. Two Indians seen after dark; Elick [Alec] fired at them. It has been cold all day.

Saturday, Sept. 2nd — We traveled today about 12 miles and camped at Powder River.   been cold today.

Sunday, 3d — We traveled about 6 miles when a man met us who was going through to Washington. It has been cold today. We got to the Round [Grande Ronde] about 4 o'clock in the afternoon.

Monday, Sept. 4th — We traveled 8 miles today and stopped near a stream of water at the foot of the mountains. A great many Indians came to trade. It rained all night last night.

Tuesday, Sept. 5th — Today we traveled 12 miles over the mountains and through the rain; stopped at Grand Ronde River — a beautiful place surrounded by pine trees. It rained all night last night.

Wednesday, Sept. 6th — We traveled today 20 miles over very bad roads. We met the soldiers who were going back to fight the Indians. I was very lame at night when we stopped walking.

Thursday, Sept. 7th — Today we traveled 15 miles, which brought us to the Umatilla Valley. We camped at the foot of the mountains near a spring; a great many Indians near.

Friday, Sept 8th — We started this morning ahead of Mr. Ebey. They were looking for their horses. Mr. Cannon took the road to the dalles; we came on the road to the Sound. Mr. E [Ebey] caught up with us in the afternoon. We stopped near a spring 10 miles from the foot of the Blue Mountains. Mr. Yantis and Mr. Kirtland camped near.

Saturday, Sept. 9th — It was late this morning before we started, on account of Mr. Ebey's horses that were gone. We traveled 15 miles and camped near a creek. Mr. Yantis camped on the opposite side of creek.

Sunday, Sept. 10th — We traveled today 15 miles and camped on Walla [Walla] River. Crossed it at noon. Mr. Yantis had an Indian guide. We traveled about 15 miles.

Monday, Sept. 11th — We started this morning early and traveled about 5 miles, & reached Fort Walla Walla, but could not get ferried over until tomorrow. We crossed the Walla Walla River 4 times before we got to the Fort.

Tuesday, Sept. 12th — We got ferried across the Columbia

River today; paid 8 dollars a wagon, one dollar a head for cattle. Traveled 3 miles up the river and camped near Mr. Yantis folks.

Wednesday, Sept. 13th — We started this morning early and traveled about 15 miles up the Columbia River. Mr. Yantis folks had not started when we started.   camped on the river bank. Plenty of Indians around and good grass.

Thursday, Sept. 14th — We traveled 14 miles today, and camped on the river again; forded the river in the morning — the Yakima River.

Friday, Sept. 15th — We traveled 17 miles and camped near very poor water; could not get water fit to cook in.

Saturday, Sept. 16th — We traveled today 8 miles. We lost our way, which made it 14 [miles] that we traveled, and when we got to water it was very poor, but some better than the water we had last night.

Sunday, Sept. 17th — We traveled 8 miles today and camped at a spring — good water and grass. We hauled wood about a mile. An Indian came to the camp and stayed all night.

Monday, Sept. 18th — Traveled twelve miles today. The Indian who stayed all night with Mr. Ebey came out to meet us. It was after dark before we got to the river.

Tuesday, Sept. 19th — We traveled about 10 miles today, and camped. Met Mr. Meeker on his way to meet his father. The Indians brought potatoes to sell, but Charlie and William did not get any.

Wednesday, Sept. 20th — We traveled 12 miles today and camped in the first pine woods we have seen since we left the Blue Mountains. The road leaves the river here to turn to the right.

Thursday, Sept. 21st — We have traveled 15 miles today, up a gradual ascent, and down a tremendously bad descent to the foot of the Cascade Mountains, where we refreshed ourselves by drinking out of the Naches River; camped near the river on the east side of the Cascade Mts.

Friday, Sept. 22 — We traveled 10 or 15 miles today, up the Naches River & crossed it 14 times;[3] very bad crossing —swift current and very rocky.

Saturday, Sept. 23 — We traveled 10 or 11 miles today; crossed the river 11 times, and camped where we had good grass.

Sunday, Sept. 24th — We crossed the river 32 times before we met Mr. G. [Goodell, Sr.] and were about to cross it again when he rode up. It was joyful times to meet him. We traveled about twelve miles and camped, it began to rain before we got through supper and rained nearly all night.

Monday, Sept. 25th — We traveled 8 miles & camped where the men were at work on the road.

Tuesday, Sept 26th — We traveled 2 miles and camped in the woods. Mr. G. and I rode on in the morning, and he killed a grouse for supper. Mr. King camped a half mile from us. He came up to our camp at night.

Wednesday, Sept. 27th — We traveled about 15 miles and camped. Mr. Judson's wagon turned over, coming down a very bad hill. King's company came up with us about this time. Dick upset his wagon twice coming down the same hill. We crossed Green Water several times in the afternoon; camped in the road; no feed but brouse for the cattle.

Thursday, Sept 28th — We crossed White River 5 times today. Mr. Whitsell and Mr. Kirtland's man passed us today to go after provisions.

---

[3] Lest anyone think that the number of crossings of the little Naches River was excessive, note the remembrance of James Longmire in which he says that they crossed it 68 times in 1853. "Narrative of John Longmire," *Washington Hist. Quart.*, XXIII (Jan., 1932), 47-60, especially 59.

Friday, Sept. 29 — Mr. G. and William left us today &
went on to feed. I baked the last of the flour that Mr. G.
brought. Mr. Ebey gave Mr. Judson's and Van Wormer
some crackers for supper. We were in hopes we should get
through to grass today, but we had to camp in the woods
again.

Saturday, Sept. 30th — Mr. Ebey drove his loose cattle
through, ahead of the wagons to grass. I have just got
through to the prairie down the Cascade Mountains. The
wagons are back, but they will soon be up. They have 8 bad
hills to come up. They came up in about 2 hours after we got
through. Mr. G. & Wm. left here this morning. Charley and
Melang [Melancthon Goodell] then walked 4 miles to get
the flour that Mr. G brought.

Sunday, Oct. 1 — We traveled 4 miles today to near a house
where a man lived who had provisions to sell. He charged 2
dollars a bushell for potatoes, 16 dollars a hundred for flour.
Mr. Judson & Charley bought some more flour.

Monday, 2nd — We have had very bad water today, several
hills to climb, & a bad swamp a quarter of a mile long. Mrs.
Judson & I walked through, Winfield [Ebey] turned over
near the swamp & spilled all the milk. We crossed the river
this morning for the last. There was a log that was laid across
the river half a mile down the river from the ford where we
went across afoot.

Tuesday, Oct. 3d — We traveled only 2 miles today and
camped near the ford of a river; passed two new houses where
no one lived & one where Mr. G. left some potatoes & meat
for us, but could not get any flour. Mr. Whitesell passed us
today on his way to Stillicum [Steilacoom].

Wednesday, Oct. 4th — We forded Puyallup this morning
once. We traveled 10 miles and camped where Mr. Judson

& Ebey did on the top of a hill. Mr. Meeker overtook us at the foot of the hill. Was going on after a team to take hay to the cattle in the mountains.

Thursday, Oct. 5th — We traveled 15 miles today over prairie — good roads, bought 10 pounds of flour.

[*Goodell*] October 6th. This morning Mr. Judson and Charlie got up and started on and crossed the river before breakfast. They thought they would find better feed for their cattle, but they were mistaken. Some left us about noon for home. I think we camped about a quarter of a mile from the Nisqually River. It was a rather lonesome place, just in the edge of the prairie, the woods very dark. I suppose we have got almost to our journey's end. If we had good fresh cattle we would get there tomorrow night very easy.

[*Austin*] Friday, Oct. 6th — We traveled 12 miles today and camped about a mile from a mill where we had to go after water.

[*Goodell*] October 7th. This morning we were almost froze. There was a very hard frost last night. The ground was as white as though there had been snow. We started very early and came within twelve miles of Grand Mound Prairie and stopped at noon. William bought a half bushel of potatoes. We expected that we should not get home until Sunday, but at noon we saw Malancthan coming with a horse team so we hurried ourselves out of the ox wagon and got on board the coach. Holden [Judson] brought out 3 yokes of oxen for each team so we finally all got here Saturday night.

Malancthan brought us in, in a hurry. Mother Goodell had supper all ready when we got there. She had oysters, chickens, potatoes, cabbage, cranberries, blackberries, custard, cake and everything good. O, how glad I was to sit at a table and eat like folks and to sleep in a house on a bedstead.

[*Austin*] Saturday, Oct. 7th — Wm. bought 55 cts. worth of

potatoes of a squaw, but we did not eat any of them.
Malangthen G. came after us with the horses and wagon and
[took] all the women home with him but Mrs. Judson. She
stayed till Holden drove through.

[There are no Goodell entries until October 22nd.]

[*Austin*] Sunday, Oct. 8th — Today Emelyne [Emeline]
and I went over Phoebe's [Phoebe Judson's] & Lucretia
came back with us and stayed till after tea.

[*Austin*] Monday, Oct. 9th — Today I took the things out of
the wagon. Emeline washed.

[*Goodell*] October 22nd. Grand Mound Prairie. Today
there has been preaching here. Mr. Whitworth from Olympia
preached. His text was from Heb. 11 Chap. 4th verse.[4] It has
rained by spells all day.

[Two entries written many years later in Anna Maria
Goodell's diary after a voyage from Washington Territory to
the east coast:]

Sept. 15th., 1865. One year ago today I landed in N.Y. from
the steamer Northern Light. We went to the Park House
and staid till Friday 4 P.M. We had a very pleasant trip
home and no rough weather.

Sept. 17th. One year ago today I reached Vermillion, but
would hardly know the place. I was glad enough to find
myself and children and baggage all safe.

I hope I shall be more contented for the next year to come
than I have been for the past year.

[Notes in the back of Elizabeth Austin's diary:]
    (seen on a tombstone); "He died with poison opening a
    cow."

---

[4] The King James Bible rendition of this verse is "By faith Abel offered unto God a
more excellent sacrifice than Cain, by which he obtained witness that he was righteous,
God testifying of his gifts: and by it he being dead yet speaketh."

A verse written on the grave of a young man who died on the 2nd of August. We camped here the 7th.

"He was a youth far from home,
With friends he chanced to be;
No kindred nor relation,
To know his agony."

Written by Mary Jane Judson & Anna C. Yantis:

As I sit musing here alone,
And watch the evening shades fall,
And think upon the years now gone,
Like setting sunbeams from the West
My spirit sinks beneath its eaves,
Until hot tears mine eyes o'er flow.

Home! Home Who can that place forget,
Though severed far by sea or land,
The wanderers eye is often wet,
As thoughts bring back the household band,
And though afar our feet may roam,
Our hearts untravelled cling to home.

Wood River Aug. 24, 1854

ELLENOR HUNDLEY
Courtesy of Mrs. Dortha Kimball, Safford, Arizona.

From Utah to Texas in 1856

ℰ Ellen Hundley

INTRODUCTION

Margaret Ellenor Hundley[1] was her name, Ellen for short. She had been born Ellenor Harris, daughter of James and Francis J. Wooldridge Harris of Abbeville, South Carolina, on March 27, 1821. She attended a girls' school and was known as a "perfect grammarian" by her school mates and family. The Harris family moved to Grimes County, Texas, in 1830 while it was still under Mexican rule. This part of southeastern Texas was part of the cotton kingdom of the old south, a land of large plantations and black slaves. Her father died in the Battle of Golead in the revolt against Mexico in 1836. Her older brother died in a Mexican war camp. During the same year her mother died at Christmastime. This left four Harris sisters on their own: Margaret Ellenor, Martha, Lucy and Eliza. In honor of their father's and brother's service and deaths the Republic of Texas gave to the surviving sisters a huge land grant of 8,888[2] acres, which was divided into four plantations, and the slaves were portioned out. These plantations were near the village of Anderson, the seat of Grimes County.

Just before her mother's death, Ellenor had married Lewis Goodwin on November 6, 1836. To them were born six children

---

[1] Mrs. Dortha Kimball, Safford, Arizona, letter of Oct. 31, 1986, says about her great-grandmother; "Notice the spelling of Ellenor. My grandfather insisted it was that way and not Eleanor, and she was called Ellen."

[2] If this acreage seems outrageous, please note that land grants given by the Republic of Texas under a provision of the consitution of 1836 were a league (4,428 acreas) to each family head. William Ransom Hogan, *The Texas Republic, a Social and Economic History* (Norman, Oklahoma, 1946), p. 10.

over the years following: Lewis James, b. Sept. 3, 1838; Mary Francis, b. July 16, 1840; Alice Gray, b. May 15, 1842; John Robert, b. Jan. 24, 1844; Joseph Kirkpatrick, b. June 21, 1846.

Some time before 1850 Lewis Goodwin died. We don't know when or how, but Ellenor was listed as a single woman in the 1850 Federal Census of Grimes County.

On January 6, 1851, she married again, this time to Thomas Augustus Hundley (b. Dec. 31, 1824), whom she always referred to as "Mr. Hundley" in her diary. His former wife, listed as 27 years old in the Federal Census of Texas of 1850, was Mary Jane Hundley. They were both Alabamans. The census listed their children as Panina, b. Mississippi, 5; Nancy, b. Mississippi, 3; and Alice, b. Texas, 2. What happened to these children we don't know. They don't appear in Hundley records so-far located.

Thomas and Ellen Hundley's first child, Thomas William "Billy," was born Feb. 11, 1853, according to Mormon generation records.[3] A second son, Elijah was born October 6, 1855.

Sometime in the early 1850s the Hundleys seem to have met Mormon missionaries and were attracted to their faith. Preston Thomas, a well-known pioneer of the Church of Jesus Christ of Latter Day Saints, may have been the one who brought the new message. He carried out several missions in Texas.

It seems that the Hundleys were reticent about actually joining the new church. For one thing, they were slave-holders. This practice was not approved by the Mormon establishment. It would appear that they went overland in 1855 to scout out the land in the Salt Lake area.

The diary which we transcribe here was written on their return trip to Texas in 1856. There are no typical Mormon usages or references in Ellen's diary. She never refers to men and women as brothers or sisters. This omission is particularly noticeable in her reference to Preston Thomas, whom they had known in Texas. In her mention of this highly revered Mormon leader, whom they met on the trail on July 14, she does not use the appellation, "Brother," an unheard-of omission for any Mormon.

---

[3] We were able to study these records on microfilm at the South Salem, Oregon, Stake Library, Church of Jesus Christ of Latter Day Saints.

The overland journey began in Grantsville, Utah. They traveled in reverse over the usual Mormon trail through Emigration Canyon, past Fort Bridger and via what she called "the Missoura route" (June 16) to Fort Laramie. At some point they turned up the South Platte River and went along the east side of the Rocky Mountains southward in what later became Colorado. They reached Cherry Creek near the later site of Denver on July 8. The rest of their journey took the Arkansas River route, in reverse to its usage several years later in the Pikes Peak gold rush. They traversed Kansas and eventually turned south through Indian Territory (present Oklahoma) into Texas and on home to Grimes County.

Soon after their return they became Mormons and sold out their property in land and slaves, planning to traverse their 1856 route. By this time Denver had been etablished and named, and they stopped there to take part in the gold rush. Another son, Jefferson Davis, was born there on November 28, 1860.

It was not until 1862 that the Hundley family reached Heber, Wasatch County, Utah, where they settled for life. Heber lies in a beautiful Alpine-like valley amidst high mountains. It was in those mountains that James Hundley worked as a logger, helping to harvest pine, spruce, fir, and Douglas fir.[4] It was when he was chopping saw logs that he was injured in an accident, and he died soon afterward on July 18, 1870. His place in the family was taken by Ellenor's son, John Robert Goodwin, who lived out his life until August 22, 1900. He had fought for four years in the Confederate army.

Ellenor carried out the work of a typical frontier mother. The children and grandchildren remembered how she washed and ironed, carded, spun, and wove. They raised wheat and ground it in a coffee mill for bread. For a time she taught school in Park City.

She was also very active in the Church. She was a primary teacher, relief society teacher and relief society president for many years. The Hundley home was a gathering place for young and

---

[4] United States Forest Service, *Wasatch National Forest* (Wash., D.C., Feb. 1952), *passim*.

old. She died in her 80th year at the home of her daughter, Mrs. Lucy Rebecca Murdock, on April 7, 1900. A family memorial to her reads. "Rich in love of all who came in contact with her. Rich in services of love and devotion and an abiding faith in the Gospel. Never once murmuring under distressing circumstances she was always rejoicing in the goodness of the Lord."

We are grateful to the Brigham Young University Library, Provo, for the use of their microfilm of the Hundley diary. Mrs. Dortha Kimball of Safford, Arizona, is a kind of family historian, and she has shared with us her knowledge of that subject, and also a typewritten biography, "Margaret Ellenor Harris Hundley." This document has been a mine of information. Mrs. Kimball also provided us with the portrait of her ancestor.

FROM UTAH TO TEXAS IN 1856

May 13, 1856   This day we bid fare well to our friends [in Grantsville] and started on our way to Texas   we traveled 22 miles and reached the cave[1]   we had considerable rain and hail on us   we camped at the cave

May 14   we still remained at the cave waiting for the company to start.   we washed some

May 15.   we still remained at the cave   Alice May 14 years old to day   Lewis come home from the city

May 16   Still at the cave   Mr Hundley went into the city returned in the evening bringing letters from our friends in Texas

---

[1] For identification of this cave the Public Inquiries Office of the Geological Survey in Salt Lake City recommended Orrin P. Miller as an authority on the caves of the area. He is president of the Tooele County Historical Society, Tooele, Utah. Mr. Miller has been quite helpful. He suggest that Deadmans Cave, half way between Tooele City and Salt Lake City was the locale most often used by the pioneers as a camping place. It is twenty miles southwest of Salt Lake City, just south of the Great Salt Lake. Deadmans Cave was used by the pioneers and not the more famous Black Rock Cave because the former has a good source of water nearby. It is 40 by 30 feet with an arched roof of 15 feet.

May 17   at the cave   spent this day in writing to our
friends

May 18 Sabbath day   still at the cave   getting tired of the
place

May 19   washed at the cave   Alice went to the City
Lewis returned from the City with 3 letters

May 20 [and] 21   Still at the cave

22   left the cave and traveled 23 miles   passed through salt
lake City but did not make any stop.   camped at emigration
Kanyon 7 miles east of the City

May 23   Mr Hundley and Lewis went back to the
City   Mr Hundley returned and we started on   had
considerable trouble crossing the little mountain   had to
hire team to take us up   camped between the little and big
mountain   had good water and feed for our horses. 5 miles

May 24   Started to go over the big mountain   traveled 7
miles had a great deal of trouble having to unload our
waggon and pack it on horses[2] and by hand   we got in a mile
of the top and had to camp   no feed for horses here   it
rained and snowed on us   good water

May 25 Sabbath   we hired help and came over this big
mountain   paid 5 dollars for help about a mile   here we
suffered a great deal of fatigue having to walk all the
time   we traveled about 7 miles camped at a creek   good
water and tolerable feed for horses   we had plenty of snow
to east on top of mountains

May 26   Stayed on the creek and washed. Waiting for the
company to come   on lonesome times   in the east Kanyon

May 27   this morning we moved on about 3 miles to good
grass and stoped to wait for the company to come up   we
had frost and ice every night.   snow plenty in sight

---

[2] This was a horse-drawn wagon train. Far and away most of them traveled by ox
team.

May 28   we moved on about 2 miles and stopped still waiting for the company   in the evening Mr. Gorden his wife Mother and Sister come up with us and camped

May 29   started to go on to [Fort] Bridger   got as far as weber and had to stop on account of the river being up   we crossed one creek in east Kanyon 12 times besides several other little streams of water to day   we come 12 miles

May 30   we lay by to day   I washed some. The men commencd building a raft to carry us over the river   the mail come to the river but did not cross   2 men swum the river on horses and went on to the City

May 31   to day we lay by   the men finished the raft but we did not cross on account of the wind being so high

June 1 Sabbath morning   this morning they put in the raft   they made 2 trips and the third time the rope broke and she went down the river with the mail bags and 3 or 4 men on her   went down 3 miles and lodged on the same side she started from.   the men took a waggon and went and got the mail   part of it got washed off   3 or 4 bags and they never found it

June 2   the raft was gone and the men took one of the mail waggon beds and corked it and finished crossing the mail and 4 waggons for us   it looked very dangerous to see women and children cross such a stream in the manner we did but however we all got across safe   the mail men were very kind in assisting us over   Mr Johnsons waggons got up with us to day

June 3   this morning we packed up and started again   Will Sprouse went back to the City after Lewis Goodwin   we had a great deal of trouble with our horses at the hills   they would not pull   I suffered a heap of fatigue walking and carrying my child and trying to catch the waggons   we traveled 15 miles and camped in echo Kanyon   we crossed

several creeks during the day   we had good grass and water
for our horses

June 4   a heavy frost and plenty of ice   we traveled on
very well   crossed bear river and camped on this side near
the bank   we crossed several small creeks   all good water
we came about 30 miles   J york come up with us to day.

June 5   we started this morning   come about 2 miles and
broke our wagon tongue in a bog hole   had to go a mile to
get a pole to fix it   we traveled on about 20 miles and
camped on a creek   good water but poor feed for horses
Cub Johnson came with us to day   muddy creek.

June 6   we traveled on about ten miles to day   passed fort
Bridger   camped just this side and made a new waggon
tongue   crossed severel streams of water

June 7   this morning started   crossed blacks fork   again
traveled 2 miles   nooned at a creek muddy   went 15 in the
after noon and camped on hams fork   poor feed and water

June 8 Sunday morning   come on and nooned at green
river   come 33 miles and crossed green river   camped on
this side

June 9.   to day we lay by and the women washed   Lewis
and Will and Alma Taylor come to us in the evening

June 10   this morning Mr Gordon and family left us and
went on the Missoura route   we traveled 10 miles farther
and camped on the river   we had very bad road all
day   crossed big sandy in the morning

June 11   we left green river this morning and traveled over
a barren hilly country   bad road and no water   we come 30
miles and found a good spring and grass for our horses   here
we camped

June 12   to day we still had a very bad road a great many
deep ravines to cross and heavy saluratus beds   we came 10

miles and nooned on beeder [Beaver] creek   had water
saluratus; we crossed 2 very small streams of water in the
forenoon   we come on about a mile and found a cold
sulpher spring white good water; and good road; we come on
10 miles and camped   no grass and very little water alkali
and had to bring it a mile

June 13   this morning we traveled over 20 miles and still no
water but alkali and grass still on a barren sandy desert   we
come on camped on beer creek   some of us got a little sick
drinking the bad water; after we camped some of the company
went about a mile and found a white sulpher spring   cold
good water which was quite a treat

June 14.   we come on to the spring and lay bye to let our
horses rest and shoe some; here they killed 2 mountain sheep

June 15 sunday morning   we started again and traveled
over bad road sometimes having to make it as we went
crossed several dry creeks and deep ravines still a barren
sandy desert; we traveled on 30 miles and not a drop of water
for our horses   we still come on till 11 o clock at night and
still no water   we stopped here and turned out our horses
and went to sleep   come 50 miles in the day and night

June 16.   we started on again and traveled 15 miles and still
no water for our horses nor ourselves   we began to
suffer   the little children was crying and the grown ones
nearly as bad   we stopped and some of the men went to
hunt water   after a long time they found a snow bank that
had caved in the side of a deep ravine   they found it by the
moist dirt on top   dug down and found the snow   they
brought us enough to have a little to wet our parched
throats   it was half mud but we was glad to get it   our
horses was about give out and we come near losing
one   traveling hard 2 days and one night with not a drop of
water and hardly any thing to eat   after the men come to us

with the water we left the road and here they took the ax and
broke up the snow and we melted it and gave it to our horses
and made us some coffee and to look at it you would think it
was half cream   2 of Cub Johnsons mules give out; it was
very hard work getting to the snow as the banks was very
steep but it was fortunate for us we found it for our horses
would have died and we would have nearly died ourselves
one of the mens tonge was so dry and swollen he could not
wait for water but sucked the wet mud   this was T. Taylor

June 17   we traveled 20 miles to day still over a heavy sandy
road on the desert without any water   in the evening we
found a salt lake of water   the stock could not like it; they
dug around the edge of the lake small wells and found fresh
cold water for ourselves and our horses   we had no grass but
salt grass and this our horses would not eat   they had to
guard our horses all the time to keep them from getting
bogged and one or two did get bogged so deep that you could
scarsely see them except their heads

June 18   to day we lay bye to let our horses rest as they were
all about give out   in the morning they killed an antelope
about 10 o clock they killed another

June 19   still lay bye on account of our horses

June 20   still lying bye

June 21   to day we traveled 20 miles and found a good
spring and good grass   here we camped   the road was good
part of the time and part was heavy sand still on the
desert   we camped at the foot of some red mountain   to
day they killed an antelope

June 22. Sunday morning   we crossed over the red
mountains   a rough rocky road   traveled on 5 miles killed
a buffalo   come on 5 miles and camped   good grass for our
horses   lake water   this day we left the desert and entered
the mountains

June 23   this morning we come over a very rocky road high rolling mountainous country   we traveled 20 miles and nooned at a lake   we come on 10 miles and camped on a dry creek   we found some water standing in holes in the bed of the creek

June 24   we come on 20 miles over a hilly rough road   crossed a great many deep ravines and steep bad places   3 small creeks   very good water   we reached the platte[3] about 3. o clock in the afternoon and camped   in the evening about 150 Indians Shoshones come up to us and camped all night with us   they were very friendly   they all had good horses   we had good grass

June 25   this morning we forded the platte and all got over safe and come on 15 miles and nooned on a creek   good water   we had bad road.   we come on over the mountains 10 miles and camped between the Elk Mountains   good water but poor feed   Cub killed an antelope on the platte

June 26   still traveling in the mountains   plenty of snow on the sides   bad enough road; but beautiful scenery   the high mountains all colored with green trees and the snow on the sides; we come on by a bed of snow about 4 feet deep on the road side   we had plenty to eat and snow water to drink   here the road was boggy and bad   good deal of water standing in it   just this side we crossed a very large rocky creek   we traveled 15 miles and camped   good cold water   tolerable feed   here we found some ripe strawberries

June 27.   this morning we had the roughest road of any we had traveled   rocky   we crossed a large rocky creek and several small streams all good water   we passed through timber and seen a great deal we come 20 miles and camped on a small creek   good water and grass   plenty of mosquitoes in the mountains

---

[3] This was the South Platte River, which has its rise in the Colorado Rockies.

June 28.   good road with the exception of some steep rocky hills   we crossed several streams of water   4 creeks in going a half a mile   fish creek   we traveled 30 miles and crossed a river the name we did not know   Larama camped over on this side good water and grass

June 29.   Sunday morning   we come on 5 miles and met 3 trains from Arkansas   Going to Calafornia with sheep and cattle   we come on 30 miles and camped in the black hills   we crossed several small creeks   in the evening the horses ran away down the hill and broke the tounge of the waggon   We had to stop and make a new one in the pines.

June 30   to day bad road steep rocky hills and ravines crossed several creeks   come on 40 miles to powder river   provision short

July 1 tuesday   lay bye to rest our horses   the women washed   they killed an Antelope   out of provision living on game

July 2 wednesday   traveled 30 miles   crossed 2 large creeks   good water camped on a small creek   poor water and feed   killed an antelope   there was a cherokee train camped just below us[4]

July 3 thursday   this morning 3 of our company left us and turned back with the train   Alma and T. Taylor and George

---

[4] Cherokees had answered the lure of California gold in 1849-1850. In the latter year some of them had discovered color in Ralston Creek, near present Denver. Others followed from Indian Territory (Oklahoma) over the following years culminating in the William Green Russell expedition, which spread the news of gold in the Pikes Peak region to the whole world. Russell's wife was a Cherokee who told him about the possibilities. The Cherokee-Russell prospecting expediton was made up of both Indians and whites and traveled to Cherry Creek [present Denver] in 1858. It was not unusual for travelers to cross paths with Cherokee trains as the Hundleys did on this day. For an in depth study of the Cherokee impact on the Pikes Peak gold rush see LeRoy R. Hafen's classic introduction to *Pike's Peak Gold Rush Guidebooks of 1859.* *Southwest Historical Series,* IX (Glendale, Calif., 1941) pp. 21-80. A note should be added that through the years the name of the mountain named for Zebulan Pike has been spelled both with and without the apostrophe. The accepted spelling today is "Pikes Peak."

Brady   we come on and nooned on a rocky creek   traveled 30 miles and camped on a small creek

July 4   come on 10 miles   crossed the Platte and nooned on this side   killed an antelope

July 5   still lying bye on the Platte   we washed to day   they killed an antelope and a deer   met 2 arkansas trains

July 6   still lying by to rest our horses   Sunday; this evening they killed 3 deer and one antelope

July 7 monday   we started on again   this morning met 2 arkansas trains with about 1000 head of cattle   traveled 25 miles and camped on cherry creek   good grass and water

July 8 tuesday   lay bye half the day   come on in the evening.   met some mexicans packed with flour going to trade with the Indians   we traveled 15 miles and camped at the head of cherry creek⁵   passed a mexican camp on C C

July 9 wednesday   this morning 2 californians come back from a train that we met this side of the Platte and come back with us   to day we traveled 40 miles crossed black squirrel creek   come over a high rolling country but good road camped at the muddy spring   sorry grass

July 10 thursday   this morning we met 3 arkansas trains with more than 1000 head of cattle   we come on and nooned on the fountain Cabuoya⁶   traveled 20 miles and camped on fountain cabuoya

July 11   traveled 25 miles good road   reached the Arkansas river and camped   good grass   here was a trader camped

---

⁵ The city of Denver stands at the confluence of Cherry Creek and the South Platte River. In Clyde Brion Davis' words, Cherry Creek "now trickles between concrete retaining walls through the city of Denver. *Rivers of America Series: The Arkansas* (N.Y., 1940), p. 29.

⁶ *Fountaine qui Bouille* or Fountain Creek derives its name from the boiling spring of Manitou, just west of Colorado Springs. Hafen, *op. cit.*, p. 103.

on the opposite side of the river with some provision   the
men went over and bought some corn and coffee and tobacco
and beans and a little meal   this was fortunate for us as we
had been living on wild meat for some time and some was
getting sick

July 12   to day we had some bread for dinner; lay bye to day
to trade and rest our horses   plenty of mosquitoes

July 13. Sunday   this morning we started on again   Cub
Johnson and all left us except one young man to go through
Mexico; and we come on ourselves   we passed some
Mexican and one white man camped on the road side   we
traded some with the men bought a little flour and some
more beans and some fine beef. Cub Johnsons folks were
afraid to pass through the Indians   we come on 30 miles
and camped on the river   thousands of Mosquitoes

July 14 Monday   to day we met Preston Thomas[7] and
company going to the vally   we traveled 20 miles and
camped on the river

July 15 tuesday   this morning our horses was gone back the
road home 8 or 10 miles on account of mosquitoes and it was
late when we got them so we lay bye and did not travel any

July 16 wednesday   to day we passed Bents old fort[8]
traveled 20 miles and camped   good grass   no mosquitoes

---

[7] Preston Thomas was a prominent Mormon leader who took Texas as his missionary
field.

[8] This is now a National Historic Site on the Santa Fe Trail 8 miles west of Las
Animas, Colorado. It was built in 1833 by William Bent and became a principal
commercial trading station on the way west along the Arkansas. The adobe fort stood at
the juncture of Purgatoire Creek with the Arkansas. The full name of the creek in
Spanish was *El Rio de Las Animas Perididas en Purgatorio* (The River of the Lost souls
in Purgatory). David Lavender describes it thus: The rectangular fort faced eastward
toward approaching caravans, its front wall 137 feet long, fourteen feet high, and three
or more feet thick. The northern and southern walls, of the same height and thickness,
were 178 feet long. At the southeast and northwest corners rose round towers eighteen
feet tall." William Bent abandoned it in 1849. *Bent's Fort* (Garden City, N.Y., 1954),
pp. 136-37, and *passim*.

July 17. thursday   reached Bents fort[9]   come by 27
wickeups shians [Cheyennes] 50 come out to the waggon but
treated us friendly   we come to and met 6 more on horse
back.   there was 5 wickeups at the fort   Rappehoos
[Arapahoes] friendly   we camped this side of the fort   nice
neat looking Indians and neat wickeups   come 20 miles

July 18 friday   this morning left the fort   come to 15 miles
and nooned   2 Apaches come to us and eat dinner and a
Rappahow and his squaw come on to travel with us to the
agent.   here we seen an Indian wrapped up in his buffalo
robe buried up in a tree   the Indians come on and camped
with us   we traveled 23 miles to day

July 19 saturday   traveled 20 miles   passed the Apachy 8
wickeups   none come out to the waggons   the old Indian
come by and brought another squaw with him; 20 here we are
with no company to pass through the Indians but one young
man and this old Indian and his 2 squaws   lonesome times
and nothing to eat but beans and hominy and that to cook
every night   no grease nor meat to season it with

July 20 Sunday   this morning we met a white man and an
Indian comeing from the agent to gather all the Indians
together to make them presents   we passed a place where
the Indians had killed a little white boy and burnt his
waggon because some poeple had killed an Indian on the
other road the Missoura route near fort Karney   the old
Indians chief that was traveling with us went with Louis and
showed him the spot where he was killed   he was with the
Indians that killed him   we come on and met the Agent[10]

---

[9] Bent's New Fort was on the north bank of the Arkansas opposite present Prowers,
in present Bent County. Lavender estimates it to have been about 100 feet per side, *op.
cit.* Dr. G.M. Willing describes it in 1859 as being "built of rock — ferrunginous
sandstone — taken from the neighboring river bluffs, with a main entrance to the north
with barracks for the garrision and ample accommodations for traders." LeRoy R.
Hafen, *op. cit.*, IX, p. 101.

[10] We have not been able to identify this agent. The standard work on the subject is of
no help. Flora W. Seymour, *Indians Agents of the Old Frontier*, (N.Y., 1941).

and his train and 100 Indians just at camping time   we all camped at the same place   here the agent told us it was not safe for us to be alone as there was 7000 Kyoway [Kiowas] camped just below us on the river and they were mad and fighting among themselves and we had better go back with them to Bents fort and wait for company   this was bad news to us but it was better to do that than for us all to be killed or robed and taken prisoners; the Agent was very kind and let us have some flour coffee and sugar

July 21 monday   this morning we turned back with the train to Bents fort   at noon the agent gave the Indians a beef and it made me shudder to see their cruelty to a poor dumb brute   they skined it alive   we come on and all camped together   it made me feel awful at night to look round and see the Indians camped all around us and such a few white men and no women but Alice and myself besides squaws.   we was 60 miles from the fort when we met the agent

July 22 tuesday   to day we passed the Apaches   the chief come out to us dressed very fine in his war dress and sword   he treated us very friendly and made all his men behave themselves   there were 400 come to the waggons the agent gave them their goods and provision and they appeared very much pleased with them   the old chief come on and stayed all night to look at their wickeups as we passed them   looked like a little town

July 23 wednesday   we come on near the fort and camped plenty of Indians with us

24 Thursday   we come on and camped out side the fort the whole place covered with Indians   Bent would not let us have a house in the fort

25 friday   still at the fort   we went down to the village and bought some mockasins

26 saturday   at the fort.   the Indians had a dance inside the fort   they had a Utah squaw prisoner and 2 Utes scalps   they were all painted and dressed out in their feathers and war capes; they made the prisoner dance with them and pointed their lances at her   they had the scalps on 2 sticks and held them up and danced with them and rubbed them on the ground they enjoyed themselves finely; the old squaws danced as well as the young and sung all the time they danced   it made the cold chills run over me to see their actions and hear them war hoop and yell   they were dressed very fine; after their fashion with their beaded buckskin dressed all fringed off   the old squaws carried the scalps they were painted black as a crow and the men that beat the drums were painted black   there was about 1000 at the dance.   this morning we seen a dog killed and dressed ready to eat   they are a favorite dish among the squaws   they had been suffering for food and waiting for the agent to come   had killed some of their horses to eat after the dance   the agent made them some presents and gave them some provision

27. Sunday   at the fort waiting for company

28 still at the fort

29 at the fort spent an awful night   the Indians brought in a pawnee scalp and they danced sung yelled and beat their drums all night long   we could not sleep a minute for them   I was frightened out of my life nearly

30 still at the fort

[July] 31   at the fort today   some of the comanches & Kiaways come up here   we had Rappahoes Kiaways commanches shanees black feet Uts Apaches Shians and Mexicans   the sight of a white face looked good for you could look no way but what there was Indians

August 1 [and] 2 still at the fort

Sunday 3   this morning we started on again with a train from the fort   we come on 5 or 6 miles and camped

Aug. 4 monday   to day we lay by   part of the oxen was gone in the evening   they found them and we went on   our horses were gone back 3 or 4 miles on the road and Mr Hundley had to walk after them   the train went on and left us all but one man   we was frightened all most to death surrounded every where by Indians   we passed about 1000 wickeups commanches and Kiaways the worst Indians that was   they took one yoke of oxen and killed them

Aug. 5   this morning we met about 3 or 4000 Indians   they looked like an army   they behaved themselves very well and did not interupt any thing but I was afraid of them

Aug 6.   to day the waggon Master and his driver a Mexican had a fight and the master made the driver leave   are camped on the [Arkansas] river

Aug. 7   to day we got to where we met the agent   there was a Kiaway overtook us at noon   he said he was looking for Pawnees that there was a company of his men a war party coming on to have a fight with them   this was sad news for I began to think we was nearly out of danger of Indians.   the Indian come on and camped with us   I was uneasy all the time as he was looking for his men up

Aug 8   we come on again this morning   the old Indian still with us   we traveled 20 miles and camped

Aug 9   this morning the Indian left us and went back   the Agent and Mr Bent over took us at noon   2 carriages and one baggage wagon;   we come 20 miles and stopped

Aug 10 Sunday   this morning got a very early start and traveled very well   at noon the train killed a beef   we traveled 15 miles   ten thousand million of grass hoppers

Aug. 11   we come on as usual   we got into the Santafee road this morning   the mail passed us at noon   the whole

plain full of grasshoppers   at Dinner Mr Bent sent us a
green peach pie which was quite a treat on the plains   we
traveled 25 miles and camped on the river   here we have
rain every day and night on us

Aug. 12   this morning the Agent left us and went on with
the mail   we passed fort Adkison here[11]   took up 2 dead
bodies   the Mother and her daughter and carried them
with their friends   they had been dead 4 years   rainy bad
weather

Aug 13   traveled on very well   plenty of grass all along the
river

Aug 14   rainy wet morning   to day we lay by on account of
rain   quite cold

Aug 15   this morning Mr Bent left us and went on   we
started on again at noon   we seen some buffalo a good ways
off   met a santafee train   they killed 4 buffalo   our train

Aug 16   come on   as accident camped on coon creek   no
grass

Aug 17   Sunday   nooned on pawnee fork 10 miles from
coon creek   Come on and camped at pawnee rock traveled
25 miles today

Aug 18 monday   reached fort walnut[12] 250 miles from fort
bent

Aug 19   to day we lay by   the train left 44 head of cattle
and we had to stop here   we seen thousands of buffalo   they
killed 2

---

[11] Fort Atkinson stood on the Arkansas near present Larned, KA. A contemporary
wrote of it, "The fort itself is of adobe, or sun-dried brick, roofed with canvas,
containing fair accommodations for the garrison, and defended by a few small field-pieces
and the usual armament." "The Siege of Fort Atkinson," *Harper's New Monthly
Magazine*, Oct. 1857, pp. 638-48.

[12] This was Allison's ranch at the juncture of Walnut Creek and the Arkansas.
William B. Parsons described it in the Lawrence, Kansas, *Republican* as "a large
building made of logs of equal length, set endwise in the ground." Quoted in LeRoy R.
Hafen, *op. cit.*, p. 325-26.

Aug 20   still at the fort waiting to find the oxen   to day we
went out and found some of the finest plums and grapes I
ever saw   we had some fine pies which was very good after
so long a famine   in the evening we come on a while down
the river and camped to good grass

Aug 21.   still lying by   the oxen gone   here there was 2
large santafee trains passed us

Aug 22   this morning Mr Hundley went out and killed a
large buffalo the finest that had been killed   we all went out
to look at it   was the first one the children had ever been
close to   we could see thousands all around us   we caught
some fine fish at the fort   in the evening we started and
traveled 25 miles to cow creek   we traveled all night nearly

Aug 23.   to day we lay by   2 trains passed us

Aug 24 Sunday   to day we left the train and started on by
ourselves again   we traveled on 20 miles to little Arkansas
and camped

Aug 25   come on 25 miles and camped on little turkey
creek   here we reached the Osage nation and we have to go
through them alone over wild wilderness country

Aug 26   to day we lay by to wait for Levers   he was with
the train

Aug 27   this morning we left the santafee road and started
on to the nation   we traveled 30 miles and camped on the
Coon

Aug 28   come on to day 20 miles and nooned on little
cottonwood creek   bad banks but the prettiest grass I ever
saw   we traveled 10 miles and camped on a creek. 20 miles
to day   after we stopped and got supper we concluded to go
on a few miles   we come about 5 and staid all night   to day
we seen about 100 wickeups   old ones   an Indian city

Aug 29   to day we come on to big walnut creek   here it
commenced raining on us and we had to stop   we staid

about 2 hours and found the creek was rising very fast and we thought we had better cross over so we come over and the bank was very steep and slippery and the horses could not pull so we had to unload our waggon in the rains and just throw every thing out in the mud   we had an awful time of it and we come about a quarter of a mile and broke our wagon tongue off short, so here we had to stop in the rain and mud in the dreary bottom and make a new one.   wet and cold as we could be little children and all   we finished it and come 15 miles

Aug 30   to day we come 7 miles to little walnut creek and it was so high we could not cross and we lay by the rest of the day   in the evening Mr Hundley killed a small deer   rich land   hundreds of old wickeups all around but no Indians

Aug 31. Sunday   this morning we crossed the creek and traveled 22 miles   we crossed 3 or 4 creeks during the day   all had timber on them   at noon we stopped on a creek and found some fine plums

Sept. 1   traveled over a high rolling country   nooned on a small creek beautiful scenery all around us.   we come on and in the evening we stoped and got supper and come on 5 miles and camped on a high ridge   traveled 25 miles   lonesome times in the wild wilderness   one lone little family and one young man 17 years old

Sept 2   to day come 15 miles and nooned on a black Jack ridge   we passed water twice in the morning; a small spring on the ridge   traveled 35 miles to day and part of the night

Sept 3.   traveled 25 miles to day   there was an Indian dog come to us at noon and about 10 O clock at night it come to us again   we knew there was Indians close about so we tied up our horses and watched them

Sept 4   this morning we traveled over a beautiful country

high hilly and pretty scenery all around   in the morning there was some Osage Indians come to us but they were very friendly   we give them some sugar and coffee and tobacco we crossed several creeks during the day

Sept 5.   come on to day to the Verde grees [Verdigris] found the river very low but the banks very slippery and bad   had to get a yoke of oxen from Mr Coody[13] to pull us   camped here

Sept 6   lay by to let our horses rest   Mr Coody gave us some nice water melons which was quite a treat

Sept 7   still lying by Sunday

Sept 8.   had a fine mess of beans for dinner

Sept 9. 10. 11. 12. 13   Still lying by at Mr Coodys   here they were very kind to us in dividing vegetables with us and watermelons and milk. Mr Hundley was taken sick here with chills and fever and was very sick

14. Sunday   this morning Mr Griers train come up with us; to day Mr Hundley was worse than he had ever been before

15   to day we started on again   traveled 15 miles   some bad road   crossed 2 or 3 creeks

16   traveled 20 miles to day   some very bad road   camped on a creek just this side of Hicks[14]   nooned on a creek to day   Mr Hundley missed his chill

17   traveled on very well   some bad road

18   to day very bad road

19   to day we crossed the Chickensas river 80 miles from Verdigrees

[13] This was at the ranch of Richard and Susan Coody on the Verdigris. In the years following it became a gathering place for parties going west to the Colorado mines. Hafen, *op. cit.*, pp. 41, 48-49, 51, 300.

[14] This was the establishment of George Hicks, who later became quite influential in promoting and leading companies to the Pikes Peak mines. Hafen, *op. cit.*, p. 300.

20   lay by and washed   the men went to fort Gipson[15] to buy provision   here we got some apples

21 Sunday   started on again   got along very well

22   traveled on very well   come 20 miles

[September] 23   this morning crossed the canadian   40 miles from arkansas   in the evening crossed the canadian again   come down the big rocky hill

24   bad rocky road

25   very rocky road still   Lewis very sick

26   to day some bad road

27   some rocky road still   crossed 2 large creeks

28   Sunday   lay by   rainy wet morning   Lewis sick monday   traveled on very well   some hard road   crossed one very large creek and one toll bridge

29   to day come on very well   passed through Boggy ville [Boggy Depot, Oklahoma]   heavy sandy road   toll bridge

Oct. 1.   to day we come in 2 miles of red river and camped   Alice was very sick here

Oct 2   crossed red river   come on about 4 miles and camped at a spring   Alice still very sick

Oct 3   passed through Sherman [Texas] 14 miles this side of red river   Alice had a chill and was very sick

Oct 4 Sunday   come on to western

Oct 5   lay by to get flour   Joseph Billy Alice all sick and Teresa

6   still lying by   all sick

7   lying by waiting for flour

8   started on again   traveled about and stopped   rainy day

[15] Fort Gibson was an important frontier post. It served as a military center for the whole of Indians Territory, a place where treaties were signed. There is now a town of the same name.

9   traveled on very well   passed another mill

10   no accident to day   mad[e] a very good days drive

11. Sunday   to day passed through Dallas and crossed Trinity river   we left Mr Greers train to day   at night they over took us again and we all camped together

12 monday   came through [unreadable word] 16 miles from Dallas

13 tuesday   [unreadable word] in morning   got a late start   traveling about [unreadable word] camped   Mr Hundley was very sick all night

14 Wednesday   traveled on very well   Mr Hundley [unreadable word]

[Note: There are three more entries: 15, 16, 17, and all are unreadable. Also there is another page of written material, all in a different hand, and not related to the content of the diary.]

Delaware to Utah, 1857

❧ Sarah Maria Mousley

INTRODUCTION

Sarah Maria Mousley was the third child of eight born to Titus and Ann McMenemy Mousley in Newcastle County, Delaware. In her middle name the "i" is pronounced as the word "eye" and accented. The surname is pronounced with the "Mous" sounded like the "Mos" in Moses. They were descendants of the founders of the Delaware colony, the Swedes and Finns, who settled there in 1638 and over the years following. She was a mature young woman of 29 years when the family made the 1857 crossing to Utah. They traveled by train to Iowa City and by wagon train from there to Salt Lake City. Sarah had broken off an engagement to a young man in the east because he would not convert to Mormonism. One brother, Lewis, had already migrated to Utah in 1856, and, according to the diary as they neared the end of their journey, they learned that he was living "on Weber river forty miles from the valley."

The year 1857 was a time of troubles for Latter-Day Saints both in the eastern states and in Utah. It was a time when much anti-Mormon sentiment was being whipped up in the newspapers. American nativism reacted to the coming of great numbers of Mormons from Europe. During the presidential election year, 1856, the "Mormon Question" was on the front burner. The Republicans declared in their platform that they were opposed to the "twin relics of barbarism," slavery and polygamy.

President James Buchanan decided that a show of force was necessary, and a military expedition was ordered from Fort Leavenworth to Utah. They got away in mid-July. There followed what has been called the "Utah War," characterized more by bluster than by actual fighting.

The remarkable thing is that Sarah Maria Mousley showed little knowledge or concern about these events. Her concerns were for the most part with her family and with her traveling companions. Their journey paralleled the route taken by the military units, but they seem not to have made contact.

Sarah did tell of meeting handcart travelers whom they accompanied at times during the long journey. This was the second year of that remarkable exodus of westering Mormons.

During the long trip they often stopped at the newly-established way stations set up by the Church to give aid to the overlanders. This was a new feature of western travel.

Sarah Maria and her younger sister, Ann Amanda Mousley (age 21 years), were united in plural marriages on the same day, July 18, 1858, to a dynamic Mormon leader Angus Munn Cannon, an Englishman from Liverpool. There is a family tradition that Cannon was planning only to marry Amanda, but that Brigham Young would only give permission for the wedding if Angus would marry Sarah Maria, who would thus become the first and legal wife. Sarah bore six and Amanda ten children over the years that followed. Later there were added two more plural wives. Altogether Angus was the father of 27 sons and daughters.

It was on January 20, 1885, that Angus Munn Cannon, President of the Salt Lake Stake of the Church of Jesus Christ of Latter-Day Saints was arrested and placed under bond on charge of unlawful cohabitation. He was arraigned on February 11 in the Third District Court and pled not guilty. The trial took place in April, and on May 9th he was sentenced to six months imprisonment and a $300 fine. He was placed in the Utah Penitentiary. Over the next months his and other cases were carried to the United States Supreme Court. It was a test case. He declared that he would associate with all of his family or none. He was released from prison on December 14, 1885.

The Salt Lake *Tribune*, with a quaint sense of humor, immediately announced his release with a play of words on his name, "Anguish Can Again." Whatever it might have meant to some, it was certainly an "anguish" situation for Sarah Maria and others in a large family.

We are grateful to the Utah State Historical Society for making the Sarah Maria Mousley Cannon diary available to us. We are also grateful to Mrs. Robert G. Snow of Salt Lake City for encouragement in the publication project. Mrs. Snow is a descendant of Angus and Sarah Maria Cannon. She was the one who carefully made the typescript from the original hand-written version of the diary, which has since been lost. She told the editor that she tried to copy the diary exactly as written, often using a magnifying glass to be sure of her observations.

SOURCES

Principal sources for the above introduction are as follows:

Leonard J. Arrington and Davis Bitton, *The Mormon Experience* (New York, 1979), especially Chapter 9, "The Kingdom and the Nation," pp. 161-84.

LeRoy R. Hafen and Ann W. Hafen, *Handcarts to Zion* (Glendale, CA, 1960).

Descendants of Sarah Maria Mousley Cannon, especially Mrs. Robert G. Snow, Salt Lake City, and Barnard S. Silver, Moses Lake, Washington.

MOUSLEY FAMILY MEMBERS WHO MIGRATED TO UTAH:

"Grandma" was Elizabeth Caythers McMenemy, Ann Mousley's mother.

Titus Mousley (May 3, 1790 - Aug. 5, 1865) was born in Wilmington, Delaware and died in Salt Lake City. He was Sarah Maria Mousley's father. He was listed as a farmer in the 1860 Federal Census of Utah. The census also indicates that he was evidently a successful farmer; for his real estate is valued at $3000 and his personal property at $1400.

Ann McMenemy Mousley (Feb. 11, 1799 - June 2, 1882) was born in Cecilton, Maryland, and died in Salt Lake City. She was the wife of Titus and mother of the following children:

Margaret Jane Mousley (Aug. 12, 1819 - May 30, 1880), had become
the wife of Joseph Foreman (b. 1818), who became a farmer in the
Salt Lake City area. The 1860 census lists six children, including
Margaret, who was two years old, born in "Nebraska." This was the
baby who's birth is referred to in Sarah Maria's diary on July 14, 1857,
with the words, "just after our encampment for the night we were
called to receive a little stranger in our midst who if fortunate would
yet call me Aunt."

George Washington Mousley (Aug. 9, 1825 - Dec. 8, 1867) was listed
as the "Principal S.L. Academy" in the 1860 census. His wife was
Eliza W. and there were three children.

Sarah Maria Mousley (July 21, 1828 - Mar. 12, 1911, b. Centreville,
Delaware), was the writer of the diary.

Lewis Henry Mousley (Feb. 9, 1833 - June 23, 1913, b. Centreville,
Delaware), had already gone to Utah with Philemon C. Merrill's
company. He married Mary A. Crossgrove on March 3, 1858. He
lived a long life and was ordained a bishop and in 1900 a patriarch.
He served a term in the Utah penitentiary for unlawful cohabitation
and paid a fine of $300. Andrew Jensen, *Latter-Day Saint
Biographical Encyclopedia*, II (Salt Lake City, 1914), pp. 107-08.

Martha Ellen Mousley (Sept. 24, 1830 - July 26, 1898, b. Wilmington,
Delaware), became the wife of James Ashburton Crossgrove in 1861
in Salt Lake City. There they lived until 1872 when they moved to
the vicinity of Draper, a few miles south of the city. He became
well-known as a fruit grower. She is called "Nellie" in the diary.
Ibid., p. 300.

Ann Amanda Mousley (June 10, 1836 - Mar. 19, 1905, b. Centreville,
Delaware), along with Sarah Maria became plural wives of Angus
Munn Cannon on July 18, 1858, in Salt Lake City. *Ibid.*, I, pp.
292-95. She is referred to in the diary as "Amanda."

Wilhelmina Logan Mousley (Oct. 11, 1840 - Jan. 16, 1918, b.
Centreville, Delaware), married David Henry Cannon, a printer, in
1859. He left immediately on a mission to England. He became an
active Mormon leader in St. George Utah. She is referred to as
"Willie" in the diary. Davis Bitton, *Guide to Mormon Diaries &
Autobiographies* (Provo, Utah, 1977), pp. 56-57.

Thomas E. Mousley, b. Jan. 21, 1825, was a cousin of the younger
Mousleys. His parents were Reuben and S.H. Mousley. It was his
wife who gave birth to a baby on September 4th while on the journey.

Ellatheria Dupont Peria (Mar. 22, 1835 - June 12, 1918) was a native of
Brickhill, Md, and a cousin of the Mousley young people. Her
mother was Margaret McHenry, a sister of Ann McMenemy
Mousley, their mother. Sarah Maria says in her diary that sometime
in May Ellatheria was married to William Davis Robinson (Aug.
19, 1836 - Sept. 10, 1901), who had just been baptized a Mormon on
Mar. 13, 1857. The wedding took place on May 26, 1857, according
to Fourth Generation Records of the church, in Iowa City. He had
been born in Chester, Pa. The latter years of their lives were spent in
American Fork, Utah. They had five children,. Jensen, *op.cit.*, III,
p. 501.

PERSONS NAMED IN THE DIARY:

John Andrews was a 33 year-old Irish weaver who came over with his
wife, Elizabeth, and four children from the British Isles. On Sunday,
June 21, their little boy fell out of the wagon, and a wheel passed over
his body. We know he recovered for he is listed in the 1860 census as
a 10 year-old, born in Scotland.
Miner Grant Atwood was stationed at Deer Creek [modern Glenrock,
Wyoming], to aid immigrants. He later became a missionary to
South Africa. Davis Bitton, *op. cit.*, p. 15.
"Mrs. Bowman" is so-far unidentified.
"Br. Cuningham" is unidentified.
David Buel Dille, which the diary spells "Dilly," was on his way home
to Utah from a British Mission, 1853-1857. He was with the
handcart migration of that year. LeRoy R. and Ann W. Hafen,
Handcarts 1856-1860 (Glendale, CA, 1960), p. 153. According to
the 1860 census the Dilles were living on a farm near Brigham, Cache
Co.
Joseph Foreman is listed with the Mousley family members, as the
husband of Margaret Jane.
Martin George is so-far unidentified.
George Ginge (spelled in the diary "Gingy") is listed as a single man in
the 1860 census of Utah. He was a 45-year-old miner, born in
England, and living in Virginia City, Carson Co. (present-day
Nevada).
Sallie Hare is so-far unidentified.
James Henry Hart, b. June 21, 1825, in England, was a single man. He

later married Sabina Scheib in 1861 in Salt Lake City. He was a lawyer. They settled ultimately in Bear Lake, Idaho, where he became a newspaper editor, a legislator, and a judge. Information from Third Generation Records of the Church.

Jacob Hoffheins was captain of the wagon train, which was remembered as the Hoffheins Company. Sarah writes the name "Hawfines."

Huffaker is so-far not identified.

"Br. Jones" is too common a name to identify.

There were two brothers, Seth and Robert Langton, who with their families went to Cache County and settled near Brigham. Hubert Howe Bancroft, *Utah* (San Francisco, 1889), p. 597.

Matthew McCune and wife, Sarah Elizabeth Caroline, had an amazing story to tell. He had been serving in the British army in India, and they learned about Mormonism from two young men, Benjamin Riches and George Barber. The upshot was that they accepted the new faith and were on their way with the Delaware Company in 1857. They settled first in Moroni, Sanpete Co. McCune went on several missions, one to Burma, and others to England. They made their permanent home in Nephi, Joab Co. Probably the boy mentioned as "Harry" in the diary was their 17 year-old son, Henry, so-named in the 1860 census. Andrew Jensen, *op. cit.*, III, p. 161.

William Davis Robinson and his wife, Ellatheria, are identified in the family list.

Captain Jesse Bigley Martin led the very first wagon train that season, arriving in Salt Lake City on Sept. 12. He was returning from a British mission. Hafen, *op. cit.*, p. 157.

There were too many Millers for identification.

James P. Park was the President of the Sixth Handcart Co., made up of 154 handcarts. They arrived in Salt Lake City on Sept. 12. Hafen, *op. cit.*, p. 153.

Too many Sharps dot the pages of early Mormon history.

Patriarch John Lyman Smith (1828-1898), was ordained to that post on Oct. 8, 1848. Hosea Stout wrote in his diary for that date, "Conference met. The authorities passed the usual ordeal. Father John Smith appointed Patriarch of the whole Church . . . " Stout, *op. cit.*, p. 332. He was a cousin of founder Joseph Smith. Bitton, *op. cit.*, p. 324; Robert B. Day, *They Made Mormon History* (S.L.C., 1968), pp. 19-20.

Erastus Snow was an important Mormon leader, who was returning to Utah in 1857 after an extended stay in the east. Bitton, *op. cit.*, p.

332, comments on Snow's "Autobiography," which is in typescript in the Historical Department of the Church in Salt Lake City.

George J. Taylor was the 22 year-old son of John Taylor.

John Taylor was an important pioneer Mormon leader, future third President of the Church. He was returning to Utah after several years in New York publishing a newspaper called *The Mormon*. Jensen, *op. cit.*, I, pp. 14-19.

Thomas Sirls Terry was returning from a two-year mission to the eastern states. He had crossed the plains in 1847 to Utah with the pioneer group. Bitton, *op. cit.*, p. 356.

William Wilkes and his wife, Elizabeth, and their three children were among the English immigrants of 1857. They settled near Brigham, Utah, in Cache Co., according to the 1860 census. He is listed as a "laborer" with $250 in real and $20 in personal property.

Phineas Young was a brother of Brigham Young. He had migrated to Utah in 1847 with the pioneer group. He was a "printer, saddler, and mail carrier." He was returning from a mission to England. Stout, *op. cit.*, p. 210, fn. 5 by editor Juanita Brooks.

SARAH MARIA MOUSLEY'S DIARY

Left home or rather my former home[1] on the   day of May for Utah. landed in Philadelphia the afternoon of the same day & started for Baltimore through Wilmington as President Taylor had made arraingements for our going by that line of railway on Friday the   and on the following Tuesday landed in Iowa City, Iowa, stoped at the Irving house kept by Mr. Stanton for near three weeks at which time our goods having all come to hand we started for the camp of the saints with the view of starting across the plains and making the camp our home untill such times as we would start being very much detained on account of a remarkable late spring, cattle not coming etc, I never knew or appreciated the merits of mormonism as since in the wisdom of Gods providence I have been thrown so

---

[1] Wilmington, Delaware.

continually amidst the enemies of truth and consequently I am not priviledged to withdraw from their society. joyful were my feeling although many privations in view when the time rolled on to again mingle with the people whose aim was to do the will of God and obey his commands. the day on which we reached the camp our spirits were enlivened by the presence of President Erastus Snow whose smiling countenance was recognise by all those who had formerly listened to the words of truth that ever fell from his tonge he remained with us at camp untill Wednesday the May and on Tuesday Pa bought from him a farm of one hundred acres situate in the immediate vicinity of Salt Lake City price three thousand Dollars and the afternoon of the same day President Snow solemnised the marriage ceremony of Wm Robinson and Cousin Ellatheria D. Peria[2] The following Saturday Washington [Mousley] drove his carriage into the city with a hope of meeting President John Taylor, which he did, as his son George was undisposed from having ruptured a blood vessel the previous day President Taylor remained with us untill Wednesday organising our company which consisted of ninteen ox wagon's and two carriages the company was organized as follows Captain Hawfines [Jacob Hoffheins] as Captain of the company, Martin George as Captain of the first ten and G.W. Mousley as Captain of the second or Delaware ten Joseph Foreman as Chaplain Br Mccuein [McCune] Captain of the guard and Titus Mousley Captain of the herdman and on the following Saturday afternoon we made a start for Florence[3] with very wild cattle inexperienced drivers etc. our journey consisted of five miles. the following day which was Sunday

---

[2] See under Ellatheria Dupont Peria in list of family members above.

[3] Florence, Nebraska, was a new town first surveryed in 1853. It was incorporated by the legislature of the new territory in March 1855. It became an important gathering point for emigrating Mormons. It is now at the northern edge of Omaha. Lilian L. Fitzpatrick, *Nebraska Place Names* (Lincoln, 1967), p. 56.

in the afternoon we started again   the cattle were something
better than the first day.   the next morning Monday took
an early start but did not travel far on account of
inexperienced cattle and drivers   Tuesday morning started
again after a very pleasant nights rest in the camp["ground"
crossed out] there was a man the owner of the ground came
and priviledged us to take fuel as much as we needed and
desired some of the priesthood to administer to a brother
whose name I think is Fisher and whom was sick
Wednesday Morning May [June] 10   started precisely at
the appointed hour which was seven O clock   Captain
Mousleys ten leading   traveled well   camped at twelve o
clock   the last ten had not all come in — we waited over two
hours for those behind and Washington started accompanied
by Br George J Taylor in search of them   found them fast in
the mud broken an axil and consequently the company was
obliged to camp for the remainder of the day whilst they put
in a new axil for Br Gingy [Ginge]
Thursday [June] 11.   started about half past eight detained
by the broken wagon of yesterday   passed through the most
beautiful country   some handsome houses were to be seen
and evidence of good taste   passed through a handsome
villiage called Brooklyn [Iowa] at which place Pa's carriage
stoped   we entered a store and were soon asked where are
you   travelling   Pa   told   them   Utah   they
said you had better stay and assist in building our villiage to
which Pa replied no indeed   he did not sell his former home
to allow his means to benefit the gentiles   he intended to do
all   he   could   for   the   interests   of   mormonism   encamped about two miles from the villiage above named,
Friday 12   Started at half past six in the morning   not
very clear but a prospect of rain cleared away and proved a
splendid day   stoped for dinner as usual   the company

travelled better than usual   they seem to be improving in experience   encamped on the open plain   there was water near but no fuel   we all seemed lost on that account but the goodness of God provided for our want and as an old gentleman was passing with a wagon load of wood he called to the children to come to him and he then gave them wood sufficient for cooking supper and breakfast which kindness will never be forgotten by me   numbers came to see us and ask questions with a request to stay for our evening's meeting   accordingly Jos Foreman spoke to them for a considerable time   had good attention from sensible person's.

Saturday 13.   started early and travelled within one or two miles of a handsome town called Newton [Iowa] encamped near the banks of a handsome stream just in sight of camp of a Kansas emigrants who had kept either just before or behind us

Sunday [June] 14.   left the camp a quarter of eight and passed through the handsome town spoken of yesterday encamped on the banks of a stream about Six miles from the town at six   had preaching by Jos Foreman Chaplain, to quite a congregation who seemed to have suffectient interest in the gospel to hear.   very good behaviour retired at nine oclock.   to rest

Monday 15   Started at six Oclock   travelled ten miles   at noon encamped on the banks of mud creek where we found a splendid spring   started again after dinner and travelled ten miles   encamped on the banks of a beautiful stream   had a violent thunder storm   rained violently could make no fire on account of the wet

Tuesday [June] 16   started about seven   had a very wet day yet occasional sunshine   miserable roads   got along well considering the disadvantages of the rain. We reached fort Des Moines about six oclock   encamped near the city in the rain   had a great number of visiters among whom was an acquaintance whose name is William Day from Delaware we were very glad to meet him as he is a nice man   when he was told a Mormon camp was passing through the city he followed to search for us, he came to Des Moines about six weeks ago, after wishing us a pleasant and prosperous journey and congratulations exchanged we separated,

Wed 17   this morning we found our cattle were over half strayed away   diligent search was made and at dinner we were ready to start having the good fortune to find every one of the lost cattle although so many were missing   travelled about eight miles through the worst roads we had been called to pass   encamped on the banks of a pretty stream   had a supper and meeting as usual   retired early,

Thursday 18   Started at six and passed through the handsomest country I ever behild   paria's [prairies] decked with varied flowers. and in the midst of a wide spreading pararie we observed a beautiful grove   we thought it had been trained by a skillful hand to suit the taste of the possessor instead of being in the wild domein of nature   my heart exclaimed how beautiful how wonderful thou art sweet earth. Oh how my heart rejoices in pursuing the pleasant path of duty   encamped on the edge of North Coon Creek   had a pleasant night   S

Friday 19   Started at six and crossed the Creek by ford   a splendid ford the water clear and not to deep.   crossed Middle Coon and travelled about twenty miles   had good luck and all things passed off well

Saturday 20   Started at six and travelled well   stopped to dinner   started again and made good time having travelled twenty miles   at three oclock encamped on the open pararie   had early supper and just about sunset we beheld four Missionarys from the vally   their names were [blank space]   supper was prepared for the weary travellers as they had crossed the plains to Florence by hand carts   our meetings were joyful and yet sorrowful for seperating they to labour among the gentiles, how rejoyced were their hearts when on raising a hill they beheld the Mormon Camp at its foot,   retired to rest at nine.

Sundy 21.   Started at seven   travelled well although a child of Br Andrews fell out of the wagon and the first wheel passed over his body   his name is Nephi Andrews aged about seven years   travelled the distance of about twenty miles   pleasant day   all enjoyed ourselfs well passing through a beautiful country

Monday 22.   Started at the appointed time   travelled well being cool   the cattle were lively and got along first rate   passed through the town of Lewistown [Lewis, Iowa]   quite a pretty place and rapidly improving   the people crowded round to hire some of our folks offering good wages if they would stay   some were almost ready to stay   travelled about twenty miles and encamped out of town,

Tuesdy 23   Started at six and travelled quite well   not so fast as usual   rather warmer for the cattle   passed over some great hills and pleasant vales   beautiful flowers to improve the appearance of the prospect of diversifing and beautifing the surrounding object   travelled about seventeen miles and encamped near the river called Little Jordon   had quite a shower to cool the air and the evening passed maraculously away as there was no gentile to infringe upon our right which was a treat to us as we have almost become tired answering questions people have no business to ask   after a pleasant meeting retired at ten to rest.

Wednesdy 24.   Started at six and travelled well although

very warm   halted for dinner   the cattle were almost
overcome on account of the great heat   camped for the
night near a beautiful stream

Thursday 25   Again started at six   cooler than yesterday
more pleasant for travelling   encamped for dinner on the
Missourie bottom near the spot where the Mormon soldiers
were drafted in forty six. viewed the spot where a few short
years ago in compliance with the contrys call men left their
weeping families to fight for the contry that had exiled them
from its protection on account of the religion of heaven.
encamped for the night in Bluff city a beautiful town of
considerable magnitude   were visited by a number of
gentiles and three gentlemen of our acquaintance two from
West Chester and one from New London   they were very
much surprised to see us there and yet happy to meet an
acquaintance   they were to polite to ridicule Mormonism
and yet did not fail to request Pa to stay and then with his
influence to improve their city   to this he replied oh!
no!   staid to meeting   retired in good season to rest

Fridy 26   Started at six and travelled over some of the
steepest mountains I ever could have thought it possible to
pass   met Br John Taylor who came from Florence to meet
the camp and whose happy smile illumed our way and whose
presence is ever a joy and comfort   those who are honoured
with his society encamped on the bank of the mighty
Missourie but feared it to late to ferry our wagons across the
river   were obliged to cross the river for water for culinary
purposes   Pa and Washingtons family staid in Florence as
they had entered the city expecting he would likewise do so

Sat 27   at six began to ferry the wagons across the river and
encamped on the top of the hill where there were two others
camps one of them is expected to travel with us   came on a
heavy rain which made it somewhat unpleasant   visited Br

Langton and took dinner   returned in the carriage to the
camp   remained in the wagon untill the rain was over   after
supper Willie & I accompanied President Taylor in a walk
to the highest summit around where we viewed the camp's
and the city of Florence with many other objects of beauty
and interest   retired at ten to rest

Sunday [June] 28.   beautiful clear yet warm   passed the
day in camp busey.   after ten the girls Nellie Amanda &
Willie rode with Br Taylor to visit the graveyard of the
saints near the city of Florence   it contained about six
hundred graves.   after meeting retired to rest

Mon 29.   Were very busy washing ironing cooking etc
clear and warm   just as we were about to retire we were
soluted by a splendid seranade from the citizens   the music
was splendid the evening beautiful and everything delightful,
President Taylor P[handwriting not clear] Young and three
[unclear] other bretheren took supper with us

Tuesdy 30.   Finished washing and ironing   were busy
preparing to start on the morrow.   Pa and Ma visited
Omaha city   found it really beautiful   retired to rest after
survice

Wednesdy July 1st   we bade adieu to civilization and started
across the plains in company with some of the St Louis
saints   found some of the teams who had started before
broken down having upset and broken some of the running
gears of the wagon   were somewhat detained on account of
inexperienced cattle from those teams that were added to our
number   retired to rest early not being well   President
Taylor his son George Br Miller and his boy took supper
with us

Thursdy 2   Bade adieu to President Taylor and those
associated with him as they were going with mules and
consequently much faster travelling would be done by

them   we seperated preying mutually for each others safty
and prosperity not only untill we meet in the peaceful home
of the saints but through life   travelled well considering we
had two new teams of St Louis saints in our company whose
cattle as well as drivers were inexperienced   overtook a
wagon belonging to Br Cuningham   overset   broken guide
the men went to work unloaded and mended   set up loaded
and started   travelled such a distance as to make us now
twenty-seven miles from Council bluff city   started in good
time   travelled well   reached Elk horn about six oclock
ferryed our teams across one at a time in about two
hours.   the current is deep swift and not very pleasant to
ferry   encamped for the night.

Fridy 3   started about seven or eight and travelled about
thirteen miles to the Platt river   passed the liberty pole[4] a
flourishing village right in an Indian country   a flag was
blowing and as we passed they cheered us I suppose on
account of the American flag which floats at the head of our
train   encamped beside the Platt had to use the water from
the river generally but we sent our carriage back to the village
to get water which was very good   overtook the St Louis
company who were to travel with us through the indian
country   our company now consists of thirty nine wagons
first rate people having been added to our number

Sat 4   rested from travelling   washed ironed & baked
attended two meetings and a musical entertainment consisting of dancing singing etc   prayer by President Hart
benediction by Jos Foreman   retired to rest at eleven and
represided ourself by sleep

Sundy 5   arose about five   prepared for a start   morning

---

[4] Liberty Pole was a Mormon way station near present Fremont, Dodge Co. It would
be given the second name a year later and incorporated by an act of the legislature on
Nov. 2, 1858. Fitzpatrick, *op. cit.*, p. 54. *See also* Merrill J. Mattes, *The Great Platte
River Road*, Neb. State Hist. Soc. Pub., XXV (Lincoln, 1969), p. 130.

service half past seven   started at eight   travelled all
day   pleasant fine cool day   encamped for the night after
meeting retired to rest

Mondy 6   started at seven and travelled about fifteen
miles   encamped early which gave the sisters a chance to
bake and cook which by the bye is quite necessary for comfort
and convenience   travelled slower than usual

Tuesday 7   started at half past six   travelled well   we
have seen no Indians for the past four or five days   an
incident connected with the indians I will here relate as they
have been very friendly with us   we returned the compliment in the same manner they called at our table for
refreshment and accordingly I was making lemonade which
I offered to one who had watched the process of preparing
and whom I had handed a chair   he seated himself with
great dignity and took in his hand the cup I offered but
would not touch the drink untill I would drink with him   I
began to drink from another cup but he handed his to me as
much as to say drink from this   I took it drank and returned
it   he drank and said good squaw with many gestures of
satisfaction   he drank exclaiming good good   encamped
on the Loup fork a splendid place   a good spring of water
and everything very very nice except the muscutoes which
were very troublesome

Wed 8   Started at half past six   travelled well but just as
we were about to encamp for dinner Br. Langtons team were
overset by a woman passing in front of his cattle and frighting
them   his family were in but not hurt only badly frightned,
after dinner started again and travelled well   encamped
near Beaver settlement[5] having travelled twenty good

---

[5] This was Genoa, a Mormon way station set up to give aid to their immigrants from
the east. It had been established on May 11, 1857, by settlers from Florence. On July 1
it was reported to have "97 men, 25 women, 40 children, 42 yoke of oxen, 20 cows, 6
horses, 20 hogs, two dozen chickens, 2 cats and dogs aplenty." LeRoy R. and Ann W.
Hafen, *Handcarts to Zion, 1856-1860* (Glendale, CA, 1960), pp. 151-52.

miles   met with Br Sharp formerly of our branch in
Delaware   retired at ten to rest

Thu 9   At half past eight began to ford the Loup Fork
river which was very wide and in some parts swift others
quicksandy   got across very well although some of the
Sisters who forded the river on foot were almost overcome by
fatigue through the swift current   encamped on the western
side of the river for the remainder of the day and
night.   retired to rest after meeting

Friday 10   Started again on our journey   travelled untill
about eleven oclock when a thunder storm came up   stoped
for dinner and untill the storm should be over   a difficulty
here occurred between the two companies when after a while
a reconciliation took place although a difficulty arose between
Br Taylor teamster and the Captain   I never witnessed
such a struggle which ended by the Captain tore the mans
cloths out of the wagon and left him on the plains alone   the
last the camp seen of him he was kneeling in prayer   we
travelled the distance [blank space] miles and encamped late
at night without wood or other conveniences

Saturday 11   Early this morning a committee of Elders
came from Genoa or Beaver settlement accompanied by the
man whom was left on the plains yesterday   a council was
called   the captain forced to acknowledge the great wrong
he had done promised to do better in future and lead the
people with more of gentleness   remained in camp all day

Sundy 12   Started at about seven   passed through some
very pretty contry and some places where there was not one
particule of grass as it had been burned off with the parari
fire   encamped for dinner and here visited or went to see
the corps of an aged Sister who had been subject to desease of
heart and died from fright by her husband being kicked by
one of his oxen   the kick did not injure the man but she
witnessed the scene and died from fright exclaiming my

husband will be hurt   she leaves no family except the
husband   her age was sixty three   traveled the distance of
sixteen miles and encamped for the night as there was a
violent thunderstorm coming and indeed of all the storms I
ever witnessed I think this the most distressing   however
we were forewarned by sufficient time to get supper which
had become quite a consideration to the traveller.

Monday 13   Discovered on search a great number of our
cattle were missing as also a pair of horses that belonged to Br
Huffaker of the St Louis company   search was made and
the missing cattle and horses were found   the sister whose
remains have been deposited beneath the parari sod leaves
two children in England to morn her loss   remained in
camp all day on account of having a great distance to travel
ere we come to water   had a splendid meeting this evening
retired early

Tues 14   Arose a few minutes past three   started five
minutes of six   having a heavy rain and no water in view
short of twenty two miles encamped for dinner   had good
grass for the cattle   started again and travelled on untill we
came to Parari [Prairie] Creek⁶   rode in the carriage this
afternoon as Ma was not very well and wished to ride where
she could lay down   just after our encampment for the
night we were called to recieve a little stranger in our midst
who if fortunate would yet call me Aunt. Gertie M.H.
Forman's child, a girl, very fine. Mother and daughter
doing well   retired early to rest after service

Wed [July] 15   Started off about half past six and travelled
untill we came to a ford to cross the creek   had good luck in

---

⁶ This was a favorite Mormon camping place. A year before in the official journal of
the First Handcart Company it was reported on July 31st that at Prairie Creek there was
"No wood, but plenty of buffalo chips." The next day the handcarts crossed the creek
twice with great difficulty. The carts "had to be carried over by the bethren." Hafen, *op.
cit.*, p. 205. The camp was just east of Wood River.

crossing and encamped at dinner time near water for cattle   encamped for the night on Pararia Creek

Thurs 16   Started early and crossed Pararia Creek and encamped for dinner near a place of water for cattle and crossed Wood river on an old bridge and encamped near the shore of the same   a splendid place to camp   good water and wood   retired to rest for the night.   threaten a violent storm from the thunder and lightning but the rain passed over and a cool wind refreshed us   splendid to sleep

Frid 17   Started at half past six   travelled well encamped for dinner where there was no water either for man or beast   at four or five oclock we drove to a river I think the Platt and watered the cattle   they were almost famished with druth after which we drove four miles to the Elm Creek and encamped for the night   a splendid camp ground retired for the night

Sat 18   Started at six oclock and travelled to a fine watering place   encamped for dinner   warm but more pleasant air than yesterday.

Sunday 19   Started and travelled a short distance from the old road on account of hearing of the misfortunes of Capt Martins company as they had a very bad stampeed   on account of Buffalo being so numerous the cattle became frighted as they were hitched too ready to start in the morning   they broke two wagons to pieces and lost fifteen head of cattle   we met three wagon's returning to Genoa to wait another season   each wagon had only one yoke of cattle and their load was mostly gone   sorrow filled my heart as I gazed on the wreck of misfortune. Surely the lord our God had been good to us in thus preserving us from danger and misfortune   encamped on a small stream for the remainder of the day   washed and had a splendid bath as Sunset   the lady's enjoyed it very much.

Mon 20   Started and travelled the distance of twenty three miles on account of water and then encamped after dark without grass wood or water

Tuesday [July] 21   Started at four oclock and travelled about four or five miles   encamped for breakfast near the Platt river where the stampeed of Br Martins company took place   visited the place of destruction and death as two persons were killed a man sixty four and a child four years of age   travelled well the rest of the day   encamped for the night near the river

Wed 22   Started about seven oclock late on account of looking for an ox belonging to Br Snow and which had been strayed   dined on Buffalo for the first time   encamped near the river for dinner   remained the rest part of the day in camp on account of some of the hunters having shott a Buffaloe about five miles distant   accordingly a wagon was unloaded and they started for the prise   returned about seven oclock when the meat was divided and all parties satisfied with the superabundance of fresh meat   retired late having been ironing and baking

Thursday 23   Started at six and travelled well the day being cooler than usual   encamped near the cool spring which is really beautiful and so refreshing to the thirsty traveller   the water boils up from a bed of sand so as to afford drink plenty for the cattle   surely our God is good for his mercy to us in our unworthyness in causing a fountain to burst forth as it were on the sandy desert   I feel to say Lord we will praise the[e] whilst life and thought and being last or immortality endures, retired to rest at ten   all well

Fridy 24   Arose at half past three   breakfast before the God of day had shed his resplendant ray's over the calm face of the morning   started at six and encamped near the Platt river having passed the beautifulest scenery my eye's ever

rested upon   the bluffs on each side the wild flowers
beautiful to behold the air redolent with odor the calm still
waters of beautiful lakes all, all serving alike to awake an
adoration to the God whose word we have left the happy
scenes of childhood years to repair to the mountains with the
saints of light

Sat 25   Started about half past five   cool day   splendid
for travelling   travelled the distance of twenty-two miles
some parts of which was very sandy road   encamped in
good time having forded several streams   retired early in
good health

Sundy 26   Arose early. pleasant morning cloudy and
threatens rain   travelled the distance of about two and a half
miles over sand hills the most terrible I ever beheld encamped
on the banks of the Platt river for dinner   this morning had
news from Br J. Taylor's he having passed these sand hills on
the thirteenth of this month.

Mondy [July] 27   Started early and travelled well   our
cattle very quiet to all appearance but in the afternoon of this
day I was called to witness the most terrific of all scenes a
stampeed on the plain   the cattle started all most all together
and Oh my father my heart sickens as I recall the scene and
my soul is grievd in memory of the painful occurrance   I
beheld men thrown woman leaping from their wagons
children screaming as team after team ran on in wild
confusion dashing headlong on the wild parari without
pouer to impeed their progress in the wild scene of apparent
death   God gave me presence of mind sufficient to remain
in my wagon which I did and alone except the unseen
guardian who in God's wisdon did not leave me alone but
shielded me from the shafts of the destroyer   I set or
remained unhurt and beheld the cattle stoped and their
affright calmed in answer to my fervant prayer   after the

wagon in which I had been riding was stoped and my driver
who had been knocked down and allmost knocked senceless
had overtaken me I alighted from the wagon only to witness
the most terriffic of all scenes   my sisters loved and dear all
jumped from the wagon and Nellie and Willie were badly
injured   in their fright they jumped from the wagon and
weather some of the cattle had steped in our dear Willie face
and on the side near her heart and streaming with blood and
crying for help while near her was Harry[7] fainting in view of
beholding Willie thus suffering   a little further and Amanda
was endeavoring to restore Nellie who had in falling hurt
her back and being in poor health was illy able to endure the
injury recieved. Amanda who also jumped had hurt her knee
and shoulder but fortunately the carriage had remained
behind and the horses knew nothing of the fright and yet in
all my heart exclaimed Lord we will praise thee for thy
goodness thou has shielded us from death   thou hast taught
us a bitter lesson on the power of satin and his designs to
overthrow thy saints   thou hast stood by in the hour of triel
and thy arm has protected us in a maraculous manner   and
now Oh Father we pray thee through thy son to accept the
heartfelt gratitude of all and enable us to serve thee faithfully
in time and eternity!   encamped for the night but just as we
were about to retire our cattle stampeded again; in gratitude
to Captain Terry I must say his kindness will ever claim a
memory and through the ceaseless ages of vast eternity will
in reverence as a ministring angel to those endeared and
suffering ones of my Fathers house his skill in attending his
faith and power in God and many acts of kindness by day and
night shall ever claim my faith and prayer's and should
opportunity ever offer me to turn from him a bitter cup in

---

[7] We have not been able to identify "Harry," who is mentioned several times is this
diary. He could have been the 17-year-old son of Matthew and Sarah Elizabeth
Caroline McCune, who are listed among the persons named in the diary (see list above).

life   my vow is now to do so and may God preserve him in
the truth in health strength and the pleasant preformance of
every duty untill we shall all regain the presence of our
Father from whose presence we are now exiled that we if
faithful pay dwell with him eturnally.

Tuesday 28   Arose not very well from excitement and
anxiety   remained all day in camp   were visited by Indians
noble and true they deeply sympathised with us in our
bereavement or distress of the sisters and some of them
remained around the bed where Nellie and Willie and
watched all night   one wept and said he loved the pale faces
of those by whom he was surrounded and would prey to the
good Spirit for their recovey   the girls better and the men
sixteen in number went in persuit of the cattle lost

Wed 29   the girls seem better today   remained in camp
and were visited by a tribe of young Indian children   Oh
how I love their society and although so ignorant of their
language I love to behold them   the tribe is the Siou

Thursday 30   the girls seem better but still not able to move
unless lifted   no news of the cattle untill night when a part
of the men returned for provision as some of the men had run
out of eating material   the lost cattle numbered forty of
which number Pa lost three   retired at eleven to rest.

Fridy 31   It was deemed wisdom to remove from where we
were now encamped and accordingly the cattle were divided
and we moved the distance of two miles   one of the men
returned from the persuit of cattle   his horse overcome and
fell in the river from exhastion and fatiegue   after horse feed
the horse was brought to camp

Sat August 1   Started again for a move   the men returned
without the cattle   a dead loss but fortunately we were still
able to move and rejoicing that our circumstances were as
comfortable as we were   the hand cart company passed us

yesterday and a train of ox teams united with them under the charge of Brs Parks [Park] and Dilly [Dille]   all much better in health and rejoicing   travelled the distance of fourteen miles mostly through the sands   very deep and hard for the weakened teams   all rejoiced when we were through   encamped after dusk and prepared supper by the light of the moon   retired about ten

Sundy 2   Started at six   travelled well and encamped on the banks of the Platt for dinner   the girls get along well riding in the carriage and seem much better   our camping place for dinner was Ash hollow a splendid and romantic place   encamped for the night near the Platt and here witnessed an awful thunderstorm   all much better   the girls are now getting able to help themselfs to walk   Captain Terry is as usual their attendant

Mon 3   Started at eight on account of rain early this morning   had splendid scene and travelled about twenty-one miles   encamped on Croll creek[8]   a beautiful ground splendid water   another violent thunder storm   getting along well

Tues 4   Started at half past five for the purpose of getting ahead of a train of wagons and hand cart companys who it was reported had small pox   overtook them at dinner and passed by   all in usual health and spirits and although some of the teams were overcome from heat and a long drive yet all seemed well in spirit with few exceptions   encamped for the night near the Platt

Wed [August] 5   Started at an early hour and travelled well although very warm and some of our teams went back to assist those who were weakended by the loss of cattle   I

---

    [8] This could be another name to add to the list of those given for modern Pumpkin Creek, which flows around the south base of Court House Rock. Mattes says "it is plagued by a variety of names which contine to haunt modern writers and map-makers." Mattes, *op. cit.*, p. 341-42.

know not the exact distance of travel but came in sight of chimney Rock and indeed passed some of the most spendid edifices apparently my eye ever beheld. Oh how I wish mine were a painters pencil or poets pen   I would portray if possible the beauty of the scenes through which we have been called to pass

Thursday 6   Started quite early and had a splendid day for travelling   cool a little cloudy   came opposite Chimney Rock at dinner time   stopped for dinner   passed saleratus springs   very singular in appearance   travelled the distance of twenty one miles and encamped near the Platt   very pleasant day   the girls all better   a splendid camp ground

Fridy 7   Made 13 miles to spring creek for noon and 2 miles more P.M.   camped on the Platt river

Sat 8   Storm [handwriting obscure] heavy thunder and lightning in the night   cool and fine in the morning halted and bought oxen of a trader at 11 oclock A.M.   encamped on Platt river

Sund 9   Travelled 16 miles   heavy sand   lost 1 large ox for Mrs. Bowman

Mod 10   Camped at noon opposite Laramie   one man left behind to suffer on plains by Capt McCuen owing to dissatisfaction   by driving made 4 miles   camped on the Platt   wood and water pasture scarce

Tued 11   Passed a mountainous road   no water   no grass   travelled 14 or 15 miles   great [handwriting obscure] time   some weak teams to get along   found water   scarcely any grass   late to camp   some did not get up untill next morning

Wed 12   went 6 miles and camped to feed on mountain grass   wood and water plenty

Thurs [August] 13   Laid over to feed the cattle   nor sheer [obscure] some of them

Fridy 14   Seperated from the St Louis company this morning on account of scarcity of grass   travelled well over sand and some heavy hills   encamped on a beautiful stream for dinner called [blank] a very clear and cold spring a splendid place to camp   wood plenty   shade also which is indeed a treat   crossed a river at which place it would have been hard to have encamped for the night as we could find no water although the grass was very good   Captain Hawfines sick

Saturdy 15   were detained on account of an ox of Br Taylors having been left as it was lame and could not travel fast   two of Pa's men went back to bring him along   a nice cool morning   all well   the girls better   the Captain also   overtook the St Louis company when they encamped for the remainder of the day   Br Terry visited us at dinner time   we were pleased to see him well   started at four oclock and travelled a short distance through a hail storm   cool and very pleasant   encamped for the night near a beautiful spring but before the company were all in camp the water came rolling past from a water spout that had bursted occasioning a bad smell and spoiling our nice spring water

Sund [August] 16   Started early and travelled without water for the cattle   distance about three and a half miles   the other company close behind us   encamped about three oclock for the day the company passing us three miles   Br Terry came back in the evening and remained with us all night   the camp was mostly well

Mond 17   Arose early at three oclock   started before six   travelled about eleven miles of mountainous land and struck the river at two oclock for dinner   remained till three   started again   encamped for the night near the river having found a splendid spot of grass and a nice spring of

good water   the St Louis company encamped near   all
well   about 8 miles   SM.

Tuesday 18   Arose about three oclock and started half past
five   travelled about ten or twelve miles this morning stoped
for dinner at half past one near the Platt   some splendid
grass short but good   grass improves now   very cold
mornings and evenings   Br Hart and Br Huffaker came
past searching for a camp ground   St Louis company all
well   I feel like wishing the journey over as tis so cool for
Grandma Pa and some more who are not able to endure the
cold

Wed [August] 19   Arose in good season but to our
disadvantage found about twenty head of our cattle gone
search being made the cattle found and started again having
a great mountain to assend and heavy sandy roads   met Br
Jones and Br Atwood from this new settlement that is now
being formed on the Deer Creek[9]   these men were very
much surprised to see us this side of the river   the road is so
much better on the other side of the river   we regret being
on this side as the roads are awful   scarcely passable with
our weakened teams   an express arrived from the valley for
those in the settlement as well as the camps to hasten
home   Oh how I wish for the wings of the morning to fly
away to the saints of light

Thurs 20   Started again to travell through the sand and
high hills   encamped for dinner   a splendid place   grass
good   Pa's carriage went on to the bridge [Reshaw's Bridge]
and stoped for some business such as shoeing his horses and
so on   all will come to the bridge in the afternoon
encamped for the night after passing through very heavy
sand and high mountains

---

[9] Deer Creek was another Mormon way station to give aid to the immigrants from the
east. It is the site of present Glenrock, Wyoming. Hafen, *op. cit.*, p. 151.

Friday 21   Arose early and started about half past six
travelled slowly on account of hills and sand   an express
from the valley to hasten home which was good news to
all   the Captain found two oxen   one proved a dead
one   the other a nice young steer they were on the opposite
shore and at evening we encamped near the Texas company
of Saints[10] on their way home to the valley   there were only
about eight or ten wagons and over 1000 head of cattle as
they were taking a great many with them

Sat [August] 22   Arose in good season but did not get
started untill eight Oclock as six of our cattle had strayed
amoungst the Texas herd   the Captain lost one yoke of his
that belonged to the church   he started in search of
them   Br Wilkes accompanyed him but the cattle were
found in the herd   we started on as there was a drive of
perhaps twenty miles before us on account of Saleratus
water   near thirty head of dead cattle on the road since
yesterday on all belonging to emigrants who had gone before
us on our journey   fortunately for us we came to some
beautiful springs now known as Willow Springs   The trees
have decayed and the stumps alone remained to mark this
spot   the ground around is full of lumps or mounds and will
be easily recognised on that account   the cattle were driven
over a mile to avoid bad water   the springs are splendid but
not sufficient to water the cattle   passed some beautiful
mountains red in appearance   the distance not over 13
miles

Sundy 23   Started about seven o clock on account of
herding our cattle with the Texas company came to
prospect hill really a beautiful spot   we beheld the Sweet

---

[10] There is a note in the journal to the effect that this company was captained by
Homer Duncan who was returning from a mission in Texas. Davis Bitton says that
there is a 57 page "History of the Life of Homer Duncan," in the Historical
Department of the Church in Salt Lake City. See Bitton, *Guide*, p. 93.

water mountains in the distance   rainy   at noon we came
to a nice spring of water   stoped whilst the rain should
continue   encamped for the night   all well

Mondy 24   Bought some new cattle one yoke for Pa   had
some trouble to get them seperated from the herd as they had
been purchased of the Texas company   did not start until
almost noon   came in sight of Devils gate and encamped for
the night on the Sweet water at the foot of Independance
Rock.

Teu 25   Arose early   had breakfast soon and all necessary
arrangements made for visiting Independance Rock mounted
the towering summit and viewed the surrounding objects but
feel my pen or thoughts inadequate to the task of portraying
a true picture of the awful grandue and beauty of these
scenes   encamped about three miles this side of Devils
Gate   stoped at the station near the Gate and had the horses
shod   did not travell over seven or eight miles today some
very slow teams   met some kind hearted saints at the Gate

Wed [August] 26   Arose early   had a very great storm of
wind   blew down the large tent and caused us some
disadvantages   started about seven and encamped almost
dark making only about twelve miles to-day

Thursday 27   This morning we concluded to seperate as
there were some teams or person's who would not keep up so
Pa and Br Washington concluded to take their wagons and
Br Lankton also accompaning us   the Captain seemed well
satisfied but I do not believe he was   moved along
well   passed the Texas company and get along well for as Br
Taylor said we could divide into tens whenever we should
deem it wisdom we all feel as though we should get along
better since the seperation   at dinner time Br Lankton
seemed dissatisfied and concluded to wait for the wagons we
left in the morning   had a splendid camp ground   grass

wood and splendid water being near the ford No 4 of Sweet
Water   in   the   evening   Will   Robinson,   Harry   and   I
accompanied Sallie Hare [handwriting obscure] to the other
camp for the purpose of obtaining Sallies clothes as she was
going   with   us   and   her   cloths   were   in   Mrs   Bowmans
wagon   we got her trunk and returned in peace to our
camp   they had a bad sandy camp ground   all well   distance 17 miles

Fridy 28   Started at six and travelled well about twenty-one
miles   as we encamped two young men rode into our camp
and took of the saddles from their horses & remained with us
all the night   had a nice ground and good time   get along
much better since we seperated and have good times

Sat 29   Did not start as soon as usual about seven and as
those two young men were about to leave us Pa invited them
to see us when we get home   he also enquired their names
when to our surprise we had been entertaining our Patriarch
John Smith   we travelled about two miles and came to the
sweet water where there was an abundance of most beautiful
fish   we took a net of Br Washingtons stopped the train
and began fishing   caught fish sufficient for three hearty
meals for the entire camp   as we were about done we beheld
Br John Smith and his comrade coming to us   they assisted
netting in the fish   observed how to salt them so they would
keep   we were stoped about one and a half hour and made
20 miles   about three or four was the most dreadful rocky
road I had passed   so trying on the wagons   came to camp
just a few moments after sunset   a splendid ground   wood
and water and all things well

Sundy 30   Arose early and started in good season   drove
to the station   encamped for dinner   started again and
stoped in good season on a branch of the Sweet Water   had
a splendid camp ground   all well

Mondy 31   Did not start untill about eight oclock   a

company of Indians came to our camp and seemed rather inclined to steal   encamped after going 14 miles for dinner when six boy's from the vally came to our camp and staid with us all night   plenty of game   get along well   peace prevails which is a great consideration.

Tues Sep 1   Started in good season and left our brethren whose society had been so aggreable to us   they to fulfill their mission   we to reach our home in the moutains of Israel   travelled twenty one miles and encamped on little Sandy a splendid ground   grass sufficient for our cattle not being so numerous as before the seperation

Wed 2   Arose all well   travelled fast as the weather is now cool and pleasant for travelling   we heard Br Lewis was on Weber river[11] forty miles from the valley   passed the government train the first one en rout to Utah numbering about twenty six wagons   all well and get along well under the special care of our Father in Heaven   my heart rejoices in prospect of so speedy a meeting with those from whose lips flow the words of life   encamped on big Sandy for the night   grass rather poor

Thur 3   Started half past six and came to grass about ten oclock   turned out to graze and rest the cattle   stoped between two & 3 hours   started again and travelled untill night   encamped without water on account of going by direction on a finger   heard the river was quite a distance off

Fridy 4   arose and prepared for starting   this morning Mrs. Thomas Mousley had a little daughter added to her household   quite well and able to travell   travelled about eight miles and came to Green River a beautiful place and fery   five boats on this ferry   here we encamped for the purpose of resting the cattle etc

Sat 5   Remained in camp washing etc untill afternoon then

---

[11] Lewis Mousley was her brother who had traveled overland to Utah the year before, 1856. See list of family members above, p. 160.

forded the wagons over   encamped for the night   this
ferry seems to have been a business place   good grass and
plenty of water

Sun 6   This morning a beautiful chance for a prosperous
journey and may God our Father speed us home in peace and
prosperity   Started but found we had taken the California
road and was consequently obliged to retrace our steps   this
we found out through the kindness of a Mountaineer who
directed us aright

Mon [September] 7   Traded off some of our cattle by
giving considerable money and now started to retrace our
steps and get on the right road again   travelled to Green
river ford where we had crossed and some few miles below

Tues 8   Arose early and travelled well within about ten or
twelve miles from the ford where we should have been

Wed 9   Started and nooned at the Station and travelled
quite a distance   encamped without water for the night

Thurs 10   Arose early and went to a trading post and
procured potatoes cheese and fresh beef   passed Blacks ford
Hams fork and Black ford again

Frid 11   Passed small creek   no water   11 miles Black's
ford third time   2 miles and encamped 3 miles on a
stream   all well

Sat 12   Travelled 12 miles to Fort Bridger   met St Louis
com[pany]   all well and pleased to see us   Capt Hawfines
com   he started as soon as he heard we were coming   met
many saints and remained in camp all night

Sun 13   This morning were detained by getting oxen
shod   Capt Hawfines only travelled about one mile and
then waited for four wagons of his company whom he had left
because they could not find some of their cattle which
however they found and were ready to start with him
again   President Hart's company started about ten Oclock

we started between eleven & twelve   travelled well   all
well and get along well   passed cold springs on the right of
the road 6 miles a creek and spring 2 miles   5 miles to
Muddy fork and encamped on little Muddy one mile further
Mon [September] 14   passed copperas spring 3 miles
assended a high ridge the summit of which was altitude 7,315
feet   leanthy descent and narrow pass   travelled well and
nooned but were overtaken by the St Louis and Capt
Hawfines company who had not attempted to noon   encamped two miles east of Bear river   all company's
together   Capt Terry spent the evening with us

Tues 15   arose and started at seven Oclock and kept out the
way of the St Louis and Capt Hawfines   passed the Cache
cave[12] two miles and Camped making 18 or 20 miles

Wed [September] 16   Had a very heavy rain last night
cloudy morning and started down Echo Canyon some
dreadful places to pass

---

[12] This cave was often a favorite stopping place for immigrants ever since Orson Pratt
had visited it in July 1847. It is near the head of Echo Canyon, 9 miles from the
Wyoming border. Pratt had written in his journal, "The opening resembles very much
the doors attached to an out-door cellar, being about 8 feet high and 12 or 14 feet wide."
This landmark was later used by western outlaws to hide their loot. It had been named
by trappers who cached their supplies and furs there. *Utah, a Guide to the State* (Salt
Lake City, 1945), p. 355.

JULIA ARCHIBALD [HOLMES]
Courtesy, Denver Public Library

To Pike's Peak and New Mexico, 1858
◢ Julia Anna Archibald (Holmes)

INTRODUCTION

The two letters that follow tell the story of the Pikes Peak gold rush through the eyes of a young woman who participated in it: The first letter was written by Julia Anna Archibald [Holmes], who took part in the famous Lawrence, Kansas, Company which headed for the Colorado mines in early June 1858. She told her story for the benefit of the readers of *The Sibyl*, a little paper advocating the women's movement of the 1850s, published in Middleton, New York. A strong emphasis is on the journey as a special part of that movement. Julia does not use her husband's surname, Holmes, at any time in this letter. She tells of how she wore the "American" or "Reform" dress — i.e. the Bloomer costume,[1] which was named for Amelia Bloomer, a women's rights advocate of that day.

Julia addressed her letter to "Sister Sayer," the editor and publisher of *The Sibyl*. It appeared in the editions of March 15 and April 1, 1859. "Sister Sayer" was really Lydia Sayer Hasbrouck.[2] She, too, chose to use her maiden name and not her husband's surname.

Julia's letter is saturated with her feelings about her part in the women's movement. She wore her bloomers throughout, even to

---

[1] This costume had been worn by a number of other women on the western trails. See *Covered Wagon Women*, Volume IV, 1852 to California, for a discussion of this subject (pp. 12-15).

[2] Benjamin M. Shambaugh, "Hasbrouck, Lydia Sayer," *Dictionary of American Biography*, VIII (New York, 1932), pp. 306-07; Robert E. Riegel, *American Women: A Story of Social Change* (Cranbury, N.J., 1970), pp. 204-05; Paul S. Boyer, "Hasbrouck, Lydia Sayer," in Edward T. James, ed., *Notable American Women, 1607-1950*, II (Cambridge, MA, 1971), pp. 151-52.

the top of Pikes Peak. She asked to stand watch even as the men were required to do. Her letter/diary is a classic of the American westward movement; it is also a classic feminist statement of the mid-nineteenth century. We have transcribed it directly from *The Sibyl.*

There is an interesting contrast between Julia's letter to *The Sibyl* and the second letter published in the Lawrence, Kansas, *Republican* on October 7, 1858. This was addressed to her mother, Jane B. Archibald of Lawrence who sent it to the *Republican.* In contrast to the first letter this one contains not a word about women's rights. She says nothing about the clothing she wore on the journey, nor one word about her wanting to share everything with the men, even standing guard. Her married name, Holmes, is the appellation used both by her mother and by the editor of the newspaper.

In a remarkable book entitled *A Bloomer Girl on Pike's Peak* the Denver Public Library made Julia Holmes' story available to a wider public than the original by publishing it as a "Limited Edition" in 1949. The editor, Agnes Wright Spring, made a comprehensive study of the life of the diarist. It is to this detailed study that we turn for information on Julia Holmes' life. We have chosen to publish the letter once more to make it available to an even greater readership.

Julia Anna Archibald was born in Noel, Nova Scotia, on February 15, 1838, to John Christie and Jane B. Archibald. The family moved to Worcester County, Massachusetts, in 1848. She was second to the oldest in a family of eight children. When the Kansas-Nebraska act was passed in 1854, the family moved to Kansas as members of the free state movement. They were pioneer founders of Lawrence, Kansas. They were also closely associated with John Brown and his anti-slavery movement. Jane Archibald, her mother, was an early advocate of woman suffrage.

James H. Holmes arrived in Kansas in 1857 and settled near newly blossoming Emporia on the Neosho River. He named his farm "Holmes Ford." On October 9, 1857, he and Julia Archibald were married near Clinton by a "Reverend Nute." She and her husband and her brother, Albert W. Archibald, 18 years old, decided to join a party from Lawrence for the purpose of going to the Pikes Peak mines. This was in June 1858. She takes up the story herself from then on.

After their journey, unsuccessful as far as finding gold was concerned, she and her husband traveled part way home and then turned south to New Mexico. Her letter to *The Sibyl* was sent from Fort Union,[3] New Mexico, on March 15, 1859.

Over the following years the family spent much time in New Mexico. For a period James Holmes was Secretary of the Territory, having been appointed to the position by President Abraham Lincoln.

During the late years of the Civil War the family moved to Washington, D.C. where Julia lived out her life. There were four children: Charles and June died in their early years; Ernest Julio Holmes grew up to become a citizen of Trinidad, Colorado, and Phoebe became a teacher in Washington, D.C.

It was not long after they moved to the District of Columbia that Julia and James H. Holmes were divorced. She worked in federal bureaus over the years and continued her activities in women's organizations. She died on January 19, 1887.

THE LETTER OF
JULIA ANN ARCHIBALD [HOLMES]

Fort Union, New Mexico, Jan. 25th, 1859.

SISTER SAYER. — I think an account of my recent trip will be received with some interest by my sisters in reform, the readers of The Sibyl — if not by the rest of mankind

[3] Now Fort Union National Monument, located on U.S. Freeway #25, 27 miles northeast of Las Vegas. It was established by Col. Edwin V. Sumner in 1851 at a spring called Las Posas by the Mexicans, "The Holes" by the Americans. It served as a military center of activities for smaller posts throughout the southwest. It was a key point to be defended during the Civil War. It was abandoned by the military in 1891. Chris Emmett, *Fort Union and the Winning of the Southwest* (Norman, OK, 1965), *passim*. The massive James W. Arrott Collection on Fort Union is located at New Mexico Highlands University Library, Las Vegas, NM.

—since I am, perhaps the first woman who has worn the "American Costume" across the prairie sea which divides the great frontier of the states from the Rocky Mountains. In company with my husband, James H. Holmes, and my brother, I traveled in an ox wagon and on foot upwards of eleven hundred miles during the last three summer months.

We were on our farm on the Neosho River, in Kansas, when news reached us that a company was fitting out in Lawrence for a gold adventure to Pike's Peak. Animated more by a desire to cross the plains and behold the great mountain chain of North America, than by any expectation of realizing the floating gold stories, we hastily laid a supply of provisions in the covered wagon, and two days thereafter, the 2d of last June, were on the road to join the Lawrence company.[1] The next morning we reached the great Santa Fe Road, and passed the last frontier Post Office, Council Grove. Here we mailed our last adieus, and felt somewhat sad that we should hear no more from our friends for so long a time — a period of six months, it afterwards proved, we were to be imprisoned from the world and friends. Here we learned that the train we were to join had passed the day before, and we drove as rapidly as staid cattle could travel for the next fifty miles to overtake it. Several millions of dollars' worth of merchandize is transported annually over this road from the Missouri River to New Mexico, entirely in wagons, and we now met many trains from that Territory coming to Independence for loads. These teams are composed of from five to seven pairs of cattle, attached to huge wagons, capable of carrying seventy to ninety hundred pounds of freight each. Many Americans follow freighting for a living, and

---

[1] In a "Report of William B. Parsons," in the *Lawrence Republican*, Oct. 28, 1858, he says that on June 4 their party was joined while camped on the Cottonwood by "Messrs. Hutchins, Easter, Mills, Turner, Maywood, Archibald, Holmes and wife." LeRoy R. Hafen, ed., *Pike's Peak Gold Rush Guidebooks of 1859*, in *The Southwest Historical Series*, IX (Glendale, CA, 1941) 323-24.

have made large fortunes. The price of freight from Independence to Santa Fe is ten cents per pound, so that a good team will earn $800 a load. One freighter, an American, residing in this Territory, (New Mexico,) realized last year from a single trip with eighteen wagons, from Kansas City, Mo., to Salt Lake, the sum of $12,000.

But I am digressing from the subject of my trip. We reached the Cottonwood Creek, crossing the 5th of June, where we found the train encamped. We were now fairly launched on the waving prairie. A person who has beheld neither the ocean nor the great, silent, uninhabited plains, will find it impossible to form any adequate idea of the grandeur of the scene. With the blue sky overhead, the endless variety of flowers under foot, it seemed that the ocean's solitude had united with all the landscape beauties. In such a scene there is a peculiar charm for some minds, which it is impossible for me to describe; but it made my heart leap for joy.

Finding that we were to have all day to rest, we took our cooking stove out of the wagon and cooked up provision for two or three days. Nearly all the men were entire strangers to me, and as I was cooking our dinner some of them crowded around our wagon, gazing sometimes at the stove, which, with its smoke pipe, looked quite as much out of place as will perhaps the first engine which travels as far away from civilization; but oftener on my dress, which did not surprise me, for, I presume, some of them had never seen just such a costume before. I wore a calico dress, reaching a little below the knee, pants of the same, Indian moccasins for my feet, and on my head a hat. However much it lacked in taste I found it to be beyond value in comfort and convenience, as it gave me freedom to roam at pleasure in search of flowers and other curiosities, while the cattle continued their slow and measured pace.

I was much pleased to learn, on my arrival, that the company contained a lady, and rejoiced at the prospect of having a female companion on such a long journey.[2] But my hopes were disappointed. I soon found that there could be no congeniality between us. She proved to be a woman unable to appreciate freedom or reform, affected that her sphere denied her the liberty to rove at pleasure, and confined herself the long days to feminine impotence in the hot covered wagon. After we had become somewhat acquainted, she in great kindness gave me her advice. "If you have a long dress with you, do put it on for the rest of the trip. the men talk so much about you." "What do they say?" I inquired. "O nothing, only you look so queer with that dress on." "I cannot afford to dress to please their taste," I replied; "I could not positively enjoy a moment's happiness with a long skirt on to confine me to the wagon." I then endeavored to explain to her the many advantages which the reform dress possesses over the fashionable one but failed to make her appreciate my views. She had never found her dress to be the least inconvenient, she said; she could walk as much in her dress as she wanted to, or as was proper for a woman among so many men. I rejoiced that I was independent of such little views of propriety, and felt that I possessed an ownership in all that was good or beautiful in nature, and an interest in any curiosities we might find on the journey as much as if I had been one of the favored lords of creation.

Soon after we overtook the company a division occurred on the question of keeping the Sabbath. It was Saturday morning, and was thought necessary for the train to lie over one day and make preparations for traveling. Two days, however were considered too long a delay. Some of the more conscientious christians desired the train to travel that day

---

[2]"Robert Middleton, wife and child" were listed in a roster prepared by J.F. Younker as member of the Lawrence party. *Ibid.*, pp. 62-63.

and rest the next, Sunday. But it was two days' journey to wood and good water after leaving the present camp. It was, therefore, decided that we could not on this journey rest on the seventh day, but must take some time when we were convenient to wood, good water, and grass for the cattle. The next day we moved on, and every one was looking out for buffalo. Every solitary wolf or mound of earth in the distance, was transformed by some of our most anxious and imaginative hunters into a buffalo. A few short pursuits of these delusive objects served to render our braves more cautious, and towards the close of the day the cry, "a buffalo! a buffalo!" became less frequent.

After the merits of several different camping grounds had been vigorously discussed by our several *leading* men, one was finally selected; and the corral made by driving the teams so that the wagons formed a circle enclosing a yard large enough to contain the cattle belonging to the train. The cattle were allowed to feed until dark, and then driven into the corral for safe keeping, and guarded until morning. This was the course pursued throughout the journey. The next morning the camp was aroused at daylight by a chorus of mingled yelling and screeching — music wild and thrilling as only a band of prairie wolves can make. Civilized man has his prototype in the noisy Indian, so the canine domestic has his lupine prototype, which can make comparatively savage sounds.

When camped on the Little Arkansas River, as I was searching for different flowers, a few rods from the camp, I cast my eyes across the river, and there within forty yards of me stood a venerable buffalo bull, his eyes in seeming wonder fixed upon me. He had approached me unobserved, behind the trees which lined the bank. His gaze was returned with equal astonishment and earnestness. Much as I had heard and read of the buffalo, I had never formed an adequate idea of their huge appearance. He was larger and heavier than a large oxe; his head and shoulders being so disproportionate, he seemed far larger than he really was. He looked the impersonation of a prairie god — the grand emperor of the plain. His countenance expressed terrible majesty and fierceness, and on his chin he wore hair sufficient for the faces of a dozen French emperors. His presence soon became known in camp, and in a few seconds he was coursing westward with our fleetest horses in pursuit. He was overtaken and shot within three or four miles. Buffalo now began to be a common object.

One evening we neglected the precaution to cross the stream before camping.[3] During the night a heavy rain came swelling the creek to a depth of twelve or fifteen feet, and flooding the camp, which was pitched on low ground, with several inches of water. The men were thus driven from the tents to the wagons or a more uncomfortable upright position. In consequence of this neglect, we were detained three days. During this time my husband went out buffalo hunting and returned bringing with him a buffalo calf apparently but a week old. It was a great curiosity to all; and, in the fullness of my compassion for the poor little thing, I mixed up a mess of flour and water, which I hoped to make it drink. I approached it with these charitable intentions, when the savage little animal advanced toward me and gave me such a blow with its head as to destroy the center of gravity. His hair was wooly in texture, and of an iron grey color. Unlike the

---

[3] William B. Parsons in his guidebook with a most extended title, *The New Gold Mines of Western Kansas: Being a Complete Description of the Newly Discovered Gold Mines, the Different Routes, Camping Places, Tools and Outfit, and Containing Everything Important for the Emigrant and Miner to Know,* says "And here, in starting, let me mention the rule — ALWAYS CROSS A CREEK BEFORE CAMPING. The streams rise so rapidly upon the plains that a slight shower at night might prevent crossing in the morning . . ." *Ibid.,* p. 172.

young of our domestic cows, he seldom cried, and when he did only made a faint noise. The buffalo cow as well as the bull is naturally a very timid animal, save when wounded or driven to bay. I learned that the mother of the captured calf made a heroic stand, and presented a beautiful illustration of the triumph of maternal feeling over fear. She was in a herd of many hundreds of buffaloes, fleeing wildly over the plain before the hunter. After a few miles chase the calf gave signs of fatigue. At its faint cry she would turn and come to the calf, but at sight of the hunter bounded off to the herd. This she did two or three times during a chase of as many miles, the calf falling behind more and more, and his mother wavering between fear for his life and her own, at last her decision was made, and she determined to defend her offspring alone on the prairie. She died in his defence.

While camped here, the company was thrown into great anxiety by a member becoming lost on the prairie.[4] Much search was made, and he was given up as dead, when some Cheyenne Indians came into camp bringing a note from him, stating he was at a trading post two days in advance. We feasted the Indians in our gratitude. They were large, finely formed, and noble looking men, and but for one sight with which they regaled our eyes they would not have appeared very disgusting. I refer to a habit with them which seems almost too nauseating to write of — that of picking vermin from each other's heads, and eating them with seeming eagerness and gusto.

I commenced the journey with a firm determination to learn to walk. At first I could not walk over three or four miles without feeling quite weary, but by perservering and walking as far as I could every day, my capacity increased

---

[4] J.T. Younker was the lost man. *Ibid.*, pp. 324-25.

gradually, and in the course of a few weeks I could walk ten miles in the most sultry weather without being exhausted. Believing, as I do, in the right of woman to equal privileges with man, I think that when it is in our power we should, in order to promote our own independence, at least, be willing to share the hardships which commonly fall to the lot of man. Accordingly, I signified to the Guardmaster that I desired to take my turn with the others in the duty of guarding the camp, and requested to have my watch assigned with my husband. The captain of the guard was a gentleman formerly from Virginia,[5] who prided himself much upon his chivalry, (and who, to use his own expression, was "conservative up to the eyes,") was of the opinion that it would be a disgrace to the gentlemen of the company for them to permit a woman to stand on guard. He would vote against the question of universal franchise, were it to be submitted to the people, although he was a hero in the struggle in Kansas, and must have witnessed the heroic exertions of many of the women of that Territory to secure for their brothers the boon of freedom. He believes that woman is an angel, (without any sense,) needing the legislation of her brothers to keep her in her place; that restraint removed, she would immediately usurp his position, and then not only be no longer an angel but unwomanly.

After reaching the Great Bend of the Arkansas River, we camped on Walnut Creek, where we found many new varieties of flowers, some of them of exceeding beauty. Among others the sensitive rose, a delicate appearing flower, one of the most beautiful I ever saw, having a fine delicious

---

[5] Luke V. Tierney became a pioneer of Denver. In the *Rocky Mountain News* of Feb. 1, 1860, there is the following item: "Directly opposite the Capitol [saloon, on Ferry street] is the new frame residence of Luke Tierney, one of the first settlers, a letter-writer, and the author of a little book on this country, published at Pacific City, Iowa, in February 1859." The little guidebook published by Tierney was *History of the Gold Discoveries on the South Platte River. Ibid.*, pp. 88-145.

aroma. It grew on a running vine. In an eastern conservatory it would be the fairy queen among the roses — the queen of flowers.

Yours,   J. Annie Archibald.

THE LETTER, PART II

We passed, on the 14th of June, a large number of Cheyenne and Arrapahoe Indians. Fifty men armed with Sharp's rifles and revolvers were afraid to allow the Indians to know that the company contained any women, in consequence of something which the carriers of the Santa Fe mail told them when they passed a few days previous. I was, therefore, confined to the wagon, while we passed many places of interest which I wished much to visit. Notwithstanding this care to be unobserved, my presence became known. At one time, by opening the front of the wagon for ventilation, at another by leaping from it to see something curious which two or three Indians had brought, not knowing, as afterward proved true, that we were very near a village. I soon discovered my mistake, and though I did not myself feel there was any cause for alarm, I was sorry I had been seen on account of the feeling existing in the train. It was of no use to hide now, for every Indian within a mile knew of my whereabouts. Though there was not a shadow of danger in such a company as ours, as many of us well knew at the time and as many experienced men have since informed us, it is very true that the red men have an unaccountable fancy for white women. My husband received several very flattering offers for me. One Indian wanted to trade two squaws for me, who could probably perform four times the physical labor that I could. Others, not quite so timid, approaching the wagon made signs for me to jump up behind them on their ponies, but I declined the honor in the most respectful language I knew of their dialect — a decided shake of the head.

We now had a stretch of land to pass over, of forty or fifty miles, on which there was ordinarily no water, no wood, nor any good grass. We started an hour or so before sundown, and traveled until midnight without resting. Here we halted a half hour, and made some coffee over a fire made of wood we had brought from our camp the day before. Resuming our journey, we continued traveling until after sunrise in the morning, when we arrrived at Coon Creek, which we were glad enough to find was not dry as it generally is. Here we camped, having traveled thirty miles or more.

Touching the Arkansas again, we found many new varieties of flowers, some of them of very delicate tint and odor. While camped here, we received a visit from six Californians who were returning to the states, with pack mules. Some of us who had letters prepared gladly availed ourselves of the opportunity to send word home. These men had started from the southern line of Oregon, and come around by the way of the river Gila and Lenora [Senora] — to avoid the Mormon country — a distance of near two thousand miles, in sixty days. They reported traveling in Sonora over a space of four hundred miles where scarcely a blade of grass or any water was to be found. As the train passed the Arkansas crossing, James and I went to the river to see some Santa Fe wagons cross. The river was here perhaps half a mile wide, and the bottom one broad bed of sand, with here and there a channel nearly as deep as the cattle's backs. After unloading a part of their freight, and placing perishable articles above where the water would enter the wagons, they attached twelve or more yoke of cattle and entered the swift running river. It was indeed an amusing scene. Twenty Mexicans with sharp sticks punching the cattle, shouting and tumbling in the water, the leading cattle continually endeavoring to turn back, the wagon master on horseback, swearing in Mexican, now at the cattle and then at the men — creating a wonderful confusion. There were in the wagon a number of barrels of whiskey standing on end. When in the middle of the stream, as the wagon ascended out of the channel one of these tipped out, together with some of the Mexicans' coats. After a deal of excitement to the Mexicans, and diversion to those on the bank, the whiskey and clothing were saved.

The next day, the 20th, being Sunday, we had intended to rest. We had not, however, camped ere a number of Cheyenne Indians came upon us, and we learned there was a large village a few miles above. These Indians are very friendly. They are not the best neighbors to have. Not being at all proud, they accept of anything their white brother chooses to give them, and more too, if they can get it. The next morning we traveled on to pass our troublesome neighbors. Near their village we noticed several hundred ponies. These Indians have the custom of suspending their dead in trees, where the dry air of this elevated plain speedily shrivels them up. While searching for Indians skeletons in trees, one of the men found a pair of young eagles not quite fledged, whose feathers were of a pure beautiful white.

The Arkansas river is very beautiful. Dotted as it is with many little islands, the banks in all cases adorned with flowers, and in many places lined with trees and shrubs. But the current is so swift that it is very unpleasant bathing — that delightful and grateful recreation to the dusty traveler. A number of large rattlesnakes were killed along this river. They were formerly very numerous, but have been killed off to a great extent by California emigrants and others.

On the 28th we reached Bent's Fort — a large stone structure built by a Mr. Bent for the purpose of trading for robes with the prairie Indians, and the Cheyennes in particular. The price paid for a buffalo robe at present is ten cups of sugar, about eight pounds. They were formerly bought for from one to four cups of sugar or coffee. Many of the men were so enthusiastic in their admiration of the fort that they took the liberty of getting very drunk by way of compliment, perhaps to it and the very gentlemanly man who did the honors of the house in Mr. Bent's absence.[6] After tarrying an hour or so, the merry men continued their journey, but went only three miles further that day. Up to this time our company had been remarkably healthy. This afternoon, however, several were taken ill. Among the sufferers some of the quasi moralists who so opposed my mode of dress, and woman's freedom. One of the actors in this disgraceful occurrence — the one-fourth of which I have not described — an *eminent attorney,*[7] has since returned to eastern Kansas and written a long letter on the trip, in whch he stigmatizes "strong minded women and weak minded men," and greatly fears for the morality of the world on their account. But of such stuff are generally the croakers against reform everywhere.

After leaving Bent's Fort we began to look anxiously for a glimpse of Pike's Peak. On the evening of July 3d, after camping, a sudden rain and hail storm came upon us, penetrating more or less every wagon cover, and blowing down most of the tents. The next morning we bid farewell to the Arkansas River, whose company we had kept three hunded miles. Traveling but fifteen miles, the train camped early this evening, in order to celebrate the "glorious fourth." This was done by consuming what little whiskey remained among the members. This day we obtained the first view of

---

[6] The indentity of this "very gentlemanly man" is obscure. William Bent was on a business trip east to Kansas City. David Lavender, *Bent's Fort* (Garden City, N.Y., 1954), 336-37.

[7] This was William Bostwick Parsons, a brilliant student of the classics and a lawyer from Burlington, KS. See LeRoy R. Hafen, *op. cit.*, p. 152, for a brief biography.

the summit of the Peak, now some seventy miles away. As all expected to find precious treasure near this wonderful Peak, it is not strange that our eyes were often strained by gazing on it. The summit appeared majestic in the distance, crowned with glistening white.

We were passing over an uneven road to-day, and getting a mile or two in advance of wagons, we came upon a pair of antelope grazing. Immediately dropping upon the ground that we might not frighten them, we had a fine opportunity to examine their beautiful form and motion. They advanced toward us until they were scarcely ten rods off, with eyes riveted upon us, perhaps a minute, when sudden as lightning they started and bounded away like the wind. Their smooth form, with slender, tapering legs, glossy hair, bright large eyes, their graceful, lofty and intelligent motion, left a deep impress of their beauty.

Proceeding up the Boiling-Spring River, we arrived on the 8th as near as wagons could approach the mountains.

From this time until the tenth of Aug., with the exception of two days, the train remained encamped in this locality. For one who has not experience to aid his effort, it will be quite impossible to imagine the disgusting inactivity, and monotony of camp life. Eating, sleeping, smoking tobacco, manufacturing pipes out of a soft white magnesia limestone rock, found near camp, which they also made into finger rings; playing cards a very large portion of the days, the chief game being eucre and cribbage; becoming weary of playing for fun, to add a little excitement to the game staking their guard, consisting four hours of day watch and four hours of night, each occurring about once a week. Occasionally the routine would be interrupted by alarms of Indians trying to stampede the cattle. Sometimes, too, a few of the men would wake up and start out for a trip of three of four days, perhaps in search of gold; for the summit of the mountain; or as was

more frequently the case to hunt deer, antelope, bears, &c.
On these hunting expeditions they always started in fine
spirits, but returned generally serious, without game,
reporting having seen thousands of deer and antelope, but
the timid animals would not permit them to approach near
enough to kill them. For a description of our visit to the
summit of Pike's Peak, I take the following extract from my
journal.

"Aug. 1st 1858 — After an early breakfast this morning,
my husband and I adjusted our packs to our backs and
started for the ascent of Pike's Peak. My own pack weighed
17 pounds; nine of which were bread, the remainder a quilt
and clothing. James' pack weighed 35 pounds, and was
composed as follows — tens pounds bread, one pound hog
meat, three fourths pound coffee, one pound sugar, a tin
plate, knife and fork, half gallon canteen, half gallon tin pail
and a tin pint cup, five quilts, clothing, a volume of Emerson's Essays, and writing materials made up the remainder.
We calculate on this amount of food to subsist six days. A
walk of a mile brought us to the crossing of Boiling spring
river. It is an impetuous, ice cold stream at this point, about
twelve feet wide, knee deep, with a cobble stone bottom.
Undressing our feet we attempted it several times before we
could cross, the water was so intensely cold we were ready to
drop down in pain on reaching the opposite bank. Three
miles further we reached the wonderful Boiling springs,
which Fremont has made known to the world in his
expeditions. There are but three which we noticed. The
strong carbonated waters mingled with bubbles of carbonic
acid gas, boil continually in the rocky fountains within which
they are set by nature better than they could be by art. In the
center of broad solid rocks somewhat elevated above the
ground around them, composed by the deposition of their
own waters, these springs ceaselessly boil. We speculated on

the limestone cave which may somewhere exist above the spring in the heart of the mountain, since they are constantly bringing away limestone in solution. We drank deep from these Saratogas of the wilderness, and leaving them, in another mile were vigorously attacking the mountain. The first mile or so was sandy and extremely steep, over which we toiled slowly, as we frequently lost all we gained. But by persevering and every rod laying, or rather falling on our backs to rest, we at last reached the timber where we could obtain better footing. We neglected to fill our canteens and now began to feel the want of water. We toiled on and up in hope of soon finding a spring. At one time we went too far to the left — not knowing the route — and got among some huge boulders which we soon saw the necessity of getting out of the best way we could. After finding the right track we continued, but we had lost so much time in getting among the rocks, and become so hungry, that after proceeding a couple of miles farther, and catching a glimpse of water in a deep canyon, we halted and considered the state of our case. The question was, should we descend that terrible canyon only to ascend again, or proceed on our journey not knowing when we should reach water? Our longing for water triumphed and down we rushed with such eagerness as is only inspired by suffering. We are camped here until to-morrow. It is now ten o'clock in the evening, and I am reclining before some blazing logs beside a torrent in a mountain canyon several hundred feet deep. The straight slender, tapering pines that stand around so beautiful in their death, smooth, white and sound, having been stripped of their bark by fire, calmly point to a sky more serene, and to stars far brighter than usual. The trees and the sky almost seem to strive together in preserving a deeper silence. But there is music from the foaming stream, sounds from a dozen little cascades near and far blend together — a thundering sound, a rushing sound, a rippling sound, and tinkling sounds there are; and a thousand shades of sound to fill up between them. The burning pine crackles and snaps, showering sparks, cinders and even coals around and all over the sheet I am writing on, as if to mock the tame thoughts they light me to write."

"Snowdell, Aug 4th. — We have given this name to a little nook we are making our home in for a few days. It is situated about four or five rods above the highest spring which gushes from the side of the Peak. On the cold moss overhung by two huge rocks, forming a right angle, we have made a nest of spruce twigs. Some smaller rocks form, with the larger ones just mentioned, a trough about three feet wide, and ten feet long. At the outlet of this narrow space we have built up a chimney. When we lie down the fire is burning but a yard from our feet, while we can stretch our hands over the smaller rocks into a large bank of snow. This we call our home. Eastward, we can look on a landscape of Kansas plains, our view hemmed only by the blue haze of the atmosphere, and extending perhaps two hundred miles. The beauty of this great picture is beyond my powers of description. Down at the base of the mountain the corral of fifteen wagons, and as many tents scattered around it, form a white speck, which we can occasionally distinguish. We think our location grandly romantic. We are on the east side of the Peak, whose summit looming above our heads at an angle of forty-five degrees, is yet two miles away — towards the sky. We arrived here day before yesterday about one o'clock P.M. during a little squall of snow. Yesterday we went in search of a supposed cave about three fourths of a mile along the side of the mountain. We penetrated the canyon with much difficulty, being once obliged to take off our moccasins that we might use the toes and balls of our feet in clinging to the asperities of the sidling rock. We found no cave but a tremendous amphitheater shaped space, whose perpendicular walls rose seven or eight hundred feet high. Piled around this vast circle at the foot of the walls, were granite boulders of all sizes and shapes rising against the walls like the terraced seats of a circus or theater. Deep in the center is a circular spot of green grass, with flowers, and a silvery stream winding through it. We called the place Amphitheater Canyon.

"To-day we remain at home resting, writing and admiring the mocking landscape. For with beauty and deep truth does Emerson remark, "the landscape must always appear mocking until it has human figures as good as itself."

"These whole mountains are of a feldsparic formation, with an occasional sample of quartz soil that is covered with vegetation which does not occupy one fourth of the mountain where we are. Granite boulders and stones of every size and shape, with granite gravel occupy over three fourths. Beautiful flowers delicate in texture and aroma, grow everywhere, except on the bare rocks, and even within reach of the snow.

"Aug. 5th — We left Snowdell early this morning for the summit, taking with us nothing but our writing materials and Emerson. We deviated somewhat from our course in order to pass the rim of Amphitheater Canyon. Here on the edge of the perpendicular walls, were poised stones and boulders of all sizes ready to be rolled, with a slight effort, into the yawning abyss. Starting these stones had been a favorite amusement with those who ascended before us, and it savored somewhat of the terrible. When a stone was started it seemed first to leap into the air, and passing from sight nothing would be heard from it for several seconds. Then would come a crashing, thundering sound from the hidden depths below, which seems to continue until lost in the distant lower region. From these hollow distant sounds some

of the men had supposed the existence of an inaccessable
cave below. As we proved yesterday, however, nothing but a
tremendous circular chasm exists. After enjoying this sport a
short time we proceeded directly up towards the summit.
Arriving within a few hundred yards of the top the surface
changed into a huge pile of loose angular stones, so steep we
found much difficulty in clambering up them. Passing to the
right of a drift of snow some three or four hunded yards long,
which sun and wind had turned into coarse ice, we stood
upon a platform of near one hundred acres of feldspathic
granite rock and boulders. Occasionally a little cranny among
the rocks might be found in which had collected some coarse
soil from the disintegration of the granite, where in one or
two instances we found a green tuft about the size of a teacup
from which spring dozens of tiny blue flowers most
bewitchingly beautiful. The little ultramarine colored leaves
of the flower seemed covered with an infinitude of minute
sparkling crystals — they seemed children of the sky and the
snow. It was cold and rather cloudy, with squalls of snow,
consequently our view was not so extensive as we had
anticipated. A portion only of the white back-bone ridge of
the Rocky Mountains which forms the boundary lines of so
many territories could be seen, fifty miles to the west. We
were now nearly fourteen thousand feet above sea level. But
we could not spend long in comtemplating the granduer [sic]
of the scene for it was exceedingly cold, and leaving our
names on a large rock, we commenced letters to some of our
friends using a broad flat rock for a writing desk. When we
were ready to return I read aloud the lines from Emerson.

> "A ruddy drop of manly blood,
>   The Surging sea outweighs;
>   The world uncertain comes and goes,
>   The looser rooted stays."

Leaving this cloud capped bleak region, we were soon in

Snowdell, where we remained only long enough to make up our packs. Before we were ready to say 'good bye' the snow was falling quite fast and we left our pretty home as we first saw it, in a snowstorm. We pursued our journey in all possible haste, anxious to find a good camp for the night before dark. At last when I thought I could not go a rod further, we found a capital place, a real bears den it seemed, though large enough for a half a dozen. And here we are enclosed on every side by huge boulders, with two or three large spruce trees stretching their protecting arms over our heads.

The next day near noon we arrived at camp, where we found some excitement existing regarding an attempt which the Indians had made the night before, to drive away the cattle belonging to the train.

I must now close this letter, which has already grown too long, though I have omitted many things equally interesting as those I have recorded. In accordance with a decision of a previous meeting, the camp broke up on the 10th and moved toward New Mexico. We arrived in Sangro Christi (blood of Christ) Pass, N.M., on the 18th, and after remaining there a few days, decided, so far as our wagon was concerned, to abandon camp life and spend the winter in New Mexico. When we last saw the gold seekers most of them were engaged in fishing for trout in the creek of the Sangro de Christi.

Your truly,   J.A. Archibald.

EPILOGUE:

The following items are all to be found in the same issue, October 7, 1858, of the Lawrence, Kansas, *Republican:* First there is an introduction by the editor of the newspaper; then there is an introduction written by the mother of Mrs. Holmes, Jane B.

Archibald; and third there is Julia Holmes' own letter written right on Pikes Peak during her climb of the famous mountain.

FROM THE PEAK

An interesting account of the ascent of Pike's Peak, by Mrs. Holmes, formerly of this city, will be found in our columns to-day — for which we are indebted by the politeness of Mrs. Archibald, mother of Mrs. Holmes.

In conversation with Mr. and Mrs. Archibald, we learn that they are in receipt of a letter from their son and daughter, dated August 31st. The Lawrence company, as was stated by us a week or two since, have gone to Spanish Peaks, in New Mexico, but had not found gold in paying quantities, at the latest dates. Mr. and Mrs. Holmes, with true American enterprise, had gone to Taos, New Mexico, and engaged in teaching school. This letter also states that while at Pike's Peak, the Lawrence company sent out prospecting parties over a good deal of the surrounding country, who found gold in all the streams, and at one place on the Platte in quantities sufficient, as they thought, to yield from *five* to *eight* dollars a day. It was stongly desired by a portion of the party to go directly to these diggings, and spend the winter there; but another portion were determined on going to Spanish Peaks, and as the whole company were none too numerous for safety among the Indians, they all finally went to Spanish Peaks. Cherry Creek [Denver] does not seem to have been visited by the party at all.

All these accounts do but confirm the unvarying testimony of the existence of gold all along the head waters of the Platte and Arkansas.

FROM THE ROCKY MOUNTAINS — MRS HOLMES ASCENDS PIKE'S PEAK.

Eds. Republican: — I send you the following short extract from a letter recently received from my daughter,

Mrs. Holmes, who has been traveling with her husband in the vicinity of Pike's Peak, and the western extremity of Kansas, and now probably in some of the frontier towns of New Mexico. Though not written with any view to publication, yet, as I have thought that it would very much gratify her numerous friends and acquaintances to hear from her through the medium of your paper. I send you the enclosed. Yours truly.

JANE B. ARCHIBALD.

————

Aug. 2d, 1858

DEAR MOTHER: — I write to you sitting in our little house among the rocks, about one hour's walk from the summit of Pike's Peak. It is a curious little nook which we have selected as our temporary home, formed by two very large overhanging rocks, and enclosed by a number of smaller ones, while close beside it is a large snow bank which we can reach with ease. Our couch is composed of a large quantity of spruce boughs, (cut with that little knife which you have used so much). These we arrange on the rock, upon which we spread some quilts — reserving others for covering — and by the help of a good fire which we keep burning all night, we can manage to keep the cold off very well.

Two days of very hard climbing has brought me here — if you could only know how hard, you would be surprised that I have been able to accomplish it. My strength and capacity for enduring fatigue have been very much increased by constant exercise in the open air since leaving home, or I never could have succeeded in climbing the rugged sides of this mountain. There was some steep climbing the first day, and I would sometimes find it almost impossible to proceed. I was often obliged to use my hands — catching, now at some propitious twig which happened to be within reach and now trusting to some projecting stone. But fortunately for me this did not last more than a mile or so.

We have brought about a week's provisions, purposing to remain here and write some letters, &c. This is the most romantic of places. Think of the high rocks projecting out in all imaginable shapes, with the beautiful evergreens, the pines, the firs, and spruces, interspersed among them; and then the clear, cold mountain stream, which appears as though it started right out from under some great rock —and on it goes, rushing, tumbling and hissing down over the rough mountain sides, now sparkling in the sunbeams and now hiding behind some huge rock, and now rising again to view, it rushes on, away down, down, until at length it turns a corner and is lost to our sight. Then think of the fragrant little flowers — so many different kinds, and some of them growing within reach of our snowbank: I will send you some of the different kinds. — There is one little blue flower here which, for some reason, I cannot tell exactly what, whether it is the form, color, or fragrance, but it has had the effect to carry me back in imagination to the days of my childhood, in my far down Eastern home.

But I shall not write any more now, for I mean to finish this on top of the mountain.

PIKE'S PEAK, AUG. 5, 1858.

I have accomplished the task which I marked out for myself, and now I feel amply repaid for all my toil and fatigue. Nearly every one tried to discourage me from attempting it, but I believed that I should succeed; and now here I am, and feel that I would not have missed this glorious sight for anything at all.

In all probability I am the first woman who has ever stood upon the summit of this mountain, and gazed upon this wondrous scene which my eyes now behold. How I sigh for a poet's power of description, so that I might give you some faint idea of grandeur and beauty of this scene. Extending as far as the eye can reach, lie the great level plains, stretched out in all their verdure and beauty, while the winding of the grand Arkansas is visible for many miles. We can also see distinctly where many of the smaller tributaries unite with it. — Then the rugged rocks all around, and the almost endless succession of mountains and rocks below, the broad blue sky over our heads, and seemingly so very near, — and everything, on which the eye can rest fills the mind with infinitude and sends the soul to God.

From Ashtabula to Petaluma in 1859
❦ Harriet Booth Griswold

INTRODUCTION

Although Harriet ("Hattie") Booth Griswold's diary begins with its first entry on April 25, 1859, the journey had really started in Ashtabula, in the northeast corner of Ohio near the south shore of Lake Erie. In that same first entry she gives the names of three children: Carrie, age 9; Eddie, age 7; and Hattie, age 2½ months. The census taker in Petaluma, California, wrote down her husband's name as Augustus Henry Griswold, age 32, in 1860, born in Ohio with personal property valued at $1200. Her age is also given as 32, born in New York. This family is very elusive as to critical dates and other information. We know by the 1850 census of Ohio that Augustus was the oldest of eight children of Roger and Juliette Griswold.

The original diary is in the Califoria Historical Society's collection in San Francisco. They have graciously given us permission to publish it.

There is a note accompanying the diary saying that the Griswolds lived successively in Petaluma, Oakland, and San Francisco.[1] In the 1860 census referred to above the father was listed as a "laborer." The Oakland city directories from 1876 to 1886 list him successively as a ticket collector for the Central Pacific Railroad, a miner, and an assayer. The last discovered reference, this time the Crocker-Langley *San Francisco Directory*, lists him as working in the "engineering department" of a telegraph and telephone company, in 1905. Curiously the same

---

[1] The note is signed by a John Catlin.

directory lists Harriet B. Griswold as a widow. Perhaps he died
during the preparation of the directory.[2]

The same note referred to above says that Harriet Booth
Griswold died "sometime after the earthquake." This gives us the
reason the final dates are difficult to come by: The earthquake of
1906 not only took 252 lives and destroyed 28,000 buildings, it
laid to waste the records of San Francisco City and County, and
with them went the vital statistics of thousands of people; so
"sometime before" or "sometime after the earthquake" is what we
have to say about the deaths of Harriet and Augustus Griswold.
The note also says that Harriet was the mother of eight children,
"most of whom predeceased her."

But she left us a legacy, and that is the diary with a poem for a
title: Ashtabula to Petaluma.

HARRIET GRISWOLD'S DIARY

April 25th 1859.   We left Elgin Kane, Co, Ill, en route for
California. Our family consists now of Carrie aged 9
years   Eddie aged 7 years and   Hattie aged 2½ months.
Stopped over night in Burlington Iowa, Barrett House.

April 26th   Started at 7 A.M. in the cars and arrived at
Agency [City] about 2 P.M.   took a coach and arrived at
Ottumwa 3½ P.M. where the company forms for a start. We
tried the Hotel a few days but were not pleased and now are
boarding in a private family by the name of Milligan.

May 18th   We left Ottumwa this morning about 10 A.M.
in our waggons for our expected long journey. We have four
large covered waggons one uncoverd and one two horse
hack. The day has been pleasant. It is my first experience of
riding after oxen and to night is our first camp after riding 14
miles over as bad a road as I ever saw.

---

[2] We acknowledged gratefully the work of Dr. Eugene Sill and his wife, Dorothy (your
editor's sister), for work they did in uncovering the almanac information in the Oakland
Public Library. The Sills have been long-time Oakland residents, now live in Woodland,
California.

I have neglected my Journal for some time and must commence date at Council Bluff

Saturday June 4th   We got into Council Bluff before dinner where I was glad to stop and have a little rest as well as change of clothes. There are some splendid stores in this place   the rest of the buildings are quite plain. Here we see the first Indians that we have met. I found a letter here from Brother John and one from Mrs. Dr Hubbard of Elgin.

Sunday June 5th   This has been an unusual Sunday to me   instead of attending Church I have spent the day in our waggon attending to the children and writing a letter to Brother Charles.   we are camping about one mile from town. We have been climbing one of the high bluffs where we had a fine view of the valley of the Missouri.

Monday June 6th   We crossed the Missouri on a steam Ferry Boat to Omaha City the capital of Nebraska Territory. We drove about two miles out of town to camp very near the bank of the river.

Tuesday June 7th   It took us a long time to get started to day as this is the last place of any consequence until we reach Salt Lake   This is considered the fitting out place and we have laid in our stores sufficient for five months if we should need them so long. They consist of Flour, Bacon & Hams, Dried Fruit Beans, Potatoes, Corn, Coffee, Tea, Pickles, a few eggs, and some other little things. We have just got regulated and are fairly   started on the Plain   Our Company consists of Mr John Gossage, Mr Jerome Gossage[1] and wife and servant girl nine hired men to attend to the stock which

---

[1] John and Lorena Gossage are listed in the 1850 United States Census along with five children. He is listed as a farmer, 42 years old, living in Muskingum Co., near Zanesville, Ohio. Lorena gave her age to the census taker as 42. They were both born in Vermont. Their five Ohio-born children were Mary Jane, 16; Sarah, 14; Samuel, 6; Warner, 4; and Cynthia, 2. Jerome's name does not appear.

consists 16 Horses and 135 head of Cattle. We are divided into two messes as we have two tents and two tables which enables us all to eat at once. We have a boy cook for our mess. We drive out of town for about four miles and camped for the night.

Wednesday June 8th   We started in good   seven this morning and came about 18 miles over a high rolling country, roads very smooth and hard, and we camped on the bank of the Elk Horn River   an abundance of Indians here begging for some thing to eat and ready to steal any thing within their reach.

Thursday June 9th   This morning we crossed the Elk Horn River on good bridge and have come 22 miles over a level smooth road   passed through a little town by the name of Fremont.[2] We are camping quite near the Platt River which is a very handsome stream. The Mosquitoes nearly devoured us outside of the waggons. We see no Indians to night.

Friday June 10th   Started in good season this morning stopped an hour at noon as usual,   drove until four this afternoon, and are camping by a little stream called Shell creek. This has been a pleasant day   our road has been very level and smooth on the north side of the Platte River   the river has been in sight most of the day   every few miles we find a house with some improvements about it. There seems to be no Indians. We find pretty flowers beside the road.

Saturday, June 11th   We have come about 16 miles to day, weather pleasant   this morning we met a government train accompanied by a company of soldiers going after supplies

---

[2] Fremont is one of the oldest towns in Nebraska. It had been platted in 1856 and incorporated on Nov. 2, 1858. G. Thomas Fairclough, *Nebraska Place-Names* (Lincoln, 1967), p. 54.

for the army. The roads have been fine with the exception of a few sloughs. We are camping quite near the river.

Sunday June 12th   This is the Lords day but no attention is paid to it by our company as regards rest or anything else which does not at all please me. I think we should rest a part of sunday at least. We have crossed the Loup Fort or Bruly [Brule] River[3]   a ferry boat runs half way across   ford the rest. The weather pleasant and warm. The road still level and smooth as a carpet. Have come about 16 miles, camping near the river.

Monday June 13th   Drove about 17 miles   a very warm day   camped on the river bank.

Tuesday June 14th   Had a severe thunder storm last night. Drove 24 miles to day   been very warm with good road.   we have come to the first house that we have seen since we left Loupe Fork. The mosquitoes torment us almost to death.

Wednesday June 15   Drove about 17 miles   saw no houses to day or indians.

Thursday June 16th   We stopped at noon for our lunch as usual had for our company fourteen Indian warriors of the Sioux tribe   they were fantastically dressed and are great beggars for eadibles   seem very friendly   they and the Pawnees are at war. This morning crossed the Wood river by fording   camped on its banks.

Friday June 17th   We are about ten miles east of Ft Kearny   it is on the other side of the river there being no

---

[3] Loup and Brulé are both French names. The word, loup, means wolf, and the name had been used for a group of the Skidi tribe of the Pawnee Indians. Skidi is Pawnee for wolf. *Ibid*, p. 135. There is a town named Brule (pronounced today Brull) in Keith Co., Nebraska. It was named for the Brulé Teton Sioux Indians. It means "burnt." *Ibid.*, p. 85.

way of crossing but fording   shall not see it. We overtook
Mr Freman[4] to day   two families beside his own in this
company   we shall travel together.

Saturday June 18th   We have seen Buffalo for the first
time   some of the company went out this morning but with
no success.   are camping on a small stream emptying into the
Platt. Had Buffalo steak for supper, given us by some
neighboring campers who killed it this morning.

Sunday June 19th   We have been lying still all day by a
small stream running into the Platte. It is quite hard to
realize that it is Sunday as there is nothing to see or hear to
remind us of the fact. We have necessarily been very busy
airing our bed and provisions and I have done a little
washing for the children   Mr Matt [Dr Mott?][5] and some
of the rest of the company went out hunting Buffalo and
returned about ten oclock at night with there horses loaded
with all they could carry   fires were kindled and they soon
had coffee and Buffalo steak cooking.

Monday June 20th   Have come to day about 18 miles   We
are fifty miles above Ft Kearney   Wood being scarce cooked
supper with fire made of Buffalo Chips which make a very
hot fire.

Tuesday June 21st   Drove some over twenty miles to day
camping on a small ravine   good water and grass.

Wednesday June 22nd   We got a late start this morning on
account of some of the cattle straying off   in the afternoon
passed through or by an indian village   a huge swarm of
them lined the road to get a sight of the palefaces especially
the squaws & papooses as they call all women & children
We camped about four miles from the village and had no

---

[4] Freeman is unidentified.
[5] She refers to "Mr Matt" here and on Aug. 30 to "Dr Mott." He is so far not
identified.

more than got our tents pitched when some of them made us a call including the Chief and his young son dressed in fancy style and riding ponies   we gave them a few provisions and then they went peacably away

Thursday June 23rd   We had a good start this morning but had not gone far when there was a general stampeed of all the cattle teams and all horses run off at full speed   of course we (the women and children) could do nothing but sit in the waggon and wait the result which did not happen to be all disastrous as they run but half a mile and stopped. Camping by a creek   have had two very heavy showers to day. Our road has been quite rolling passing by some high bluffs Passed two very large cold springs and also the fork of the Platte River

Friday June 24th   A very cool day   we lunched at noon near an indian village consequently saw plenty of them around. Provided ourselves with willow branches for fire wood as we do not expect to see any more timber on this [north] side of the river for about 200 miles. Camped upon the Platte river   traveled about 18 miles.

Saturday June 25th   An excessively warm day and we have had very hard roads for teams being rolling bluff with deep sand   drove about 16 miles   camped by a small stream.

Sunday June 26th   Got an early start this morning   Drove until eleven oclock and camped for the day and night upon a beautiful spring brook. An excessively hot day and refreshing to rest although we are obliged to be rather busy   too much to be called a day of rest.

Monday June 27th   Another warm day   lunched at noon on the bank of rattlesnake creek   drove 19 miles and are camping by what they call Rocky creek. A pleasant breeze this evening & slight shower just as we were ready to go to sleep   last night we heard a mighty tramping coming upon us which proved to be the cattle and horses runing into camp at full speed apparently very much frightened probably by indians — or Buffalo or perhaps wolves. It stirred us up considerable

Tuesday June 28th   An excessively warm day   the road lay over sandy bluffs and also had one terrible slough to cross. Camped on a small stream with a nice cool spring flowing into it. We find a great many coming out of the bluff and running to river.

Wednesday June 29th   We have had a delightful day and fine roads   have driven over 20 miles   forded Quick Sand Creek. The bluffs on south side of river are very rocky. A large wolf passed near the camp to night was persued a short distance but made its excape. Are camping on a slough near the river.

Thursday June 30th   This has been an excessively hot day   road very good   Some of the company returned from a hunting expedition with three Antelope for booty. It is delicious meat. Camping by the Platte.

Friday July 1st   Very warm day again   found rocky bluffs resembling ancient ruins of crumbling walls   we have plenty of company as there are long trains both before and behind us. Alkali water begins to make its appearance which is deadly poison to man & beast that drink it. Can plainly see Court House Rock in the distance. It is an immense rock covering several acres of ground   so regular in its form as to resemble a Capitol building with cupola on the top. Our roads are poorly over sandy and gravely bluff.

Saturday July 2nd   Weather extremely warm.   — good road   passed Court House rock   camped on the Platte.

Sunday July 3rd   Passed Chimney rock to day   it resembles a large round tent with a stove pipe passing through the center of the top.   from about 16 miles could find no chips to cook with   Such a little little bread Camped on the Platte.

Monday 4th July   An exceedingly hot day with good roads   can not spend time to stop to celebrate the day   Mr Gossage killed an Antelope on the camp ground ahead of the teams. It is delicious meat

Tuesday July 5th   Are staying over to day on account of the indisposition of Mrs. Gossage   have spent the day rather idly.

Wednesday July 6th   Mrs Gossage is not able to go on yet   we are about 40 miles east of Laramie. Weather still very warm. Had antelope for supper   it is very nice.

Thursday July 7th   Drove about 15 miles   an exceedingly hot day   camped near the river.

Friday July 8th   Another hot tiresome day

Saturday July 9th   We had a pretty long drive and camped in a beautiful cotton wood grove on the bank of the river about five miles east of Ft Laramie

Sunday July 10th   Laid by all day   sent letters home and received one from Mr Crosby and one from Mr. Waterburger

Monday July 11th   Drove past Laramie which is situated on south side of river and in plain view of this side   it seemed quite natural to push on once more. Had a drenching rain as we were camping by the river which was very much needed to lay the dust.

Tuesday July 12th   We have just entered upon the Black Hills or base of the Rocky Mountains. This is a great change from the plains and had been quite an exciting day. We have had several very long and steep ascents and descents but I suppose it is only a prelude of what is to come. The air is very cool and pleasant   the road in some places very stoney

The rest of the way very hard and smooth.   camped near a beautiful cool spring to the right of the road.

Wednesday July 13th   A fine day and first rate roads with the exception of a little sand in the afternoon   Drove off the main road to camp by a creek.

Thursday July 14th   Drove about fifteen miles without stopping and fi'ly struck the river, a fine road

Friday Saturday Sunday   Made short drives   the river in sight most of the way   at time roads mountainous

Monday July 18th   Lunched at noon at the [?] of the Platte. The river is here quite noxious. Drove until nine in the evening   the country is very dry and barren   found a little feed by the river.

Tuesday July 19th   Started this morning about 11 oclock found a very sandy and dusty road   drove until it was so dark we could not see and had to stop when there was nothing for the cattle to eat   took a cold bite and went to bed in a terrible thunder storm.

Wednesday July 20th   Started about 5 oclock this morning and drove about six miles before finding grass for cattle. Had breakfast and dinner together — Then went on about six miles farther and found a nice camping place by a mail station and a few indian huts. Our road was over a mountain and some of them look very picturesque being dotted with fir or pine trees and also have strokes of red rock running through them. We are camping by the Platte for the last time we now leave it and cross over to the Deschutes We do not expect to be out of sight of mountains now at all from here to California. Met some of the US Army consisting of two companies of Dragoons and forty waggons returning from Salt Lake.

Thursday July 21st   Drove about 18 miles to Willow

Spring. There are a number of very cool springs and formerly a grove of willow trees but they have all been cut down. The grass has been pretty well eat off. The road to day has been fine rolling but hard and smooth. It is almost lined with dead cattle which now and then give the air a splendid fragrance I have at hand my camphor bottle

Friday July 22nd   Am camping by wood creek   Have had a fine road to day   can plainly see Rattlesnake Mountains ahead.

Saturday 23rd   Started in good season this morning   Our drive has been a very interesting one   We took our lunch at noon by the Sweetwater at Independence Rock. The latter took its name from standing alone by itself and company celebrating the 4th July on it several years ago. We forded the river and reached the Devils Gate in time to go to it and see it   This is a gorge or canion in the Rattlesnake Mountains through which the Sweet Water flows   the latter is a swift and clear stream   The rocks on each side of this gap rise perpendicular to the height of three or four hundred feet. Have passed two trading posts. Are camping in a beautiful spot in a small horse shoe formed by the bend of the Sweet water   high rocky mountains are on each side and river on the other.

Sunday July 24th   Travelled about twenty miles to day a part of the road very rocky and in sight of the river most of the way. Passed two trading posts where white men have a log cabin and a squaw for a wife and little half breeds running about. The scenery is quite romantic, in places the mountains are mostly solid rock with no vegetation excepting an occasional pine tree. Camped very late   did not have supper until nine oclock.

Monday July 25th   Travelled about 18 miles today   the road has been fine. The weather has been very cool.   Had a cold thunder storm this afternoon. Camping by Sweet Water. Forded it three times.

Tuesday July 26th   Drove twenty miles to day   the road has been mountainous but hard and smooth — Forded the Sweet water three times. Snow capped mountains in sight & some warmer to day   camping by a branch of the river.

Wednesday July 27th   Drove over twenty miles   camped by Willow Creek   Lunched by a spring as cold as ice water and fine grass   The weather most obligeful   very cold nights — the air is very bracing   Fremont Peak in sight covered with snow.

Thursday July 28th   Drove five miles to the Sweetwater and then about three miles up the river to find good grass and have been staying over to wash clothes &c   This is the last that we shall see of the Sweetwater   it is rightly named for it is a lovely stream. Found willows on its banks to day but our principal fuel has been the wild sage.

Friday July 29th   Had a pretty long descent three miles off the road to camp by the Sweetwater once more. Had a late drive and cold supper.

Saturday July 30th   We found the summit of the South Pass of Rocky Mountains   Lunched by the Pacific Spring and Creek. We are now on the Pacific Coast and nearly past the Rocky Mountains. roads continued fine. Have to camp without grass or water for stock   shall probably start without breakfast in the morning

Sunday July 31st   Started at day break and drove to little Sandy River a small stream of good water   no grass. Got dinner & breakfast together and went on to Big Sandy, quite a fine stream.   grass tolerable. Willows upon its banks   a good road.

Monday Aug 1st   Had a fine road to day. Passed one trading post. We were about two hours behind a very severe hail storm.   We found the hail by the roadside in places two or three inches deep   We are fast leaving the summit of Rocky moutains behind us   Camping on big Sandy

Tuesday Aug 2nd   Mr Freemans company left us this morning which detained us some time separating the cattle. We go by Salt Lake, They by the Sublette cut off. Drove twelve miles to Green River a handsome stream very rapid current. Ferried the waggons   swam the cattle & horses. camped by the river   a trading post [near] by.   we find the latter every few miles   they keep stores and whiskey.

Wednesday Aug 3d   Drove sixteen miles   camped by Blacks Fork, another trading post. Road more mountainous.

Thursday Aug 4th   Made a very short drive and camped by a small muddy stream   passed one trading post   The road in many places very stony and rolling. Weather warmer. Carrie has been quite sick for a few days with a billious attack, better to day.

Friday Aug 5th   Drove about eighteen miles   crossed Blacks Fork twice   road very rolling and dusty   are nearing a snow capped mountain   camping by a small stream clear good water willows on its banks.

Saturday Aug 6th   Drove eight or ten miles and arrived at Ft Bridger   This place is in a beautiful valley of the mountains. Seven clear cool streams flow down from the mountains   four on one side of the Ft and three on the other side The houses are built of hewn logs   Five good stores a Post Office Blacksmith shop &c which makes quite a town. The road this side of Bridger is splendid. We are camping about six miles west of it by a fine cold spring. The mountains here are covered with grass and trees.

Sunday Aug 7th   Made a drive of over twenty miles. Had the most picturesque scenery to day of any that we have seen.

One very long descent stony and steep   passed several springs copperas ones.[6] Weather cold a high wind and very dusty. Mountains here are quite fertile being covered with grass and cedar trees and [?] the quaking aspen trees clustered in nooks on the mountains sides   Camped on Sulphur Creek a beautiful spring at the head of it   very cold to night.

Monday Aug 8th   Froze ice on the standing water last night. Found several of the horses missing this morning Drove on ten miles to Bear River and camped for the day   Horses found in course of the day.   plenty of grass and timber on the river bank. Found nice ripe gooseberries and currants

Tuesday Aug 9th   Did not travel to day   staid to shoe and recruit the stock   been washing, picking over berries & steamed a nice dumpling for supper. This is a handsome grove of cotton wood trees.

Wednesday Aug 10th   Last night was very cold again. Drove over twenty miles   Passed a number of fine cold springs. Crossed Yellow Creek at the foot of a rocky bluff which looked rather dangerous to passers by as there was a large overhanging piece of rock which looked ready to drop down upon passers at any moment   Also passed Cache Cave a cave in the bluff with a circular entrance large enough for a man to walk erect   some of the boys entered it and reported it to be about fifty feet deep with two chambers leading out of it which they did not explore. We seem to be descending very rapidly so that we are in a warmer climate to night   have had some very steep and crooked descents. Are now passing through what is called Echo Canyon a narrow pass with high mountains on each side   fair grass and cold spring near the camp.

---

[6] One might think that copperas was a copper compound; however, it is ferrous iron sulfate.

Thursday Aug 11th   The Echo Kanyon which we have passed through to day is miles long and is the wildest and scaryest place which I ever imagined   The Echo Creek winds through the whole length of the pass and has to be crossed a number of times   its Banks are quite steep numbers of springs flow from the mountain making little pits in some places   theres hardly room for the waggon to pass between the mountain on the one side and a ravine on the other.   scattered pieces of rock are lying about which from time to time have rolled down from the mountain.   some of these are overhanging   We took our noon lunch at the foot of one of the highest points of the mountain where the Mormons had erected fortifications to command this pass. The western end of this Kanyon is the handsomest   The mountain on the right going west rises in immense columns and towers up into a variety of shapes and sizes   As we leave this pass we go down a long and winding descent into the valley of the Weber River. The view from the top of this descent is very beautiful. Camped by the Weber river   it is said to abound in fire wood and an abundance of gooseberries currants and service berries which with [?] make a fine relish.

Friday Aug 12th   Our road to day has been entirely in the mountains   Forded the Weber River Canyon   creek winds through and has to be crossed thirteen times within eight miles.

Saturday Aug 13th   Had the misfortune to get behind a long freight train that have six yoke of cattle to a team which has hindered us very much   Have been ascending the highest mountain that we have to cross and have got part way down where night overtook us and are camping by the roadside. From the summit of this mountain we got a view of part of Salt Lake Valley   It was certainly a good sight to be [?] and be able to look over a lower range of mountains into a valley beneath. We are now about eighteen miles from Salt Lake City.

Sunday Aug 14th   Started at daylight and drove to the foot of the mountain   stopped for breakfast and dinner and then drove over the little mountain which was equally as steep as the other and more rough   Crossed a creek [?] within five miles   camped next on it about four miles from the City.

Monday Aug 15th   My Husband baby and myself rode to the City and all about it. It is situated at the foot of the mountain on an inclined plain of the valley which is twenty five miles wide and one hundred long   The streets are good and cross at right angles   each has one and sometimes 2 streams of clear spring water running through them. Brigham Youngs premises are enclosed with a handsome stone wall. The houses are built of Adobe and are neat and pretty plenty of nice fruit and shade trees   Expected to have heard from home but did not which has disappointed us much Received a letter from Mrs Waterbury.

Tuesday Aug 16th   Drove through town and out seven miles   Hired a pasture as we found no grass by the way. Had a nice relish of Melons, corn, beans, potatoes, and onions. Passed a boiling spring.

Wednesday Aug 17th   Drove about nine miles and camped a few miles from the lake. Henry and some of the boys took a boat in it and brought a specimen of the Salt from the shore. It is impossible to sink in it the waters so strong with salt   there are no fish in it.

Thursday Aug 18th   Drove nearly twenty five miles passed through Ogden City situated on Ogden river   forded the Weber river and camped about five miles from the City.

Friday Aug 19th   Started at noon having been delayed hunting cattle   Drove nine miles and camped by a large spring at the foot of the mountains   found good feed   shall remain here until the arrival of a large company behind as we hear of Indian troubles ahead   several companies intend joining to protect each other more   about forty three miles from Salt Lake City the country so far is well settled with farmers who seem to be thriving   they are certainly very tidy in their premises and green.

Saturday Aug 20th   Have been washing and cleaning up some   I feel quite anxious about the report that we hear of trouble ahead still making

Sunday Aug 21st   Still camped waiting and expecting every minute the train   The Lords day again but little opportunity of observing it as a Christian would wish to. I can imagine friends at home going to and from their place of worship and then sitting down in their peaceful quiet home to enjoy suitable reading and reflection and all the comforts of home included. If Providence sees fit to take note our journey and in safety shall be able to thank Him for His kindness and to appreciate a Sunday.

Monday Aug 22nd   Started in a company with a number of other waggons in all forty on account of trouble with Indians   we were joined together for safety to protect each other in case of attack.

Tuesday Aug 23rd   Had a very dusty road and hot day   on the whole a disagreeable time   I never felt more discouraged Am perfectly sick and tired of this journey   camped upon Bear River near the ford opposite an encampment of troops which have come here to quell the Indian disturbances Shall be very thankful if I ever have a quiet decent home again

Wed Aug 24th   Drove about sixteen miles and camped by a large Spring in the mountain side.

Thursday Aug 25th   Started at five oclock and made a drive of over twenty five miles the longest distance which we have travelled in a day since starting   camp about ten

oclock PM   Passed a Salt Spring   Had one very steep
rocky descent   extremely dusty   I do not fancy riding and
camping after dark in the Indian territory   I consider it
very dangerous and unsafe

Friday Aug 26th   Got a late start this morning as usual
after a late drive the night before. Drove six miles to find
creek with clear cool water.   travelled on its bank about six
miles and camped in good season and a clear nice place

Saturday Aug 27th   Drove about sixteen miles   lunched
by Hot Springs. The road for the last twenty miles has been
through a valley   are camping by a spring   creek coming
down from the mountain. Hare[s] are very abundant here
and are fine eating.

Sunday Aug 28th   Started about seven oclock   crossed
stony creek about noon   Roads rolling   camped early by a
small stream of good water   no feed. Drove about fifteen
miles

Monday Aug 29th   Started at daylight   drove about four
miles and found grass   got breakfast and rest about three
hours before starting again   crossed [?] Creek two or three
times. Camped early by a dry spring in the mountain
side   drove from twelve to fourteen miles [?] Elected John
Gossage Captain of the train.

Tuesday Aug 30th   Started at half past six and found water
in about five miles   Roads very steep and sideling   The
last descent five miles long and in places very stony and
dangerous. Camped on a branch of Goose Creek   The
Mountains were on all sides of us and on the whole it was a
very dangerous place to camp on   the indians could shoot
down upon us if they felt disposed and they have been killing
a number of persons for the sake of plunder. A little after
dark a meeting was called to pass resolutions in regard to the
regulation of the company in order to [?] and a good

understanding in case of an attack from indians or another
danger   Just as Dr Mott[7] was reading off the resolutions all
was silence — someone raised an alarm and confusion
prevailed   at once the Capt ordered every man to get the
arms and arrange themselves as they best could   as for
myself I was frightened nearly to death and was curled up in
the waggon with my children around me trembling with
fright   But thank fortune it proved to be a false alarm   one
of the men for amusement had been throwing slings stones
which buzzed by the ears of those who supposed them to be
arrows and gave the alarm   After setting an extra Guard we
went to bed although it took some time to quiet down to
sleep. Drove about 17 miles.

Wednesday Aug 31st   After travelling about three miles
we reached Goose Creek   traveld about fourteen miles and
camped in good season   good grass and water —

Thursday Sept 1st   Started early   drove about three miles
farther up Goose Creek when we entered a Kanyon   high
mountains of rocks on a small branch of Goose Creek   run
through it. Passed over some high mountainous ascents and
descents about seventeen miles and camped on a high hill
without water excepting for cooking which we brought from
a spring back

Friday Sept 2nd   Drove on twenty miles and camped in
Thousand Spring valley. Road most of the way fine. The
man that goes ahead to hunt camping places met with two
Indians   They was out of sight before we come up

Saturday Sept 3rd   Continued up the valley past a large
boiling spring near the head of the valley.   on leaving the
latter passed up a ravine about two miles and camped   fine
cool water running through   cold night.

Sunday Sept 4th   road ascending for two miles   descent

---

[7] See fn. 5, above.

not steep but long   Humbolt springs [present Nevada] about seven miles from start   must camp in a valley to the left   full of springs   abundance of grass

Monday Sept 5th   Last night was very cold   lunched at headwaters of Humbolt — Overtook a large train composed of several small trains. some if not all of them were attacked by Indians and while we were on the SLC Road. They lost their waggons and most everything they had   A number of persons have been killed and several wounded. Camped by the Humbolt which is here a clear cool stream. Very cold night and morning and extremely dusty roads

Tuesday Sept 6th   A very pleasant day   made a very good drive.   camped by the river

Wednesday Sept 7th   An extremely cold morning   a cold shower accompanied by some sleet   snow probably fell on the mountains   a cold wind all day   more snow etc to night. Drove about eighteen miles   camped by the river which is wider as we go down it. Trains in sight both before and behind ours.

Thursday Sept 8th   Drove to day about twenty miles camped near sundown by the river. In the forenoon the road was in the valley   we then entered a kanyon where the river runs between mountains   forded it several times   descended to the valley to camp. Only see indians occasionaly [?] to day that were fishing by the river   speckled trout are abundant.

Friday Sept 9th   Had a late start and slow drive during the forenoon   We then left the valley and ascended into the mountains   roads very dusty and hard for the teams ascended about eight miles to the summit of ridge and camped about two miles down by a spring   weather cold but not as cold as last night. Have got out of coffee and use barley as substitute.

Saturday Sept 10th   Had a very rough rocky road in the fore noon   Crossed what is called Gravelly[8] ford and passed the first mail station this side of Salt Lake   camped by the river. Distance from Salt Lake City 430 miles

Sunday Sept 11th   Drove about ten miles over a mountain road mostly and camped by the river for the day

Monday Sept 12th   drove nearly twenty miles   camped by the river by driving off the road a mile or two. Some of the boys found an indian arrow and gave it to Eddie

Tuesday Sept 13th   Made a long drive over twenty   road lay some distance from the river   the cattle had no water from morning until night   had a slight shower and heavy rain around us on the mountains   weather to night cool. camped by the river   met the mail coach to day for the first time since leaving Salt Lake   passed second mail station

Wednesday Sept 14th   Drove about fifteen miles and camped by the river as usual. Roads very dusty and strong with alkali

Thursday Sept 15th   Drove about fifteen miles and camped early   passed over a range of mountains   some places rather steep and rocky.

Friday Sept. 16th   drove about eighteen miles   road lay in valley   passed mail station and trading post   are camped by river. Near by stood a waggon with a woman and family of children   Her husband had been gone with two men four days in the mountains to recover their cattle from the indians who have run them off   She has just learned that they have succeeded in getting back the cattle and are now near here.

---

8 Thomas H. Hunt says that travel was so hot and bad in this part of Nevada that emigrants were prone to "let it all out with a very human snarl." Harriett Griswold is far more understated. *Ghost Trails to California* (Palo Alto, 1974), p. 39.

Saturday Sept 17th   Drove about the same as usual and camped by the river in good season   road lay mostly in the valley with the exception of a few sandy bluffs.

Sunday Sept 18th   Drove until about one oclock and camped by the river   road lay over sandy bluffs and very hard for the teams

Monday Sept 19th   Road to day has been through a very barren country and dust was like ashes full half a foot deep. It is truly a desolate country   no vegetation but chaperel.   a thorny woody shrub sometimes called grease wood.

Tuesday Sept 20th   Road about the same as yesterday   a high wind which made the dust disagreeable

Wednesday Sept 21st   Weather and road the same   shall be thankful when we get out of this barren region   drove down to river to camp as usual

Thursday Sept 22nd   Found the indian pony dead this morning   Reached what is called the big meadows in the afternoon   drove down about four miles and camped on fine grass the best we have seen in long time   The river has disappeared and nothing to be seen of it but a slough

Friday Sept 23rd   Laid by to day to make hay for the desert which is about twenty miles ahead   have also been doing extra cooking and killed a young beef

Saturday Sept 24th   Drove about ten miles and camped without grass   the water as [?] the Lake grows brackish and is quite strong with alkali   left another horse beside the road to day that gave out   The soil all along the Humbolt is strongly impregnated with alkali and the dust affects animals.

Sunday Sept 25th   Drove about fourteen miles to day   part of the way on the bank of the Lake which is quite a handsome body of water where it is deep   we are now camped in or near the Sink[9] where the Lake spreads out into sloughs and sinks in the ground. The water is unpleasant to drink without the addition of acid   it is salt beside being strong with alkali. The horses have all been taken ahead to night to a half way place on the Desert to wait until we come up tomorrow

Monday Sept 26th   Started upon the Desert which is a barren stretch of country forty five miles   thirty five of which is no water and what there is poison   At night fall we reached the wells which are half way across where stock can be watered at one shilling a head, and people a quarter   this is a great relief to crossing the desert as it was before the wells were dug. The last ten miles of the way is very sandy and trying to teams   we stopped at the wells long enough to water and feed the working cattle and get our supper and then started on our night journey about eight P.M. and arrived Carson river about half after seven the next morning. Got our breakfast and drove up the River about four miles and camped for the day   very little grass on this river plenty of willows and Cotton wood. It is a fine clear stream and fine water   it is a relief to get away from the Humbolt which is horrid water to drink. The name of the place where we first struck the river was Ragtown.[10]

Wednesday 28th   Drove up the river about ten miles and camped.   road rolling sandy and rocky   A very cold rain

---

[9] The Humboldt Sink was the last dying gasp of the river as it flowed into a wide flat basin and extended itself in all directions to form a marsh containing a lake into which the river flowed. The waters are now impounded behind Rye Patch dam. Helen S. Carlson, *Nevada Place Names* (Reno, 1974), p. 139.

[10] "Trading posts sprang up at various places, particularly at Ragtown — so called, it would seem, because of its appearance — where the trail came to the Carson River after crossing the desert." George R. Stewart, *The California Trail* (New York, 1962), p. 297; also Carlson, *op. cit.*, p. 197. It was also called Ragwood Station, about 12 miles northwest of present Fallon. Evidently the emigrants threw off many of their soiled and damaged clothes here.

last night   mountains ahead covered with snow which makes the wind very cold.

Thursday Sept 29th   Drove eleven miles   road lay over the bluffs in places sandy and in other rocky   camping by the river where we find better grass than we have since left Humbolt   Gave twenty five cents for a little brown sugar that I could bought at home for four cents   Weather last night very cold indeed.

Friday Sept 30th   Drove about four miles up the river off from the road to find good grass to rest the cattle on as they seem to be very weak and tired out.   and several have died.

Saturday Oct 1st   Drove eight miles over a very sandy road   Camped early by the river.

Sunday Oct 2nd   Made a long drive about eighteen miles   road rather rough.

Monday Oct 3rd   Started rather late drove about seven miles to China town[11] and after a short time put up and I believe they expect to have a great time soon on account of gold mines which have been discovered near here, and which they are working   Got supper and then started on another night drive over mountains which were rocky and the low places sandy. Arrived at Carson City about two AM and camped until after dinner

Tuesday Oct 4th   Started about two PM   drove eight miles and camped by the river in fir grove. Weather delightful

Wednesday October 5th   Drove about ten miles and

---

[11] Anyone who studies the federal census records of 1860 and 1870 is impressed with the many, many Chinese who were scattered through the gold region. Chinese had come into the Carson valley as early as 1855 in large numbers. They did the menial labor and worked the placers only after the Americans had operated at a particular place. The best treatment of this subject is Gary P. BeDunnah, *History of the Chinese in Nevada, 1855-1904*, Master's Thesis, University of Nevada, Reno, 1966. This particular Chinatown became the later town of Dayton, Lyon County. Carlson, *op. cit.*, pp. 92-93.

reached Genoa[12] quite a busy little place at the foot of the mountain with a fine stream flowing through it   went on about five miles and camped by the river. The cattle are so weak and dying off so fast that we have got to lay over a few days before crossing the mountains which we are very near.

Thursday Oct 6th   Lay by all day to recruit the stock several more have died to day

Friday Oct 7th   Staid in the same place all day.

Saturday Oct 8th   This morning our team the horse and buggy and horses started ahead and left Mr John Gossage and four men behind with three waggons and loose stock until the latter are able to travel. Drove about eight miles   road sandy.

Sunday Oct 9th   Drove about eight miles   arrived at the entrance of Carson Kanyon   crossed the river and camped

Monday Oct 10th   Drove through the kanyon and got along nicely although it is a horribly rough road   The river comes tumbling down over the rocks with great force and noise   immensely high mountains are towering on both sides, the road very winding turning very short in many places.   to avoid rocks in some places it required the drivers and a man ahead at each wheel to get the waggon along   we finally arrived at Hope valley about half past three PM   drove up the valley about two miles and camped in a pleasant place   found two trading posts here   weather very cold   surrounded by snowy mountains.

Tuesday Oct 11th   Started this morning on our way over the Sierra Nevada Mountains   We got over the first summit at noon   stopped and lunched by a stream of water   very cold   found a small lake in a valley. The ascent of the second summit is a road cut in the mountain side   one track   The road on the whole is very good although there

---

[12] Genoa was the first American settlement in present Nevada. *Ibid.* p. 118.

are some rocks and in a few places it is broken away on the outer side. We reached at the summit about half past three PM. The sides are thickly covered with the finest pine and fir trees that ever grew. Drove about two miles down the Mt and camped   Weather extremely cold but sunny days.

Wednesday Oct 12th   Another beautiful day   our road in the forenoon down the Mt was very rocky   in the afternoon we reached the good road which runs on the Mt side   drove until nine in the evening to reach a trading post to get food for the cattle and horses.

Thursday 13th   Our road has been all day on the grade down the Mt side   Have found some of the tallest trees that I have ever seen   from two to two hundred and fifty feet high

Thursday Oct 13th   Had a long drive nearly twenty miles   road very good   part of the way we had continued upon gravel roads   Mt still very high

Friday Oct 14th   Road about the same   crossed the American River on the new bridge which is a fine one   Camped by a trading post.

Saturday Oct 15th   Started early and made a good drive road rolling but Mts get lower   passed through quite a town called Diamond Springs. Drove on about two miles and camped. Weather warm   air good.

Sunday Oct 16th   Drove about fourteen miles over a very rolling country and quite rocky and rough   we are beginning to get among civilized people again

Monday Oct 17th   Made a short drive   road very dusty has been no rain here for seven months.

Tuesday Oct 18th   Passed through Sacramento City a lively pleasant place   drove another mile and camped

Wednesday Oct 19th   Drove about thirteen miles   a fine level road.

HANNAH KEZIAH CLAPP
Courtesy, Nevada Historical Society.

A Salt Lake City Stopover, July 1859
∮ Hannah Keziah Clapp

INTRODUCTION

It would be difficult to imagine any more exciting personality in the history of the American West than Hannah Keziah Clapp, educator and advocate for the rights of women.

This woman, born a New Yorker, made her first appearance on history's page as a teacher in Ypsilanti, Michigan, in 1849 at the age of 25 years.[1] She moved on from there to Lansing, where she was principal of that city's Female Seminary. She then became a teacher in the Michigan Female College. During these years she was an active feminist, even adopting the "freedom costume," the "bloomer dress."[2]

During the spring of 1859 Hannah decided to travel over the trail to California with her brother, Nathan, and his family. The letter printed below was written from Salt Lake City to an unnamed friend in Lansing, who, as Hannah suggested, took it to the colorful editor of the Lansing *Republican*, Rufus ("Roof") Hosmer,[3] who published it on September 6, 1859. A photocopy of the clipping was kindly supplied from the Hannah Clapp Collection by the Nevada State Historical Society, Reno. The public library in Lansing has a file of the newspaper on microfilm.

The overland party on its way west paused in Salt Lake City for a few days. Hannah's letter was written on July 17, 1859. They reached California in the fall. For the next year Hannah taught in Vacaville, some thirty miles southwest of Sacramento.

---

[1] The most definitive resource for this introduction has been Kathryn Dunn Totton, "Hannah Keziah Clapp: The Life and Career of a Pioneer Nevada Educator, 1824-1908," *Nevada Hist. Soc. Quar.*, XX, No. 3 (Fall 1977), pp. 166-183.

[2] See *Covered Wagon Women*, Vol. IV, pp. 12-15; also this volume, above, p. 9; D.C. Bloomer, *Life and Writings of Amelia Bloomer* (New York, 1975).

[3] "Wielded a Strong Pen, Rufus Hosmer, an Old-Time Editor...." *Mich. History Mag.*, XXV (Winter 1911), pp. 29-33.

A year later, in the fall of 1860, she retraced her steps over the Sierra to the newly laid out town of Carson City, Nevada. It was in that territory and state that she spent most of the rest of her life. She and a friend, Mrs. W.K. (Ellen) Cutler organized a private school, Sierra Seminary. Mrs. Cutler was "a noted singer and elocutionist."[4] She departed Nevada in the spring of 1864, and Hannah advertised for another teacher who would specialize in Latin and English. Eliza C. Babcock, a native of Maine responded to the ad, and the two ladies soon became inseperable in a friendship that lasted 35 years.

In 1887 Hannah Clapp was appointed to the staff of the newly founded University of Nevada at Reno as "Preceptress and Professor of History and the English Language."[5] She also served as librarian. The two friends moved to Reno. Hannah told those gathered for a reunion thirty years later that the first faculty "consisted of the following important names, to-wit, President [Leroy D.] Brown and H.K. Clapp." She added, "This august body presided over the destinies of a microscopic student body, whom it inspired with reverence and awe."[6]

In the years following Hannah Clapp was also involved intensely in the pursuit of suffrage for women. She became acquainted with the national leaders of that movement, including Susan B. Anthony. Her work on woman suffrage all seemed to be fruitless as the legislature turned it down in 1869, 1883, 1885, and 1895. It did not come about in Nevada until 1914, six years after Hannah's death.[7]

The two companions lived together until the death of Eliza Babcock on September 19, 1899. Hannah Keziah Clapp moved to Palo Alto, California, where she lived until the day of her death, October 8, 1908.

---

[4] Henry Nash Smith, *Mark Twain of the Enterprise* (Berkeley, 1957), p. 227.

[5] Totten, *op. cit.*, p. 173.

[6] *Ibid.*

[7] Totten, *op. cit.*, p. 180; Russell R. Elliott, *History of Nevada* (Lincoln, Neb., 1973), pp. 246-247.

HANNAH CLAPP'S LETTER

EDITOR'S NOTE: The Lansing, Michigan, *Republican*, September 6, 1859: The following interesting letter from Miss H.K. Clapp was received by a lady of this city, who politely permitted us to publish, of which permisson we have availed ourselves, believing it likely to interest our readers:

GREAT SALT LAKE, July 17, 1859.

This Sunday is very much like others days with us here; although now we have the privilege of attending Mormon meeting. I embraced the opportunity on Sunday — went with my bloomer dress and hat, with my revolver by my side. Heard *Lord* Pratt,[1] and saw *Prophet* Brigham. The congregation were seated in a large room, the seats graduated from the pulpit on three sides — the back seats as high as the pulpit. The Prophet Brigham and his consellors, Kimbal[2] and Wells[3], came in a back way, well guarded by soldiery. The Lord does not always take care of his Prophets, and they are a little afraid of their heads. The twelve Apostles were seated in this pulpit, which has a close panneled wall around it, four feet high. The men come into this Tabernacle at one end door, and the women at the other. The appearance of the congregation was after their own peculiar institution — barefoot and no hoops; the men in their shirt-sleeves; emigrants in their emigrant clothes; all armed — bowie knife, and revolver.

Salt Lake City is a large place, situated at the head of the great valley; on the east, the river Jordan; and on the east and north, laterally, mountains. Its first appearance, at a distance, looked like an Irish huddle;[4] but on approaching it, it looked

---

[1] Orson Pratt (1811-1881).
[2] Heber C. Kimball (1801-1868).
[3] Daniel H. Wells (1814-1891).
[4] An "Irish huddle" would have been a conglomerate pile of something.

better. It is laid out in squares of forty rods each, streets crossing each other at right angles; and on either sides, streams of water, brought from the mountains for the purpose of irrigation, as it seldom rains here.

The buildings are made of adobe, a kind of sunburned brick; all unpainted except Brigham's *Harem*, this is painted a kind of cream. His buildings and garden occupy one square, and are enclosed with a stone wall twelve feet high, laid in lime mortar. Every rod are pillars built up four feet higher than the wall. These are the "watchmen of the towers of Zion." Over the main door of this Harem is a huge lion, carved in marble, perhaps of the "tribe of Judah." On the top of the cupola is a bee-hive. Over the main gate is an eagle, with her wings spread.

An armed guard is stationed at the gates, and all entrances into this enclosure. No one is permitted to go in unless he has business with Prophet B————. Some of our party tried to call on him, but could not gain admittance. I told them I meant to see him, still I did not wish to show him the least respect. I consider him guilty of treason against the Government, and not worthy the recognition of an American.

I sent him a note, saying I would like to see him — curiosity of course — and if he would name the hour, I would call, with *my escort*. After much questioning, the messenger brought me word that his Superior, Prophet-like Majesty would attend to my call at my earliest convenience. We were admitted into his august presence, through guard. The room was large. There were thirteen men besides himself in the room, all armed. He sat in his armed chair. In a back room were armed guards.

A man about fifty eight, of medium height, sanguine temperament, portly, sallow countenance, (effect of being housed up, undoubtedly,) arose from his chair to receive us, we knowing by this act that he was a man, &c. We had a very pleasant call. After the first few moments he seemed much interested in the conversation. We made a long call, but when we came to retire, he came to the door and asked us to call again. Among the sixty wives we did not see one. A little chap came into the room while we were sitting there, about eight years of age. I asked the little fellow what his name was. He replied, "Brigham Young the Third." His grandpa replied that "he was the eldest son of his eldest son." This is the way the Brighams are counted.[5]

The man of the house where we put up while we were in the city, "The Utah House," had three wives. The first wife was very talkative. He was one and seventy, and kept preaching to me. One day he told me that "it would be the business of the Saints, in another world, to teach those of the gentiles that had not heard the gospel in this life; but he had preached to me, and he feared if I did not embrace the doctrine I would go to hell." I think Governor Cummings[6] would consider my life in danger if he knew what I said to them. I will preach a little to the women when I get a chance, in spite of the Governor.

We called on Governor Cummings. He is a superannuated, brandy-soaked, Buchanan Democrat. Believes in the Territories controlling their own peculiar institutions in their own peculiar way. He told us that "*we* had nothing to fear of the Mormons while passing their *their* territory, if we

---

[5] Hannah Clapp evidently did not know that Horace Greeley, editor of the New York *Tribune* was in Salt Lake City at the same time as she. He, too, interviewed Brigham Young. He sent back a story about that meeting entitled "Two Hours with Brigham Young," dated July 13, just four days before the date of Hannah's letter. In 1860 he published the story of his interview with the Mormon leader in a book, *An Overland Journey from New York to San Francisco*. Greeley heeded his own advice to "Go west, young man," by traveling overland in a stage coach.

[6] Governor Alfred Cumming. His wife, Elizabeth Wells Randall Cumming, wrote observant letters east telling about her journey west and experience in the Mormon city. Five of them were published in William Mulder and A. Russell Mortensen *Among the Mormons* (New York, 1958), pp. 302-315.

would not talk their religion with them; pass through quietly, not argue with them at all, or meddle with their religious views." Oh! I know we are in a foreign land; not American soil here! This is the "Independent State of Deseret." To be sure the United States has a Consul here, in the person of the Governor, as you would have known on the glorious Fourth; for you would have seen the American flag waving over his private dwelling, while at other places you see the Mormon flag hoisted. This was a beautiful spectacle. The spirit of '76 so burned in the bosom of some of the emigrants that I do believe if there had been a hundred of them they would have pulled down the foreign flags and hoisted the American flag.

The soldiers of this "Independent State of Deseret" came out in uniform, on horseback, marched around Brigham's harem, and he came out on the steps, *inside the wall*, and made a short speech. At the present appearance of the government, they will pour many more millions of dollars into the pockets of these rebels without bringing "one sinner to rependance." Two hundred thousand dollars, Col. Johnson[7] says, have been paid out of government funds to Brigham Young for lumber, at seventy dollars per thousand, for building the Fort at Camp Floyd. This Fort is forty-seven miles from the city. The statements I make concerning the Mormons are authentic, and if Hosmer wants them for his paper, let him have them.

Col. Johnson also says that the army coming here have not quelled the Mormons, only for the time. Sending the peace officers ahead of the army, placed the army in a position

---

[7] Albert Sidney Johnston was the American officer in command of the army that was sent to Utah to "solve the Mormon problem." He was an avowed agitator against all things Mormon. They were "traitorous rogues whose actions merited the closest and most suspicious scrutiny." Norman F. Furniss, *The Mormon Conflict* (New Haven, 1960), p. 98.

where they could not do anything — they were powerless. All of the army were convinced that this people were a guilty band of rebels, robbers and murderers. Their burning the provisions of the army — there were ten trains burned, one on Green River, the other on the other side, ninety wagons in all. The irons of sixty I saw lay, as they had been corralled for the night, on the banks of the Green River, and there they will remain, as a monument of this rebellion, until the emigrants shall pick them away, iron by iron. The log chains, or large chains, have been straightened out, and some of the men paced a hundred rods and still there was chain. Enough to rivet every rebel Mormon's neck, if they could be used.

Then when you come to pass through the canons, see the fortifications, and the savage and fiendish manner that they have prepared to mutilate and mow down the army of their own nation. Every entrance into the city is well fortified, and they had their men out by the thousands.

Again, to see, as I did, those sixteen orphan children, rescued from that dreadful massacre of emigrants, known here as the "mountain meadow massacre."[8] When I saw these children they were camped with a portion of the army, that were being marched to Lehi, about thirteen miles out of the city. We camped here, and I went with one of the officers to the camp where these children were. They were all very bright, nice looking children, from the age of five to eight or ten; not one able to tell his or her surname, with the exception of two boys — they were the oldest. They were sent back to the city, Col. Johnson, or Judge Eckles,[9] I know not which, sent to have them return, thinking perhaps they may be of use as evidence. This soldier told me he was one that was sent

---

[8] A balanced treatment of the "Mountain Meadows Massacre" is to be found in Leonard J. Arrington and Davis Bitton, *The Mormon Experience* (New York, 1979), pp. 167-170.
[9] Chief Justice Delana R. Eckels.

to the place of the massacre to bury the skulls — they found and buried 113. This is said to have been one of the richest emigrant companies that has ever passed through this Territory; they had over a thousand head of cattle.

I might write pages that these soldiers, officers, and men of responsibility have told me of Mormonism, and not one word of good can they say of them. Tell Hosmer, for me I believe them to be a lot of miserable, wicked land pirates, and I wish he would bring them to justice, or send them to Kingdom-Come, I care not which.

The women are miserable slaves, and the men are licentious knaves. Their children are numerous, but of a very poor quality, very raw, and not half witted. Not one to twenty of the women or children can read, and what is true the world over, converted; think they have all the rights and privileges they want. They told me the system is beautiful if I only understood it.

We were one week in the city. We are now camped twenty miles north, recruiting our animals, and waiting for some of our company to return from Camp Floyd. We are right in a settlement of Mormons. The women come daily to see us; none go away empty. Most of them are old country people, kind hearted, and I laugh, and sometimes ridicule their peculiar doctrine; still they seem interested in me. One old English widow, of forty-eight, has been several times. She came last night to bid me good-bye. She said she walked all the way from New York City to Salt Lake, and brought three children; was thankful that she had money enough to pay their fare. I told her she did more than I would for her religion, or a husband. She is good, but so bigoted.

We have had a pleasant journey, but this warm weather is tedious. We are camped at the foot of a high mountain, and in view of Salt Lake. They drive down on its banks and shovel up salt by the pailful, yes, by the wagon load.

We have the full benefit of the sun — not a shade in sight.
No timber except among the mountains.
Affectionately, I remain,   Your friend,

H.K. CLAPP

EPILOGUE

MARK TWAIN VISITS SIERRA ACADEMY

Mark Twain arrived in Virginia City, Nevada, in September,
1862, to become reporter on the staff of the *Territorial Enterprise*.
He held that position until May, 1864. Much of his duty was to
cover legislative and other political events in the Territorial
Capital, Carson City. In his routine reporting he used his actual
name, Samuel Clemens. At some point he began to sign his
published letters and columns "Mark Twain."

Such a letter, published on January 14, 1864, told of a visit with
a local politician, William M. Gillespie, to the school run by
Hannah Clapp and Ellen Cutler, in Carson City.

Files of the *Territorial Enterprise* before 1865 have been lost.
However, four volumes of clippings from the *Enterprise* turned
up in some scrapbooks kept by Orion Clemens, brother of the
young reporter. They were among the effects of Anita Moffett,
Clemens' grand niece, at her death in 1952. They are now among
the Mark Twain papers in the University of California Library in
Berkeley. They were published in a choice book, *Mark Twain of
the Enterprise*, (Berkely, 1957), by a competent Mark Twain
scholar, the late Henry Nash Smith of the same university.
Among them was the letter telling of the visit to Sierra Academy.
We are grateful to Elinor Smith of Berkeley for permission to
publish the letter.

MISS CLAPP'S SCHOOL

By authority of an invitation from Hon. Wm. M. Gillespie, member
of the House Committee on Colleges and Common Schools, I
accompanied that statesman on an unofficial visit to the excellent school

of Miss Clapp and Mrs. Cutler, this afternoon. The air was soft and balmy — the sky was cloudless and serene — the odor of flowers floated upon the idle breeze — the glory of the sun descended like a benediction upon mountain and meadow and plain — the wind blew like the very devil, and the day was generally disagreeable.

The school — however, I will mention first that a charter for an educational institution to be called the Sierra Seminary, was granted to Miss Clapp during the Legislative session of 1861, and a bill will be introduced while the present Assembly is in session, asking an appropriation of $20,000 to aid the enterprise. Such a sum of money could not be more judiciously expended, and I doubt not the bill will pass.[1]

The present school is a credit both to the teachers and the town. It now numbers about forty pupils, I should think, and is well and systematically conducted. The exercises this afternoon were of a character not likely to be unfamiliar to the free American citizen who has a fair recollection of how he used to pass his Friday afternoons in the days of his youth. The tactics have undergone some changes, but these variations are not important. In former times a fellow took his place in the luminous spelling class in the full consciousness that if he spelled cat with a "k," or indulged in any other little orthographical eccentricities of a similar nature, he would be degraded to the foot or sent to his seat; whereas, he keeps his place in the ranks now, in such cases, and his punishment is simply to "'bout face." Johnny Eaves stuck to his first position, to-day, long after the balance of the class had rounded to, but he subsequently succumbed to the word "nape," which he persisted in ravishing of its final vowel. There was nothing irregular about that. Your rightly constructed schoolboy will spell a multitude of hard words without hesitating once, and then lose his grip and miss fire on the easiest one in the book.

The fashion of reading selections of prose and poetry remains the same; and so does the youthful manner of doing that sort of thing. Some pupils read poetry with graceful ease and correct expression, and others place the rising and falling inflection at measured intervals, as if they had learned the lesson on a "see-saw"; but then they go undulating through a stanza with such an air of unctuous satisfaction, that it is a comfort to be around when they are at it.

[1]The bill did not pass

"The boy—stoo—dawn—the bur—ning deck—
    When—sawl—but *him* had fled—
The flames—that shook—the battle—zreck—
    Shone round—him *o'er*—the dead."[2]

That is the old-fashioned *impressive* style — stately, slow-moving and solemn. It is in vogue yet among scholars of tender age. It always will be. Ever since Mrs. Hemans wrote that verse, it has suited the pleasure of juveniles to emphasize the word "him," and lay atrocious stress upon that other word "o'er," whether she liked it or not; and I am prepared to believe that they will continue this practice unto the end of time, and with the same indifference to Mrs. Hemans' opinions about it, or any body's else.

They sing in school, now-a-days, which is an improvement upon the ancient regime; and they don't catch flies and throw spit-balls at the teacher, as they used to do in my time — which is another improvement, in a general way. Neither do the boys and girls keep a sharp look-out on each other's shortcomings and report the same at headquarters, as was a custom of by-gone centuries. And this reminds me of Gov. Nye's[3] last anecdote, fulminated since the delivery of his message, and consequently not to be found in that document. The company were swapping old school reminiscences, and in due season they got to talking about that extinct species of tell-tales that were once to be found in all minor educational establishments, and who never failed to detect and impartially denounce every infraction of the rules that occurred among their mates. The Governor said that he threw a casual glance at a pretty girl on the next bench one day, and she complained to the teacher — which was entirely characteristic, you know. Says she, "Mister Jones, Warren Nye's looking at me." Whereupon, without a suggestion from anybody, up jumped an infamous, lisping, tow-headed young miscreant, and says he, "Yeth, thir, I *thee* him do it!" I doubt if the old original boy got off that ejaculation with more gusto than the Governor throws into it.

The "compositions" read to-day were as exactly like the compositions I used to hear read in our school as one baby's nose is exactly like all other babies' noses. I mean the old principal earmarks were all there: the cutting to the bone of the subject with the very first gash, without any

---

[2]The lines are from "Casablanca," written by Felicia Dorothea Hemans, an English poet (1793-1838).

[3]James W. Nye, a New Yorker, was Governor of Nevada Territory, 1861-1864; United States Senator from Nevada, 1864-1872.

preliminary foolishness in the way of a gorgeous introductory; the
inevitable and persevering tautology; the brief, monosyllabic sentences
(beginning, as a very general thing, with the pronoun "I"); the penchant
for presenting rigid, uncompromising facts for the consideration of the
hearer, rather than ornamental fancies; the depending for the success of
the composition upon its general merits, without taking artificial aids to
the end of it, in the shape of deductions or conclusions, or clap-trap
climaxes, albeit their absence sometimes imparts to these essays the
semblance of having come to an end before they were finished — of
arriving at full speed at a jumping-off place and going suddenly
overboard, as it were, leaving a sensation such as one feels when he
stumbles without previous warning upon that infernal "To be
Continued" in the midst of a thrilling magazine story. I know there are
other styles of school compositions, but these are the characteristics of
style which I have in my eye at present. I do not know why this one has
particularly suggested itself to my mind, unless the literary effort of one
of the boys there to-day left with me an unusually vivid impression. It
ran something in this wise:

COMPOSITION

"I like horses. Where we lived before we came here, we used to have a
cutter and horses. We used to ride in it. I like winter. I like snow. I used
to have a pony all to myself, where I used to live before I came here.
Once it drifted a good deal — very deep — and when it stopped I went
out and got in it."

That was all. There was no climax to it, except the spasmodic bow
which the tautological little student jerked at the school as he closed his
labors.

Two remarkably good compositions were read. Miss P.'s was much
the best of these — but aside from its marked literary excellence it
possessed another merit which was peculiarly gratifying to my feelings
just at that time. Because it took the conceit out of young Gillespie as
completely as perspiration takes the starch out of a shirt-collar. In his
insufferable vanity, that feeble member of the House of Representatives
had been assuming imposing attitudes, and beaming upon the pupils
with an expression of benignant imbecility which was calculated to
inspire them with the conviction that there was only one guest of any
consequence in the house. Therefore, it was an unspeakable relief to me
to see him forced to shed his dignity. Concerning the composition,

however. After detailing the countless pleasures which had fallen to her lot during the holidays, the authoress finished with a proviso, in substance as follows — I have forgotten the precise language: "But I have no cheerful reminiscences of Christmas. It was dreary, monotonous and insipid to the last degree. Mr. Gillespie called early, and remained the greater part of the day!" You should have seen the blooming Gillespie wilt when the literary bombshell fell in his camp! The charm of the thing lay in the fact that the last naive sentence was the only suggestion offered in the way of accounting for the dismal character of the occasion. However, to my mind it was sufficient — entirely sufficient.

Since writing the above, I have seen the architectural plans and specifications for Miss Clapp and Mrs. Cutler's proposed "Sierra Seminary" building. It will be a handsome two-story edifice, one hundred feet square, and will accommodate forty "boarders" and any number of pupils beside, who may board elsewhere. Constructed of wood, it will cost $12,000; or of stone, $18,000. Miss Clapp has devoted ten acres of ground to the use and benefit of the institution.

I sat down intending to write a dozen pages of variegated news. I have about accomplished the task — all except the "variegated." I have economised in the matter of current news of the day, considerably more than I purposed to do, for every item of that nature remains stored away in my mind in a very unwritten state, and will afford unnecessarily ample material for another letter. It is useless material, though, I suspect, because, inasmuch as I have failed to incorporate it into this, I fear I shall not feel industrious enough to weave out of it another letter until it has become too stale to be interesting. Well, never mind — we must learn to take an absorbing delight in educational gossip; nine-tenths of the revenues of the Territory go into the bottomless gullet of that ravenous school fund, you must bear in mind.

MARK TWAIN

MARTHA MISSOURI MOORE
Courtesy, Beinecke Rare Book and
Manuscript Library, Yale University.

The Trip to California, 1860
♃ Martha Missouri Moore

INTRODUCTION

On June 1, 1860, while traveling upstream along the Republican River in Kansas, Martha Missouri Moore wrote in her diary, "The anniversary of our wedding day. One year ago to day we were married. . . Few have been the trials of my wedded life, few the sorrows that have crossed my path. There has been a loving hand that would chase away all gloom from my brow and hold it close to his bosom in moments of despondency."

Her maiden name had been Martha Missouri Bishop, daughter of James Jefferson and Frances (Brown) Bishop. She had been born in Benton County, Missouri, on October 18, 1837, so was 22 years old at the time of her 1860 journey. The wedding took place in Missouri's Dade county.

The man she married on that June 1st, James Preston Moore, was also a birthright Missourian having been born in Dade County on October 28, 1828. He was a farmer and stockman. According to family tradition he had already been to California and back several times, often acting as a guide.

With the following words, almost an afterthought, Martha wrote in her diary on May 6th, "I had forgotten to state that we had a drove of 5100 head of sheep." They had made the decision to drive the livestock to California, thinking that this would be no more difficult than caring for them over a Missouri winter.

"This seemed to us to be an incredible experience, so we talked to some of our sheep men friends about it. None of them showed much surprise as if to say, 'No problem.' One said with a shrug, 'You'd need three good dogs and one good man for every thousand sheep.' Another pointed out, 'You'd have to shear them just before starting so that their wool was short. Heavy wool would be a problem in crossing streams because it would absorb water and add to the weight of the sheep. With more wool they'd be more likely to drown.'''

Martha wrote in her diary on May 9th, "It is almost impossible to force sheep across water." On Monday, May 14th, she told of buying a shepherd dog named Chloe, "quite a pretty bitch." The next day they purchased another dog. The cost for the two was $33.00. Dogs would be the key to success of the drive. As for shepherds, they had accompanying their wagon train several young men, undoubtedly experienced sheep herders.

James Moore sold off a thousand sheep on June 7th according to Martha's diary entry for that day. This was at Fort Laramie.

By 1860 there had been a number of huge bands of sheep traveling over the California Trail.[1] They waited until after most of the other wagon trains had left as sheep tended to leave very little forage after they passed through.

What one learns from the literature of the day is that James Preston Moore had earlier taken a flock of sheep from Missouri to Tehama County, California, and had a ranch waiting for them there. Louise Barry in her classic book about the jumping-off places of the overland exodus, *The Beginning of the West*,[2] quotes from one George E. Blodget, a mail carrier, who had just returned from Fort Laramie, that he had met James Moore of Missouri "about 5 miles this side of Fort Laramie, driving about 10,000 head of sheep, which from bad water and continued travel, were dying at the rate of 40 or 45 daily." He arrived in California that year, 1852, with something over 4500 animals, having suffered a dreadful loss.[3]

Moore evidently thought, however, that the journey could be done with more success, for he returned to Dade County with plans to take another flock of sheep overland. This journey was put off until 1860. He accumulated a great many of the animals

---

[1] Edward Norris Wentworth, *America's Sheep Trails* (Ames, Iowa, 1948), pp. 138, 169.

[2] (Topeka, Kansas, 1972), p. 1095.

[3] Wentworth, *op. cit.*

and also bought up horses and cattle in numbers for the overland drive.

In crossing the country they did their best to minimize the number of stream crossings. They followed the traditional California Trail, turning off the Humboldt section of the trail in present Nevada to cross over the Nobles' Route just north of Mt. Lassen to enter the northern Sacramento Valley. They settled on Reed's Creek, near Vina, some twenty miles south of Red Bluff. There they were visited by the United States census taker in 1870. That person recorded that Moore was a "Stock Dealer" worth some $10,000. There were by then four children: Nancy, age 9; Lee, age 7, Martha, age 6; and Guy B. age 2. There would follow two more children, Fell, b. 1871, and Ray, b. 1874.

John Quincey Adams Warren, editor of the *American Stock Journal,* visited the Moore ranch in 1862 and described in a letter to that periodical in the August issue what he saw: "J.P. Moore, Reed's Creek, has 2,800 American sheep. He is crossing with ½ breed Cotswold, Merino, and South Down. The fleeces averaged 4 lbs., and the clip 9,000 lbs. He also has a few American horses and mules, and 40 to 50 head of cattle, under improvement. The land is composed of rolling hills, or what is called 'Bald Hills,' and the grazing is clover and wild oats, which are considered very nutritious for the stock."[4]

James Preston Moore died on October 18, 1880, his wife's 43rd birthday. His obituary appeared on Wednesday, October 20th, in the Red Bluff *Daily People's Choice* saying that death was caused by "a rupture of the right ventricle of the heart near the root of the pulmonary artery." The newspaper pointed out that he had "devoted his attention to growing alfalfa and pasturing stock, which made his name famous among stock men throughout the adjoining counties."

Martha Missouri Moore, who wrote the very special diary of the overland sheep drive, died only a few months after the death of her husband, on February 7, 1881. We have found so far no obituary attesting to her death. Martha's niece, Frances Bishop

[4]Quoted in Paul W. Gates, *California Ranchos and Farms, 1846-1962* (Madison, Wisc., 1967), p. 190.

Sweaney, wrote many years later after having typed out a copy of the diary, "As I sit at a typewriter copying from the yellowed pages, I seem to sink into a reverie and out of the shadows there comes a small, dark figure of a lady dressed in the style of the '60s, who seems to beckon to me and urge me to set out again on the old trail. I wish I might, and perhaps I may."[5] So say we all.

On May 8th Martha wrote in her diary, "Mr. Dicus & Lady came up in the evening they belong to our crowd but haven't been with us until today." These were Samuel Calvin and Margaret (Maggie) J. Dicus (pronounced Dy-cus). They were old friends who had decided to go with the Moores to California. Mrs. Discus must have been pregnant for much of the journey, for their first son, William H. was born in 1860 in California. They would have two more boys, Charles, b. 1863, and George, b. 1886. The Dicus family settled in Butte County on arriving in California. They moved to Vina, Tehama County, to become neighbors of the Moores in 1870. They operated a general store in Vina for fourteen years. They ranched and raised stock. Samuel Dicus is listed as a farmer in the 1870 federal census of Tehama County.

The Martha Missouri Moore diary is in the Beinecke Rare Book and Manuscript Library at Yale University. We gratefully acknowledge the kindness shown to us by that library in supplying us with a microfilm of the manuscript and in giving us permission to use it.

We also gratefully acknowledge the indispensible help given us by two Tehama County local historians, Ruth Hughes Hitchcock and Andrew J. Osborne, both of Red Bluff. They have both shared with us their knowledge of the history of their county and especially of the Moore and Dicus families. Ruth Hitchcock has prepared a book entitled *Leaves of the Past*, which has been made available to the reading public by the Records and Research Department at the California State University at Chico. This is a major source on the history of individuals and families of the Tehama County area. The Moore and Dicus family information

---

[5] This comment is found in a typescript accompanying the handwritten diary in the Yale collection.

referred to in the above introduction came mostly from these sources.

MARTHA MOORE'S JOURNAL

1860 May 2nd Wednesday.   After bidding home & friends farewell we started on our trip to Cal. We overtook the train at Mr. Doughertys where there were quite a number of persons gathered to bid us good bye. Pa, Ma, Nan, Tommy, George & Zeb come to Mr. Simpson's our first camping place with us. It was a sad parting when the time came to bid them good bye and may God speed the day when we shall meet again.

May 3rd   Still camped at Simpsons. Mr. Moore absent hunting horses that ran away from us this morning. Uncle Billy Snadon, Tom Snadon and brother Zeb left for home at nine. We struck the camp at 11 o'clock and went up to Simpson's pasture where the hardest storm overtook us I have ever felt   It pelted us two hours when it as suddenly ceased as it came upon us. I went up to Mr Simpsons wet and muddy and spent the night   Mr. Moore came home in the evening but did not bring the horses, John Biddle having brought them before 11 in the morning.

May 4   Had a fair start the day being mild and pleasant we traveled over some beautiful country thickly settled with fine farms. Camped on a slew at the side of the road   Made 33 miles. I rode Jim this morning for the first time.

Saturday 5th   Come to Roops Point in Benton Co [Missouri] a distance of 13 miles. Carried water 1½ miles to cook with, not good at that. The season is very dry everywhere.

Sunday 6th   I rode Fan over to Drywood where we

camped   during the day we passed a little place called Shanghai. I had forgotten to state that we had a drove of 5100 head of sheep. Found some gooseberries at the roadside, which I cooked for supper   They were quite a treat.

Monday 7th   Mr. John Renfro & Dicus rode into camp this morning with the startling news that we had let 1000 head of sheep get away from us at Simpsons and we must wait until they could catch up with us again. The weather is very unpleasant   The wind blew harder today than I ever felt it.   camp life isn't very agreeable when the wind blows a hurricane.

Tuesday [May] 8th   Still waiting for the sheep. It was cold all day no fire to warm by nor wood to make any. The wind blew so very hard   I could not get out of the wagon for fear of being blown away. Mr. Dicus & Lady came up in the evening   they belong to our crowd but haven't been with us until today. Also Brother Frank & Zeb. I was glad to see them, it seemed like home again.

Wednesday 9th   Left Little Drywood with 4800 head of sheep having experienced the loss of some three hundred. Pa overtook us today before noon   Crossed Big Drywood   it took us three hours. It is almost impossible to force sheep across water. They wont go by good nor foul means. We camped in a fine valley of grass. Pa took supper with us and stayed all night.

Thursday 10th   The road very rough in many places the day intensely warm, come through Fort Scott in the afternoon. Pa treated us to a glass of iced Lemonade which was really good. Camped this side of town on the Mormiton [Marmaton].

Friday 11th   Pa left for home this morning taking Zeb with him. I disliked to part with them and more especially to go

away without one.   but then the best of friends must part
and I am no exception to the general rule.

Saturday 12th   Left Mormiton and came to Clear Creek
when we stopped for the day. This creek is literally covered
with cedar and is very good water. I wove Mag [Dicus] a
cedar wreath while sitting on the ox yokes this evening. The
weather quite pleasant.

Sunday May 13th   Left camp early   Traveled over a
barren scope of country 20 miles from where we camped to
Deer Creek   found fine grass & water hole   fish for supper.
Everybody mad because it was late when we got into camp

Monday 14th   Called a few minutes to see Hannah Flinn
and her babe   They live close by the road side   Saw Frank
Flinn and some more of our acquaintances   Camped on
another fork of Deer creek. Today Mr. Moore got a
Shepherd dog Chloe. quite a pretty bitch.

Tuesday 15th   Passed through Leroy [LeRoy, Kansas]
very pretty little place. Mr. Moore got another large
shepherd dog today, the two cost him $33. Saw the wonderful
phenomoma Mirage today west of Leroy where small cottages
look like two story houses Nooned on a little creek in the
prairie and camped on the Neosho river. We have traveled
over some beautiful country and very thickly settled
considering five years ago it was the home of the savage and
wild beast.

Wednesday 16th   Left Indian creek in the morning passed
through Geneva a small town   Camped on the Neosho.
Distance 10 miles.

Thursday 17th   Waited some time in camp for lost
cattle   Mag & I went to see the river   after wandering
around some time we found the desired place. Bought some
butter from two little girls iced and very nice   Come through

Ottumwa [Kansas]   it rained nearly all day   camped on a little bottom in the prettiest kind of place.

Friday 18th   Were moving early, passed through two small places did not learn the name of either   camped on the Neosho.

Saturday 19th   were moving at ½ 7   Crossed a small creek when the sheep got separated from the wagons causing no little trouble.   camped in a hollow.

Sunday [May] 20th   Left camp at ½ past 8   crossed two streams of running water. The sheep drove slowly. This is Sunday but we observe no rest here. May the Heavenly Father remember his erring children in mercy. Mag & I gathered some gooseberries to stew. Some Indians came to camp tonight the first we have seen. To the boys who have never seen any they are objects   to me a nuisance   Camped on Bull creek.

Monday 21st   Passed through Council Grove crossed the Neosho river with out little trouble. Had quite a conversation with a strange lady. I found her very pleasant   Nooned on a small creek   The weather is very hot. Camped on the river again tonight, the sun has set in beauty. Distance 11 miles.

Tuesday 22nd   Left the Neosho traveling over a barren scope of country with no settlements, the dividing ridge between the Missouri and Arkansas rivers   We struck Clark's Creek in the afternoon traveled down a lovely valley   passed a few settlements camped on the same stream. The water is slightly impregnated with sulphur and the best creek water I ever drank. The night bids fair for rain.

Wednesday 23rd   The rain we expected came and kept everyone busy until 12 oclock   I got up and dressed to get the hands some brandy. Left camp at ½ 7   Crossed the creek in a beautiful bottom   After crossing the road wound over the hills. This little valley is hedged in by hills and the inhabitants see nothing beyond their own little world. Camped on Caw [Kaw] river in sight of Fort Riley.

Thursday 24th   Lay over intending to overhaul some meat & other things. Mag & I did up our washing. I blistered my hands & arms so much for my first experience. The sun shone intensely hot and the wind so very high it was impossible to get about. Walked two miles for a drink of water.

Friday 25th   Waited on the river bank in the broiling hot sun expecting every moment the sheep would cross the river, but the sheep were very contrary and there was no getting them across. Was visited by Mrs. Perry who spent the morning quite pleasantly with us. Mag & I called at Mrs. Toppins camp, a whole lot of East Canada folks were there.

Saturday 26th   Left camp early, crossed Kaw river on a bridge of boats and come up through Fort Riley   a more beautiful place I never beheld   Situated in a valley surrounded by hills, the houses are all built of stone, presenting a neat and lovely appearance. Stopped at the Settler's to purchase some things   as we ascended the hills on leaving I looked back upon the Fort nestled in that lovely vale. The scene was enchantingly beautiful, imagination could have pictured it the work of fairies, not of human hand. Lo! in the distant hills or above every thing else arose a tomb a land mark for the nation.

> Soldier rest, thy warfare o'er
> Sleep the sleep that knows no waking,
> Dream of battlefields no more[1]

Camped at a large spring of good water, found plenty gooseberries. At Fort Riley we took the road up the Republican, it being nearer and better.

---

[1] Walter Scott, "The Lady of the Lake," Canto 1.

Sunday [May] 27th   Were detained in camp until 2 oclock
P.M. on account of missing horses. Two young men brought
Jim the black horse in and we sent and got the ponies. It
looked very much like stealing. Camped in a lovely valley on
the Republican Fork of Kaw river.

Monday 28th   The wind was very high this morning   one
will certainly get their share of dirt that leads this life.
Nooned on the prairie   a drove of horses passed us while
nooning   they looked very nicely   Two splendid match
grays how I wish they were mine. Camped on the
river.   made 12 miles.

Tuesday 29th   Morning cloudy & cool. Of all the nights I
ever spent last night was the worst. The wind rocked my
wagon so much there was danger of tilting it over   In vain I
wooed the goddess sleep   she would sit lightly on my
eyelids for a few minutes when a sudden jerk would make one
as wide awake as ever. The day was very unpleasant and we
were all glad when night come. Camped on a little
creek   found gooseberries   also plenty of wood, water &
grass. Made 12 miles

Wednesday 30th   Detained in camp for lost horses   Did
anyone ever see such a time as we have with our horses. It is
enough to worry out the patience of Job. The sun shines out
like the face of an old friend this beautiful morning. Camped
on the Republican   found plenty of wood, water &
grass.   distance 10 miles.

Thursday [May] 31st   a rainy day   everything goes wrong
lost 7 head of sheep. Passed a new made grave. What a train
of sad reflections it awakened on a trip like this. Left home
with bright anticipations and glowing hopes of a future, only
to find a grave by the roadside. This is the end of man "dust

thou art and unto dust thou shalt return."[2] is the irreversable sentence against all material matter.

Friday June 1st   The anniversary of our wedding day. One year ago today we were married. Have the joyful anticipations of that bright morning been realized? Has the canvas which was extended in glowing and ornate cólors faded from view & left heart sickening desolation? or has the way been strewed with flowers and the paths along the way leading into channels of pleasure. Few have been the trials of my wedded life, few the sorrows that have crossed my path. There has been a loving hand that would chase away all glooms from my brow and hold me close to his bosom in moments of despondency. I passed on the sweetly gliding stream whose course has been through life's sunniest vales, no dark sands have marred its limpid beauty, or adverse winds disturbed its peaceful flow. May kind Heaven add her protecting care and direct our way through paths of peace and pleasantness giving us at last a final admittance into the abode of light

> Where the wicked cease from toubling
> And the weary are at rest.[3]

Camped on a branch of the Republican   plenty of wood water and grass. Made 14 miles.

Saturday 2nd   Left the Republican today after traveling up it one week. The day exceedingly warm.   camped on the high prairie without any water, Thought the times very hard. Made 14 miles.

Sunday [June] 3rd   Sabbath on land & sea! And its influence is not entirely lost on man out in the wilds of

---

[2] Genesis 3:19.
[3] Thomas Campbell, "Pleasures of Hope."

civilization.   he forgets his reverence for God's holy day; yet the thought of it coming over him causes him to pause and reflect and for a moment worldly cares are forgotten and Sunday in all its quiet happiness streams upon his heart. Left camp 10 minutes after 4 A.M. Come to water at ½ past 6, when we stopped and got breakfast & watered our stock. Come 6 m. farther to Salt Creek where we camped for the night   got some good spring water and gooseberries.

Monday 4th   A beautiful morning. The birds sing sweetly among the trees. Mr. Moore rode in the wagon all day a little indisposed. Camped on tributary of the Blue, wood water & grass, found a great many gooseberries   Made 14 miles.

Tuesday 5th   Crossed the Blue without any trouble & came into the main California road. Quite a hurricane come up in the evening and the weather from intensely hot became suddenly cool, so much so I had to put my shawl on and was cold at that. Had a shower in the evening. Camped on the Blue.

Wednesday 6th   Mr. Moore and I rode a head of the sheep to the station where we met some very pleasant folks, had a good rest. Camped out on the prairie without water excepting what we hauled.

Thursday 7th   Left camp by daylight and got into Platte river valley by 9 A.M. The river is a perfect curiosity, it is so different from our own streams that it is hard to realize that river should be running so near the top of the ground without any timber and in no bank at all. Wrote to Mat Nevill, Mat Moore & home. Camped on the Platte some distance from the Fort.

Friday 8th   Today we come through Fort Kearney   it is not much of a place.   mud & adobi houses constitute the fortifications. I purchased a dress at Kearney City, paid 20 cents a yard. Went to the fort and camped.

Saturday 9th   A dismal morning the weather cold & chilly. We concluded to wait for a better time to cross Platte. Made part of my dress, found poor Mag crying to go home. Had rather a pleasant time while camped there, but I can enjoy my self any where   what would make any one else fret & scold I am content with.

Sunday [June 10th]   Still raining   every thing is completely soaked through. It is said Abraham dwelt in tents, he must have had more of the ambitious nature about him than I have, or a very unpleasant life   Left camp at noon and come up to the 17 mile point where we camped again. It cleared off nicely in the evening.

Monday 11th   Cool & pleasant all day. Had a nice ride on Jim. The scenery along this river is very beautiful. It is true there are no Alpine heights to strike with awe the beholder but one perfect scene of rural loveliness. The country is fast settling up. The inhabitants build themselves sod houses and manage to live on nothing. The roads are quite muddy. Camped on Plum Creek.

Tuesday 12th   Weather very warm   we had to go some two miles back across a bridge Plum creek being so much swollen we could not ford. Made only a half a day's travel. Get no wood here excepting what we haul. It was a beautiful sight to see the sand hills in the distance and the dark clouds across whose bosoms the forked lightening plays, looming up behind them threatening and pregnant with wrath to man. It rained nearly all night. Mr. Moore got little or no rest.

Wednesday 13th   Cleared off this morning the weather intensely warm. The same scenery still presents itself to our view, the broad river stetching as far way as eye can reach, lifting its bosom to heaven now circled with foam, now eddying sweeping majestically along. Camped on the Platte. It was was quite cool in the evening and everybody seemed to be in good humor, something unusual in our camp.

Thursday 14th   The morning very unpleasant, the atmosphere is heavily saturated with moisture, and the bosom of the river flaked with foam. This is a beautiful river and one would scarcely grow tired of looking at it. Were visited by some Sioux Indians   they were inclined to be troublesome.

Friday 15th   Raining again   This morning we had quite a hailstorm.   passed several dwellings and Cottonwood springs. Visited some graves on a rising mound just in the distance. Death is the great fate from which there is no escape and it comes alike to all men.   even out in this wilderness where there are so few and often passing strangers.

Saturday 16th   The blue sky is dotted with white clouds the dew drop hangs from every leaf and blade of grass   the birds sing enchantingly in yonder leafy spray   the wind fans my cheek refreshingly and all tends to make a scene of rural loveliness. Mr. Moore & I went to the top of Fremonts peak, we could see far away in the distance.   the river lay calm as a babe in its untroubled slumber while the South Platte poured its turbid waters into its depths. Camped on a slough. Walked two miles for a drink of spring water.

Sunday [June] 17th   The wind blew a hurricane last night   I certainly thought it would blow the wagon over. I found my clothes out of doors when I went to dress. The day was calm & cool and we nooned on the prairie. I lost my watch key   I felt bad enough about it to cry. Stopped at Fremont Springs and got a good drink of water. We camped at the ford on the South Platte.

Monday 18th   Commenced crossing the sheep this morning and succeeded in getting them all over in one day. We considered ourselves quite lucky only drowned four. Were visited by some Sioux Indians. Camped on the north side of S.P.

Tuesday 19th   Morning chill & murky but it cleared of in the forenoon and the sun was intolerably hot. A great many of the sheep are lame and some dying of poison from drinking water out of Alkali holes   discouraging. Camped on the S. side of North P. Water much better but no wood yet.

Wednesday 20th   Morning very pleasant   the sand hills stretch far away in the distance and the turbid Platte moves on in its untroubled way. The road monotonous as ever. We lay over half the day   The boys did up their washing and I finished my dress   Found wood on an island in the river and swam it over. Made 6 miles.

Thursday 21st   Started early to Ash Hollow   Struck the sand hills at noon and traveled some ten miles in them but we found no Hollows   had to camp in the hills 3 miles from wood or water. Mr Moore packed water on a mule   it did not come till after dark and I was very thirsty. We saw five antelope in one evening ride   two of them quite near us.

Friday 22nd   The sky thick clouded and the air very chill. Left camp at ¼ past 7   came to the river at ½ past 10   we came over the sand hills all day. Camped on the bank of the river.   got a cedar tree out of the river that the beavers had cut down, for fuel.   made 14 miles

Saturday 23rd   We struck the sand hills at noon & after laying in a supply of Cedar wood we come into Ash Hollow at ½ past 5. Passed the spring but did not get any water. I was bitterly disappointed. The Hollows have always been associated with dread in my mind.   lurking savages sulking coyotes and deeds of crime which made my blood chill. I was therefore surprised to find them as they are a scene with which no one would connect a remembrance of the murders said to have been committed here. After supper we visited Gen. Harney's[4] fortifications which were thrown up in haste to protect them against the Sioux Indians The river has caved in and taken with it part of the wall while the rest are fast tumbling to decay. It is hard to realize that the tramp of six hundred men has been heard here where everything is now so very quiet   nothing is heard excepting the shrill scream of the Kildee and the murmering of the Platte.

Sunday[June]24th   Mrs. Dicus and I clambered over the hills hunting curiosities and looking at the beautiful scenes. It is Sunday but there cometh no rumor of peace here. It is Woa, go on there, gee here with all the noise and bustle of camp life. A very hard rain come up in the evening.   unless one has witnessed a thunder storm on the Platte one can have no idea of its pitiless fury.

Monday 25th   This morning cloudy and very wet.   we have certainly had no dust to contend with since we come upon the Platte, for it has rained upon us every few days. The road was very sandy all day and the recent rains had filled the road full of Alkali water   Camped on the bank of the river.

Tuesday 26th   The gnats and mosquitoes are innumberable along here   Mr. Moore reports Court House Rock in the distance. Camped on the Platte   made 12 miles.

Wednesday 27th   The sun arose this morning o'er as lovely a landscape as I ever beheld.   rode horse back all day   A large freight train passed us at butte creek. We struck the

---

[4] Brigadier General William Shelby Harney was in charge of the Department of Oregon from 1858 to 1860, when he was given charge of the Department of the West, stationed in St. Louis. *Dictionary of American History*, VIII (New York, 1932), pp. 280-281. Howard McKinley Corning, *Dictionary of Oregon History* (Portland, 1956), p. 107

mail route again today not having been on it since crossing
South Platte. We came 60 miles from the Hollows in four
days. Come in sight of Court House Rock and camped
opposite it tonight.

Thursday 28th   The Court House Rock looked beautifuly
this morning pictured against the dark cloud that loomed up
behind it. The Chimney rock appears in the distance like a
steeple tall and slender. Camped opposite this noted rock
tonight. Distance 15 miles.

Friday 29th   Visited the Chimney Rock this morning in
company with Mrs. Dicus and Mr. Moore. We ascended
the rock to where the chimney sets off and could get no
higher   The boys went up the shaft   they looked like mere
doll babies up so far. The rock is composed of a kind of clay
easily broken & will soon all crumble to pieces. Camped two
miles above the stage station everybody mad and swearing.

Saturday 30th   The roads were fine today not being
troubled much with sand. We are camped tonight in Scotts
Bluffs. This is the most beautiful scenery we have been
among. The valley surrounded by mountains whose sides &
tops are covered with pines and cedars the rippling stream
make up a scene enchantingly lovely. I thought if there is
peace to be found in the world the heart that was humble
might hope for it here. Made 15 miles   The sheep were
scattered all over the canons

Sunday July 1st   Passed an excellent spring of water   how
I wished I could take the fountain with me. Come in sight of
Laramie's Peak at noon   Had quite a shower in the
afternoon which was very refreshing. Got into camp
late   everybody was mad as usual. Made 15 miles

Monday 2nd   Crossed Horse Creek this morning   passed
the stage station, a white man living with an Indian

squaw   Camped on the Platte again tonight   the water is much colder and better than it was before. Made 8 miles.

Tuesday 3 rd   Come over the sand hills this morning into a lovely bottom where we nooned. found excellent spring water & fine grass.   camped at the head of the bottom.

Wednesday 4th   This is our glorious Independence Day. In the stillness of the morning methinks I hear the notes of the star spangled banner floating upon the breeze but stars and stripes unfurl not their soft folds here   The only music heard is the mad wind soughing and sighing through the sand hills.   camped on a slough found plenty of wood water & grass. Got some excellent spring water at the station.

Thursday 5th   Laid over to wash. I don't believe I was ever so tired in all my life. I am so sore all over I can scarcely move. We had a pleasant place under the trees and soft water to wash with. Come 4 miles to the next bottom where we camped for the night.

Friday 6th   Were visited this morning by Mr. Low,[5] one of Mr. Moore's old acquaintances,   come 4 miles to Laramie's Fort. Had an awful time crossing the sheep. Wrote to Ma. The stream is very swift and when up very dangerous. Camped one mile above the Fort in short grass   plenty of wood and water.

Saturday 7th   Laid over today while Mr. Moore disposed of a thousand head of sheep at five dollars a head. Wrote to Uncle Mat, Nevill, sister Temp & cousin Agnes   Tried to bake some light bread, but did not succed very well. The day was spent quite pleasantly.

Sunday [July] 8th   Left camp early, the road rough and hilly through the Black Hills the weather much cooler than usual. Nooned under a cottonwood in a small bottom on the

---

[5] Unidentified

river just above Mr. Low's train. Several of the Sioux Indians were around begging as usual. camped on the river 1 mile above the stage station. plenty of wood & water grass poor. Made 12 miles

Monday 9th   Left camp at ½ past 7   come 1 mile and a ½ to Lime Kiln Springs to the right of the road. Had some fine mountain scenery today in many places we could see as far as the eye could reach. Laramies Peak rose beautifully in the distance. Camped on Little Cottonwood   Raining and very unpleasant underfoot. I forgot to mention that at Laramie we took what is called the river road.

Tuesday 10th   Left camp at ½ past 8   were passed by Mr. Low's train in the morning. Crossed a small branch 2 miles from where we camped   took a left hand road through the hills. The road was hilly but smooth   came to water at three P.M. and crossed another little branch at 5. Camped at two fine springs by the roadside, grass scarce. Were passed by two Indian chiefs who asked for a drink.

Wednesday 11th   Left 10 dead sheep this morning poisoned by wild cherry bushes. Come 3 miles to the stage stations on a small creek. Took a left hand road, crossed a spring branch in a steep canon twice   Nooned on the side of the hill below some groves of pine & cedar. Were passed by the stage and pony express.⁶ Passed a small ravine in which there was water at 3 in the afternoon. Camped on a dry creek   water and grass scarce.

Thursday 12th   Left camp at ½ past 8   come into the old road at 10 A.M. There is some delightful scenery among

---

⁶ This was the first year of the Pony Express, the life-span of which was only 18½ months. The classic reference for the Pony Express is Waddell F. Smith's *The Story of the Pony Express*, published by the Pony Express History and Art Gallery (San Rafael, CA, 1964). See also Rowe Findley, "A Bukaroo Stew of Fact and Legend, The Pony Express," *National Geographic*, Vol. 158, No. 1 (July, 1980), pp. 45-71. Fred Reinfield, *Pony Express* (Lincoln NE, 1966).

these hills. Nooned on the dividing ridge   grass scarce. The
pine trees that so luxureantly covered these hills grow less
and less every day. Come 5 miles to a little creek where we
camped for the night   plenty of wood & water no grass at
all, this is the barest camp ground we have had. Made 14
miles.

Friday 13th   The morning comes in intensely hot   were it
not for the clouds which generally over shadow the sun in the
afternoon we would certainly melt. Will this interminable
travel never end? But why complain? Man's days are few and
full of trouble as a morning flower he flourisheth. This is one
way of getting rid of time. Crossed a stream in the morning
another at 10. Come through an everlasting chain of hills
whose sides are as bare of verdure as the great Sahara desert.
Many of these hills are composed of red clay & tall cliffs of
rock. What wonderful workings of Nature could have
produced this phenomenon   God is mysterious in all His
ways   His wonder working wisdom. Camped in a narrow
wood & spring water, good grass on the knolls   made 15
miles.

Saturday 14th   Left camp at ½ past 8 and come to water at
10 A.M. a small branch,   Come 1 mile farther to a fine
stream of water where we nooned. Camped on the prairie at
½ past 4 P.M.   good grass but no water   hauled wood.
Saw a lovely apparition in the shape of a woman riding horse
back. She was very pretty and prettily dressed. Made 10
miles.

Sunday [July] 15th   Left camp ¼ to 7 and come to a fine
spring branch before 8,   crossed Box Elder at ½ past 9 &
come out on the prairie to noon   One of the largest steers
died today of murrain.[7] We are now through the Black Hills
having been just one week among them. As I look back they

---

[7] This was the current term for anthrax.

rise with bristling ruggedness as if to shut out forever from my sight the home of my childhood and those friends whom I love so well. And when I look down upon the turbid Platte as swiftly within its crumbling banks rolls on to join its gray flood with that of the King of waters. I sigh to think that it of all I see is moving toward the home & friends of my youth. Camped on the bank of the Platte, wood and water, grass poor. Made 12 miles. Heard a wolf howling over the river the first I have heard since leaving home. The sound was dreary and dismal and Campbell's lines soon came to memory.

> And waft across the waves tumultuous roar
> The wolf's long howl from Onalaska's shore.[8]

Monday 16th   Came to Deer Creek at 8 oclock A.M. where Mr. Moore did up his shopping.

> Distant lands enchantment to the view
> And robes yon mount in its asure hue.[9]

No where is this so truly realized as on the broad prairies of the west where one can see as far as vision can penetrate Camped on the bank of the Platte under some beautiful shade trees.   plenty of wood, water, & grass. Made 4 miles.

Tuesday 17th   Moving at 7 A.M. Were passed by Mr. Ross'[10] sheep train having the same number that we have. Rained in the evening and we camped below Mr. Ross on the river. Found plenty of currants but it was too wet to gather any.

Wednesday 18th   Left camp at ½ past 6 A.M.   came 4 miles to the bridge   crossed at 10   Had some excellent ice water. Nooned on a little bottom   had fine grass. Camped on the bank of the Platte just above the upper bridge. Fan & the grey horse very sick all night. Made 17 miles.

---

[8] Campbell, *op. cit.*
[9] *Ibid.*
[10] Unidentified.

Thursday 19th   Over sand hills & hollows until noon certainly the roughest country I ever saw, bare & desolate a fit habitation for the home of the red man and the sulking coyote. At 3 P.M. we left the Platte having traveled up it 1 month & 11 days. It was like parting with an old friend to leave the river. Camped on the sand hills between the river & Willow Springs   No wood, water, nor grass. Made 15 miles.

Friday 20th   Were moving early   came to the Willow Spring branch at 9 A.M. where we nooned. This is quite a pretty place. Came to the Willow Springs at 1 P.M. We did not stop only to wait on the sheep as there was a rain coming up. Camped on a little creek 7 miles from the springs. Had tolerable grass & fine water   sage for fuel   Made 15 miles

Saturday 21st   It rained incessantly all fore noon having rained all night before   We had rather a gloomy time   Struck camp at 12 & come some 8 or 9 miles out on the prairie, had fine grass, no wood nor water excepting what we hauled. Camped in sight of Independence rock & Devil's Gate.

Sunday [July] 22nd   It is a Sabboth morning but we were moving early. Passed Independence rock at 10 A.M. & crossed Sweetwater soon after. I think this rock much prettier than Chimney Rock & one thing certain it is going to stand as long as time lasts. Passed the Devil's Gate at 5 P.M. and camped just above it on fine grass & good water. Made 15 miles.

Monday 23rd   Were detained in camp some time to get wood this morning. Visited the Devil's Gate the most noted curiosity along this road. This is indeed wonderful to look at and one stands in awe of Him Who tore asunder the mountains and holds the winds in the hollow of His hands. But why attempt a description. All that I could say would not add to the sublimity of the scene. It speaks for itself. Passed a great deal of Alkali water this morning. Nooned on Muddy Creek had Alkali all round us but the grass was very fine Camped on the bank of Sweetwater fine grass & willow wood made 16 miles.

Tuesday 24th Passed the stage station 1 mile from camp Plenty of Alkali everywhere. the road very rough and unpleasant to travel over. Nooned on Sweetwater in the bend of the river. Nothing new or strange, the mountains look bare & cheerless, and the days are intensely hot. Camped opposite a mountain two miles from the entrance to Three crossings Had plenty of wood water & grass. Made 15 miles.

Wednesday 25th Mag & I took a ramble over the mountains. there were many strange things and many to excite our curiosities. and it afforded us a pleasant relief from the monotonous jogging of the wagons. Crossed the river three times this morning saw plenty of names cut upon the rocks, but none that I knew. Those that have gone across in earlier years friends & acquaintances have left no trace of their footsteps here. Nooned above the third crossing came over the mountains in the evening, were overtaken by a very hard rain Camped on the bank of Sweetwater. Quite a number of trains are camped along Made 12 miles

Thursday 25th [26th] Raining again this morning. Crossed the river 1 mile after starting. Come to the ice springs 3 or 4 miles after leaving the river. The water along the road is very poisonous. Came in sight of the Wind river mountains after leaving the river. These mountains are covered with snow the year round. Passed a warm spring in the evening. Camped 1½ miles from the river on the sand hills Made 15 miles.

Friday 27th Over mountains and canyons until we reached

the river at 9 A.M. where we nooned. The boys caught a fine mess of fish with a seine. Left the river at 3 P.M. over mountains all evening until I am sick and tired. Camped at some springs to the right of the road in the mountains, heard the wolves howling all night. Made 12 miles.

Saturday 28th   Were moving early over a mountainous country.   crossed several branches   Passed an old blacksmith shop where we found a lot of newspapers, though dates in February and March they were eagerly gathered by the boys. Nooned on Strawberry creek, found grass & water plenty. Crossed Rock Creek at 4 and camped on Willow Creek at 5 P.M. Made 15 miles.

Sunday [July] 29th   Found a nice mess of strawberries this morning. The weather is quite cold so much so as to be very unpleasant. Struck the river at 9 A.M.   here we nooned. Took the Lander route[11] at starting and come 6 miles to Willow Creek. Plenty of wood, water & grass   some of the prettiest flowers I ever saw.

Monday 30th   The weather cold, crossed a spring branch soon after starting, come to the river some 10 miles after leaving camp   crossed it and camped on a little creek after 5 P.M.   plenty of wood, water & grass. Made 13 miles

---

[11] Colonel Fredrick West Lander had surveyed and put in a great deal of work on a road from South Pass to City of Rocks during his service with the Army Engineers from 1857-1859. His description of the route in an *Emigrants Guide* in 1859 is quoted as follows in W. Turrentine Jackson, *Wagon Roads West* (Berkeley, 1952), pp. 207-208:

You must remember that this new road has been recently graded, and is not yet trodden down; and, with the exception of the grass, water, wood, shortened distance, no tolls, fewer hard pulls and descents, and avoiding the desert, will not be the first season as easy for heavily loaded wagons as the old road, and not until a large migration has passed over it.

All stock drivers should take it at once. All parties whose stock is in bad order should take it, and I believe the migration should take it, and will be much better satisfied with it, even the first season, than with the old road.

See also E. Douglas Branch, "Frederick West Lander, Road-Builder" *Mississippi Valley Hist. Rev.*, XVI (Sept., 1929), pp. 172-187.

Tuesday 31st   Traveled up the creek we camped on until noon when it suddenly disappeared, passed a slight ascent over a rocky ridge and we were through the South Pass. Crossed Sandy whose foaming & dashing torrent was rushing to join its mad waters with those of the Pacific   Camped on a little branch   fine grass and good water.

August Wednesday 1st   It rained during the night and the morning was damp & chill   it continued showery all day. Come over mountains to Big Sandy where we nooned found a nice mess of strawberries. Passed a grove soon after starting, over a barren desolate country   stopped at the first grass we saw some distance from the road   no water.

Thursday 2nd   Ice in the wash pan and great demand for shawls and over coats. Come 1 and ½ miles to Little Springs where we laid over until noon. Started on the 18 mile desert   come 9 miles and found plenty of water & grass, sage for fuel to the left of the road.

Friday 3rd   The weather cold enough for December   over a desert country to the No Fork of Green River. Crossed it safely & nooned on the stream   caught some fine fish out of its pearly depths. Drove 5 miles to the main river where we camped for the night. Made 14 miles.

Saturday 4th   Crossed the main river with but little trouble. Nothing about the stream to excite terror though so many sad accidents have happened here. The water is so very clear & cold. Camped on Clover Creek 12 miles from Green river. Raining and wet all evening,   another of our best steers died this evening. Mr. Moore was very unwell.

Sunday [August] 5th   Came 9 miles to Big Spring Creek where we camped for the day it being Sunday. So unwell all day I could not enjoy anything   found some strawberries Plenty of willow wood, water & grass.

Monday 6th   Crossed a little creek soon after starting and come into the mountains at 9 A.M. Traveled up Beaver Creek some 2 or 3 miles where we nooned   found plenty of gooseberries. Camped at the Block House built by the company that worked on the road. It is situated at the head of a most lovely valley and would make a fine summer residence. Made 13 miles.

Tuesday 7th   Over mountains, down canons on heights that make one dizzy to look down   such has been our road all day & tonight watchworn & weary we are camped in a valley where there are plenty of strawberries but not much else. Made 10 miles.

Wednesday 8th   The heaviest kind of frost lay upon the ground this morning yet the flowers & strawberries lift their heads lovingly to the sun untouched by the cold. The road very much as it was yesterday the scenery in many places delightful, but everyone is getting very tired. Camped on Smith's Fork at the head of the canon   No grass plenty of wood & water.

Thursday 9th   Waited in camp for lost horses. The Indians attacked us while there   every cheek was blanched white as driven snow, and we were running everywhere to get out of the way. They shot Hunter one of the teamsters through the arm, thigh and ankle. Mrs. Dicus and I ran to the willows where we hid until Mr Moore sent us word he was starting the teams. We hastened away thankful that our lives have been spared, but the roads were miserable and to mend the matter Dawn upset my wagon. We stopped to put everything in which detained us one hour longer. Camped on Salt river at dusk. Mr. Moore stood guard all night.

Friday 10th   Down Salt river to the trading post where we nooned. They gave us some fresh bear meat which was very good. Camped on Salt river   everyone on the lookout for Indians   Plenty of wood, water & grass

Saturday 11th   Passed over the lovely bottom of Salt river   entered the mountains in the afternoon, the way rough & tedious   Camped on Salt Springs. The salt is quick thick every where and we laid in a supply   made 14 miles

Sunday [August] 12th   Were moving early,   nooned at the entrance of Kinnikinnik canon[12] commenced the ascent in the evening. The mountains were steep and precipitous on both sides and we were till late in the night getting through. Camped among the pine everyone frightened at the idea of staying all night in such a place. A storm come up in the night making the dead pine creak and grown adding misery to our already miserable situation. Went to bed supperless.

Monday 13th   Started at 4 A.M. and come into grass valley by 9 when we got to breakfast, staid until afternoon and come to large grass valley where there is a lake several miles long. Camped on a small tributary of the lake   weather cold enough for winter, plenty of mosquitoes

Tuesday 14th   Were moving by 5 A.M.   come up by the lake in which there were plenty of ducks, did not succeed in getting any. Were met by the soldiers going out on their scout. Nooned on Thistle creek and I did up my washing. Camped on the open prairie 2 miles from water. Made 12 miles.

Wednesday 15th   Traveled through an open country,

12 Kinnikinnick is an eastern Indian word meaning something that can be smoked. It could be tobacco, sumac bark, red dogwood bark. There is a plant called by that term, *Arctostaphylos uva-ursi*, a small trailing shrub with reddish bark and leathery leaves. It is related to the manzanita. Leslie L. Haskin, *Wild Flowers of the Pacific Coast* (Portland, 1934), pp. 261-263.

crossed a small creek in the evening   camped on a little branch of clear, cold water.

Thursday 16th   Sent poor Hunter[13] to the fort this morning. Nooned on Thistle creek. Mr. Moore traded for some new cows. Crossed the Portneuf River on a bridge. camped at a spring branch at the mouth of the canon.

Friday 17th   Come through the canon   I was scared all the time   had a rough road all day. Crossed Rosses fork at 3 P.M. Camped on one of its tributaries, plenty of water & grass.

Saturday 18th   Come into Snake river valley soon after starting, nooned on a small creek   the weather very warm and the dust almost intolerable. Camped on a tributary of the Portneuf, had the nicest campground since leaving Platte. Made 15 miles.

Sunday [August] 19th   Come upon Coln. Howe's[14] camp at 9 A.M. It looked very nicely nestled under the hill on the banks of the Portneuf river. It had an air of comfort about it and one could almost imagine that a home in the wilderness was a pleasant one. We camped below them at a nice spring and fine grass. Received an invitation to [go] over & hear the band play and take tea with Howe, which we gladly accepted   the evening passed pleasantly and the tea and roast beef were fine. Went back to camp very much refreshed.

Monday 20th   Laid over today expecting to get an escort of soldiers to travel with tomorrow. I wrote to Pa & sister

---

13 Unidentified.

14 Col. Marshall Saxe Howe of the 2nd Dragoons had been stationed at several forts in the West over a number of years. In the late 1840's as a Major he was in charge of the American fort at Albuquerque, and during the late 1850's was, as a Colonel, in charge of Camp Floyd near Provo, Utah. He was now stationed at Fort Hall near the confluence of the Portneuf and Snake River. Frank McNitt, *Navaho Expedition, the Journal of a Military Reconnaissance from Santa Fe, New Mexico, to the Navaho Country Made in 1849 by Lieutenant James H. Simpson* (Norman, OK, 1964), pp. 151-154; Harold D. Langley, *To Utah with the Dragoons* (Salt Lake City, 1974), pp. 111-113.

Temp.   Col Howe called this morning. My wagon was very much turned up and Mag was washing. Went over and spent the evening very pleasantly with him.

Tuesday 21st   Left camp at ½ past 7   did not get the escort of soldiers as we expected   I dread going off alone in this wild country but we can only appeal to God for protection and hope for the best. Nooned on the Portneuf river, weather intensely warm. Crossed the Banok [Bannock] at 3 P.M. Camped on the banks of Snake river valley once more and drove our stock down to graze.

Wednesday 22nd   Left camp at 20 minutes after 6 A.M. Come some 4 miles to where the Harrington[15] party were killed by Indians & Mormons last year. Oh! God protect us from such a fate. There were nine persons buried in one grave   the wolves had torn it open and several pieces of bone were scattered round. Old clothes, broken dishes & parts of the wagon were there. With a saddened heart I turned away glad to escape from a scene to horrible to picture. Nooned at a sink hole spring   fine grass. Passed the American Falls on Snake river   they were quite a curiosity. Camped on a small creek 3 miles from the Falls. Made 15 miles.

Thursday 23rd   Were moving at 6 A.M. over the roughest country imaginable. Nooned on the bank of snake river

---

[15] The Harrington party was another name for the Miltimore company; 19 persons led by Edwin A. Miltimore and Milton S. Harrington. There were six men, three women, and ten children. On August 31, 1859, they were attacked about 25 miles west of Fort Hall. Martha Moore says that nine of them were killed. According to Brigham D. Madsen, in *The Shoshoni Frontier and the Bear River Massacre* (Salt Lake City, 1985), pp. 105-6, 249, eight died in the melee. There is some evidence that a few renegade white men took part in the attack, although it is doubtful that any of them were Mormons. Milton S. Harrington survived and later made a deposition telling of the attack. Those who survived turned back and returned to their home state, Wisconsin. Larry R. Jones, Historian of the Idaho Historical Society, Boise, has been helpful in pointing out this reference to us. Madsen's book is exceptional as a source on Indian-White conflict in Southern Idaho.

plenty of grass. Camped in a little valley after crossing Fall creek at 4 P.M. Made 3 miles from the Falls. Made 15 miles.

Friday 24th   Left Snake river 1 mile after starting   come to Raft river at 11 A.M. where we nooned   Come down Raft river to fine grass where we camped. Made 12 miles.

Saturday 25th   Up Raft river to the third crossing where we nooned.   left it and come to the junction of this road and the Hudspeth cut off.[16] Camped at the mouth of the canon after dark. Made 17 miles.

Sunday [August] 26th   Come up through a canon to the last crossing on Raft river where we nooned. This is the noted Mormon range where most of the their deeds of horror have been transacted and one holds their breath while traveling here. Mr. Moore lost his watch   Camped at the head of Raft river   fine grass. Made 5 miles.

Monday 27th   Over hills & hollows to a lovely valley where we nooned.   crossed several streams of water in the afternoon and camped 3¼ miles from City Rocks   plenty of wood, water & grass

Tuesday 28th   Entered the canon soon after starting   held my breath while there. Here is much for Natures admirers to study out and muse among for hours but so many deeds of horror have been perpetrated here it afforded me no pleasure to be among them. Camped at Granite Springs, plenty of wood & grass [blot] much   Made 15 miles.

Wednesday 29th   Had an awful rough road over to Goose Creek where we nooned. Traveled up Goose Creek in the evening   Camped in a lovely valley   grass fine,   thought of Indians all night. Made 14 miles.

---

[16] They did not turn off onto the Hudspeth cut-off, which had been used and named by Benoni Morgan Hudspeth and his brothers in 1849. Mrs. Paul Campbell, "Benoni Morgan Hudspeth," *Idaho Yesterdays*, Vol. 12, No. 3 (Fall 1968), pp. 9-13.

Thursday 30th   Were moving early   crossed two prongs of the creek in the forenoon and come to the canon at 3 P.M. Mr. Moore saw a dog, heard some one talking and went to examine before we entered. We saw nothing but a frightful looking place and were glad to get through. Camped in a valley near the head waters of the creek   Made 15 miles.

Friday 31st   Were awakened at midnight by Indians rolling down rocks trying to stampede the horses. Every body was in a short time trying to get a sight of them but the scamps ran off in the mountains and after firing twice troubled us no more. Passed Rock Spring at 3 P.M. and camped in an narrow valley some 5 miles from Thousand Spring valley. Made 15 miles.

Saturday September 1st   Were moving early. Come to Thousand Spring valley at 9 A.M. Nooned at the first water. Camped at the Rush Springs   water & grass weather cold enough for December. Made 15 miles.

Sunday 2nd.   Had quite a rest in camp and come to the Boiling springs where we nooned. The water is hot enough to cook an egg from 3 to 5 minutes. I could only bear my hand in it a second. This is a strange country made up of strange things and inhabited by beings stranger still. Camped some 8 miles from the springs at the foot of the mountain at some springs to the left of the road. Plenty of water & grass. Were visited by some Shoshoney Indians at the springs.

Monday 3rd   Moving early through the divide between the Thousand Spring valley and Humboldt river   down hill until we struck a small branch where we nooned the headwaters of Humboldt. Camped on the same branch. Kept a sharp lookout for Indians.

Tuesday 4th   Over sand hills all morning   had a rough time. Nooned at sink hole on the left hand road having taken this road to avoid going through the canon. Camped in a lovely valley plenty of sage, water and grass. Were visited by a band of Shoshone Indians, all friendly and begging. Made 15 miles

Wednesday 5th   Took a wrong road in the morning and were winding around all day. Nooned in a wide bottom some 3 miles from Bishop's Creek. Crossed Bishop's creek at 3 P.M. Camped on Humboldt river some 4 miles from the creek. Had fine grass   it was more than waist high. Met with bad luck this afternoon   Will Hudspeth's[17] revolver fell from the holster and fired. The ball entered his horse's side killing him in some three hours. Made 15 m.

Thursday 6th   We are now to try the dread realities of this river famous for frogs, Alkali & Indians. Nooned on the bank of the river the weather very warm. Traveled down a lovely valley which would be delightful indeed were it not for the dust that rises in such dense clouds as to almost suffocate one. Camped on the bank of the river,   two Indians staid with us over night. Made 15 miles.

Friday 7th   Crossed North Fork some 2 miles after starting   the road was rough all day, and very dusty. The ground was covered with frost this morning and the weather quite cool. Nooned on the river   had a warm place. I bought some Mountain Trout from an Indian, which were quite a treat. Camped on bank of river. The guard thought they heard Indians in the night. Made 18 miles.

Saturday 8th   Passed some Boiling Springs soon after starting. The smoke from them rose up so thick & fast we thought it was the dust from another train. Had a fine road all morning over a level country. Haven't seen any Indians all day   I presume they are keeping dark for night atrocities. Nooned on the bank of the river. Crossed the river and

---

[17] Will Hudspeth was a cousin of Benoni Hudspeth, for whom see footnote 16 above.

camped at the entrance of the canon fine grass and plenty of it. Made 16 miles.

Sunday [September] 9th Crossed the river again at the entrance of the canon, crossing it three times while in there. The way was rough and the sides steep and precipitous and I for one was glad to get through. Nooned below Moga Creek.[18] Crossed Moga in evening and camped below the hot springs at the foot of the mountain The grass was short and wood scarce. Made 14 miles.

Monday 10th Commenced to ascend the mountains early, the march was toilsome and fatiguing. Nooned in a small valley and I procured some fresh venison from a Shoshonee. Passed some springs to the right and left of the road in the afternoon. We had a rough road to trabble over down Gravelly Ford. Camped at the ford were visited by a lot of Indians. Made 17 miles.

Tuesday 11th 10 miles over the hills into the valley again here we nooned. The road was rough all evening and we camped by the river side more or less Indians at camp all the time. The night is very cool. made 16 miles.

Wednesday 12th Nothing new or interesting this river is very much like the Platte, low hills in the distance, the river fringed by willows with Alkali bottoms. Camped 2 miles above Stoney Point & had a good camping place at least the Indians didn't trouble us. Made 14 miles.

Thursday 13th Passed Stoney Point early and we were glad to get by, took the hill road which took us some distance out of the way so we did not noon but took the first camp road to the river. The day was raw and very

---

[18] We have corresponded with and talked on the telephone with Thomas H. Hunt, the author of *Ghost Trails to California* (Palo Alto, 1974), about the meaning of this word and agree with him that she means "Maggie Creek." Whether she heard it wrong or saw it in writing that was incorrect we don't know.

disagreeable. Camped at 3 P.M. Plenty of Indians around and I procured a fine mess of fish. Made 14 miles.

Friday 14th   Moving early down the river.   drowned 11 sheep in an Alkali slough   nooned on the river. Indians round   what a nuisance they are! Camped on the river   our road lay over the hills in the afternoon. Made 15 miles.

Saturday 15th   Still down the river   how I did wish it would give out   nooned in the bend of the river a short distance from the hills   the day very warm. Camped on the river at the foot hills on the Piute [Paiute] line   Made 10 miles.

Sunday [September] 16th   Made 6 miles over the hills into the valley again, where we nooned. It is Sunday but there cometh no rumor of peace here. Camped on the bank of the river in a pretty place. Two suspicious looking men rode into camp after night telling us the Shoshonee were killing a train behind us.

Monday 17th   Passed those suspicious characters early they gave us a good deal of information about California but who can believe anyone out in this wilderness. Nooned beside the lagoon   some Piute Indians round. Our road lay over the hills in the evening and it was late when we camped in the valley. Aroused in the night by Mr. Qualls riding into camp at midnight and desiring us to remain where we were encamped until he could catch up with us. They had got into trouble with the Indians and wanted more company. Made 18 miles

Tuesday 18th   Lay over today and we spent it clearing up everything generally. Every body was tired when night come.

Wednesday 19th   Were moving early over sand hills nooned on the bank of the river. Had a very sandy road all

afternoon   camped at the lower end of a little bottom.
grass scarce   made 14 miles.

Thursday 20th   Road hilly and very sandy in many
places   nooned on the river. Left the river   come three
miles after starting   Camped in the desert without wood
water or grass   made 15 miles

Friday 21st   Moving by daylight   struck the river at ½
past 8 A.M. where we rested an hour. Come to Lassen's
Meadow at noon where we encamped for the night. Made 8
miles.

Saturday 22nd   Bid the Humboldt a final farewell this
morning   glad to leave in safety a river so noted for peril.
Started on the desert to try its dread realities   stopped long
enough to eat dinner and arrived at Antelope Springs by 2
P.M. These springs have been nicely fitted up for emigrants
and much pains taken with them. Mag and I visited some
graves on the hillside   two women buried near the same
time, it seems hard to [bid] earth & friends farewell so near
the land of gold yet "He doeth all things well." Drive 2 miles
to grass where we encamped for the night. Made 14 miles.

Sunday [September] 23rd.   Left camped after 8 A.M.   had
a hilly road all morning and in the evening very dusty
through the barrens.   arrived at Rabbit Hole springs at 4
P.M. This is a beautiful country place and were it
surrounded by good country would be a noted place of
resort. As it is there is nothing but a barren sandy desert
uninviting to man or beast. Took supper and left at 8 P.M.
to the Hot Springs. Stopped at midnight and rested until
morning. Made 22 miles.

Monday 24th   Moving by daylight, took breakfast at 11
A.M.   rested some three hours and arrived at Hot Springs
at 4 P.M. We were bitterly disappointed when we arrived

here finding neither grass nor water fit to use. Left at midnight.

Tuesday 25th   The breaking of morn found us at Granite Creek having drove constantly since midnight Here we took breakfast and rested until 2 P.M. We found no water fit to drink, and arrived at the Boiling Springs at 4 P.M. here we encamped for the night. These springs are some of nature's most wonderful works, while they seethe and hiss in their caldrons man stands and trembles at the mighty works of God. You can peer far away in the depths of the water, see the jutting rocks and hear the gurgling of water, yet one feels a relief when they turn away from a vision so terrible, a feeling of security comes over them that they did not feel while gazing into their boiling depths. Made tea & coffee of the water but no one could drink it   it was so very salty.

Wednesday 26th   En route for Deep Hole Springs by daylight   arrived there at 9 A.M.   distance 7 miles over a rough barren country. Took breakfast and I am sure everybody did it justice having had little or nothing since leaving Granite Creek. There is excellent water here and a nice camp ground for tired and worn out stock and wearied man.

Thursday 27th   Left camp early for Buffalo Springs. Struck the desert soon after starting. Nooned at Moore's cut off. The road was rough in the afternoon and cold winds accompanied by rain blew in our faces all evening rendering every thing very disagreeable   Camped in swale to the left of the road   plenty of grass but no water   Made 14 miles.

Friday 28th   Drove some 2 miles to Buffalo springs where we watered everything.   nooned at the foot of the mountains on Smoke Creek. Our road lay over mountains, some heavy sand hills and a good many stones in the road. Come into the canon where the sides of the mountains were steep and almost perpendicular   it made me think of where I dreaded canons and the feeling of dread still come over me for there was only a narrow road wide enough for one wagon. Camped in a valley surrounded by mountains. Two Piute Indians stayed all night with us   Made 14 miles.

Saturday 29th   Morning chill and murky made 4 miles to Rush Creek where we nooned. Over the mountains into Rush Creek canon a rough road into the valley where we encamped for the night. Made 8 miles.

Sunday [September] 30th   The sun rose beautifully clear this morning and we were moving early for Mud Springs the road in many places rough   arrived there at 10 A.M. Tomorrow we expect to get to Honey Lake and we will be coming out of the wilderness   sure enough I for one will be very much rejoiced   The roughest road I ever come over, I never was so tired of jolting in all my life, camped among the sage without grass or water. Made 16 miles.

Monday October 1st   Were moving before daylight the morning very cold, ice in the wash pan.   this is October sure enough. The road rough and tiresome   I was glad to see Honey Lake Valley in the distance. It is a beautiful place.

Note written on a separate sheet of paper — As if to describe a photograph:

> Adobe house, on Grandfather [?] Moore's land
> near Vina   Arrows in walls.

Editor's note: The diary ends with their arrival at Honey Lake. The way followed from there was the Nobles' Route over the Sierra, through the Nobles' Pass and around the north slope of Mount Lassen to the headwaters of the Sacramento River. They settled near Vina just south of Red Bluff.

INDEX

Adobe buildings: 248
Agriculture and crops: *see* irrigation, livestock
Ague: 27
Alcoholism: *see* liquor
Alkali: 140, 224, 238, 281
American Falls (of Snake R.): 59, 287
American River (CA): 242
Andrews, John and Elizabeth: 161, 168
Andrews, Nephi: 168
Animal Springs (NE): 91
Antelope: 38-39, 52, 109, 141-42, 144, 205, 273; meat of, 224-25
Antelope Springs (NV): 293
Anthony, Susan B.: 246
Anthrax (Murrain, hollow horn): cattle disease, 32, 53, 57, 59
Apache Indians: 146-48
Arapaho Indians: 146, 148, 201
Archibald, Albert W.: 192, 194
Archibald, John C. and Jane B.: 192, 212
Archibald, Julia: *see* Holmes, Julia
Arizona: 203-04
Arkansas River: 135, 144-45, 149, 151, 200, 202-04; *see also* Little Arkansas River
Ash Hollow (NE): 42, 180, 273
Atwood, Miner G.: 161, 183
Austin, Elizabeth "Libbie" (Pelton): 78, 102, 108, 112; children, death, 80; marries H. Roeder, 80; rheumatism, 103-04

Babcock, Eliza C.: 246
Balm of Gilead trees: 68, 70; *see also* cottonwood
Bannock River (ID): 237
Bashaw, Joseph and Mary: 22
Beam, George Wesley: 83, 116, 118
Bear River (UT/ID): 55-56, 113, 138, 230, 233
Bear River Mts. (ID/UT): 54
Bears: meat of, 284
Beaver Creek (WY): 140
Beef: 238

Bellingham (WA): 79-80, 82
Bent, William: 145-56, 149-50
Bent's Fort: old, 145; new, 146-49, 203-04
Berries: *see* strawberries
Birch Creek (OR): 75
Birds: 274; meadowlark, 41
Bishop, James J. and Frances: 259, 264
Bishop's Creek (NV): 290
Black Hills (WY): 46, 225, 276-78
Black Squirrel Creek (CO): 144
Blacks Fork River (WY): 139, 188, 229
Blacksmithing: 45, 53-54, 57, 282
Blodget, George E.: 260
Bloomer, Amelia: 9
Bloomer costume: 9-10, 191, 194-96, 245, 247
Blue Mts. (OR): 124
Blue River (KS/NE): 36-37, 270
Boggy Depot (OK): 154
Boiling springs: in CO, 206-07; in NV, 289, 294; in VT, 232; *see also* hot springs
Boise River (ID): 68-71, 119-22
Bolster, James F.: 82
Boxelder Creek (WY): 276
Bozarth, Urban E.: 85
Bradley, Dick: 117-18
Brady, George: 144
Bridges: 96, 99, 220, 271, 279, 286; on American R., 242; of boats, 267; of Indians, 33, 96; Reshaw's, 183
Brigham Young Univ. (UT): 136
Brown, Leroy D.: 246
Brule River (NE): 221
Buchanan, Pres. James: 157
Buffalo (Bison): 49, 141, 150-51, 175; described, 197-99; meat of, 48-49, 176, 222; robes, 204
Buffalo chips: 39-40, 100, 222
Buffalo Springs (NV): 294
Bull Creek (KS): 265
Butte County (CA): 262

Cache Cave (UT): 189, 230
California: overland parties to, 217, 245,

California (*cont.*)
259; road to, 57; University, Berkeley, 253
California Historical Society: 217
Camp Floyd (UT): 250, 252
Canada: 81-82, 267
Canadian River (OK): 154
Cannon, Angus Munn: plural marriages, 158, 160
Cannon, David Henry, 160
Cannon, Sarah: 117
Cañon Creek (ID): 63
Carson Canyon (NV): 241
Carson City (NV): 240, 245; Sierra Seminary, 253-57
Carson River (NV): 239
Carter, Joseph and Laura: 17, 30, 39, 53, 62, 74
Castle River (NE): 102
Castle Rocks (NE): 103
Cattle: die, 63-64, 72-75, 184, 227, 240-41; drovers, 164, 219; droves of, 10, 35-38, 143-44; price of, 30; shoeing of, 109; sold, 47; stampede, 175, 177, 223; stray off, 167, 179; traded, 43, 286
Cayuse Indians: 75
Cedar trees and wood: 40-42, 57, 265, 273
Chamberlain, David and Martha C.: 20, 61
Chapman, Addison B.: 20
Chapman, George and Eliza J.: 20, 59, 63
Chapman, John H. and Martha: 20, 59, 65-66, 68
Chapman, William and Mary Ann: 21, 63
Cheese: 57; *see also* milk
Chehalis County (WA): 85
Cherokee Indians: 143
Cherry Creek (CO): 135, 143-44
Cheyenne Indians: 146, 148, 199, 201, 203
Chicago (IL): 87
Chickens: *see* sagehens
Chickensas River (OK): 153
Childbirth: 160, 174
Chimney Rock (NE): 44, 103, 181, 224, 275
Chinatown (NV): 240
Cholera: 107
City of Rocks (ID): 282n, 288

Clapp, Hannah Keziah: portrait, 244; death, 246; feminist, 10, 245-46; letter of, 247-57; as teacher, 245, 253-57
Clapp, Norman: 246
Clark, Caroline Hopkins: children, 151-52; death, 152; diary, 152-62; Mormon convert, 7, 151; pregnant, 152
Clark Fork (of Yellowstone R.): 62
Clark's Creek (KS): 266
Clear Creek (KS): 265
Clemens, Orion: 253
Clemens, Samuel L. (Mark Twain): 253-57
Clover Creek (WY): 283
Colorado: 135, 143-44; gold rush to, 191
Columbia River: 125
Comanche Indians: 148-49
Coody, Richard and Susan: 153
Cook, Jacob "Missouri" and Jane Ann: 21, 43, 52, 58, 61, 67
Cook, Thomas L. and Harriett: 21, 59, 63, 69, 75
Cooking: utensils, 30; *see also* stoves
Coon Creek: in IA, 167; in KS, 150, 202
Copperas Spring (UT): 189
Corliss, George W. and Lucretia: 80, 84
Corn: in UT, 232
Cottonwood Creek: in OK, 151; in WY, 195, 277
Cottonwood trees: 225, 230; *see also* Balm of Gilead
Council Bluffs (IA): 88, 92, 171, 219
Council Grove (KS): 194, 266
Court House Rock (NE): 224, 275
Coyotes: *see* wolves
Crab Creek (NE): 102
Croll Creek (NE): 180
Crossgrove, James A.: 160
Cummings, Gov. Alfred: 249
Currants: 230-31, 279
Curry, Thomas and Mary E.: 19
Cutler, Mrs. W. K. (Ellen): 246, 253-54, 257

Daguerreotypes: 86
Dallas (TX): 155
Deadman's Cave (UT): 136n
Deaths on trails: 34, 65, 101-02, 105, 150,

173-74, 176
Deep Hole Springs (NV): 294
Deer: 107, 116, 144, 152
Deer Creek: in KS, 265; in WY, 183, 279
Delaware: 157
Denver (CO): 135, 143
Des Moines (IA): 167
Detroit (MI): 87
Devil's Churchyard (ID): 117
Devil's Gate (WY): 50, 109, 185, 227, 280
Diamond Springs (CA): 242
Diaries and journals: sources of, 16-17, 79, 136, 151, 191-92, 217, 245, 262
Dicus, Samuel C. and Margaret: 262, 264-67, 274, 281, 284
Dille, David Buel: 161, 180
Diseases: see ague, cholera, smallpox
Doctors: see medicine
Dogs: of Indians, 43, 148, 152, 159; for sheep, 260
Douglas County (OR): 22
Ducks: 59, 285
Dunbar, William: 21, 49
Duncan, Homer: 184n

Ebey, Jacob: 83, 94, 101, 105, 124-25, 127; family of, 83, 107
Ebey, Winfield: 107, 127
Echo Canyon (UT): 137, 189, 230
Echo Creek (UT): 230
Eckels, Delana R.: 251
"Elephant, seeing the": 44
Elk: 35
Elk Creek (NE): 99
Elk Mts. (CO): 142
Elkhorn River (NE): 95, 171, 220
Elm Creek (NE): 99, 175
Emigrants: returning parties, 52, 109, 202
Emigration Canyon (UT): 137
England: 21

Fall River (ID): 59, 288
Feed for livestock: see grass
Feminist movement: 9-10, 191-92, 196, 200, 245-46
Ferries: on Columbia R., 125; on Elkhorn R., 171; fees, 54, 62, 70, 125; on Green

R., 54, 111, 187, 229; on Loup Fork, 221; on Mississippi R., 31-32; on Missouri R., 219; on Snake R., 62, 70
Firearms: see guns
Fish: bought of Indians, 59, 62, 66, 290, 292; in trail streams, 38, 56, 59, 111-12, 116, 151, 186, 236, 282-83; see also salmon
Flag Creek (ID): 63
Florence (NE): 164-70
Flour: 115, 127; price of, 57
Flowers: 167-68, 177, 200, 203, 209-10, 220, 282, 284
Food: lack of, 145; see also beef, potatoes, provisions
Foreman, Joseph and Margaret: 160, 164, 166, 171
Forest Grove (OR): 83
Fort Atkinson (KS): 150
Fort Boise (ID): 70-71, 121
Fort Bridger (WY): 139, 188, 229
Fort Gibson (OK): 154
Fort Kearney (new, NE, on Platte R.): 12, 221, 270
Fort Laramie (WY): 46, 105, 181, 225, 276
Fort Riley (KS): 266
Fort Scott (KS): 264
Fort Union (NM): 193
Fort Walla Walla (WA): 124
Fountains qui Bouille Creek (CO): 144, 205-06
Fremont (NE): 220
Fremont Peak (WY): 228
Fremont Springs (NE): 272
Fuel for fires: see buffalo chips, sagebrush, wood
Furs: of prairie dog, mink, wild cat, wolf, 40

Gaines, Gov. John P. (OR): 21, 76
Game, wild: see buffalo, deer, elk, grouse, sagehens
Gates, Levi and Emeline: 83
Geese: 39
Genoa (NE): 172
Genoa (NV): 241
George, Martin: 161, 164

Giesy, Howard B.: 17
Gillespie, William M.: 253, 256-57
Ginge, George: 161, 165
Glenrock (WY): 183
Gold: 28; coins, 27; prospectors, 74, 76; rush to Pikes Peak, and CO, 191-215; washers for, 240
Golead (TX) battle: 133
Goodell, Anna Maria: children, 81-82; death, 81; diary of, 86-130; marriages, 81
Goodell, Frederick A.: 81, 89-91, 93, 100, 118
Goodell, Jotham W. and Ann: 82, 126-28
Goodell, Melancthon Z.: 80, 127-29
Goodell, William Bird: 81, 88-89, 93-94, 104-05, 108-09, 112, 116; drowned, 81
Goodell (Goodale) family: 79n, 82
Goodwin, John Robert: 135
Goodwin, Lewis: 133, 139
Goose Creek (ID/UT): 60, 234-35, 288
Gooseberries: 95, 230-31, 266-68, 270
Gossage, Jerome: 219
Gossage, John and Lorena: 219, 225, 234, 241; children, 219n
Grand Mound (WA): 79, 83, 128-29
Grande Ronde River and Valley (OR): 77, 123-24
Granite Creek (NV): 294
Granite Springs (ID): 288
Grant, Capt. Richard: 84, 114, 118, 120
Grantsville (UT): 135-36
Grapes: 151
Grass: *passim*; in plenty, 57; scarcity on trails, 278
Grasshopper Creek (ID): 65
Grasshoppers: 65, 149-50
Graves: on trails, 36, 53-55, 60, 64-65, 97-100, 102, 268, 272, 287, 293
Gray, Joseph and Mary: 21, 24, 30, 74
Great Lakes: shipping on, 80-84, 86
Great Salt Lake: 232; salt from, 232, 252
Greeley, Horace: 249n
Green River (WA): 126
Green River (WY): 53-54, 111, 139, 187, 229, 251, 283; trading post at, 54
Grimes County (TX): 133-34
Griswold, Augustus Henry: 217, 232

Griswold, Carrie: 229
Griswold, Eddie: 237
Griswold, Harriet Booth: children, 217-18; diary of, 218-42
Grouse: 126
Guidebooks: 124, 178
Guns: 10, 27, 68, 71, 201, 247

Hail storms: 272
Hams Fork River (WY): 54, 112, 139, 188
Handcarts: 158, 161, 168, 179-80
Hardy, Ebenezer C. and Mary: 84, 117
Hare, Sallie: 161, 186
Hares: 234; *see also* rabbits
Harney, Gen. William S.: 274
Harrington, Milton S.: 287n
Harris, James and Frances J.W.: 133; children, 133-36
Hart, James Henry: 161-62, 171, 183, 188
Hasbrouck, Lydia Sayer: 191
Hay: 238
H.C. Page (ship): 80
Headley, Thomas and Sarah Ann: 84, 111, 116
Heber (UT): 135
Hicks, George: 153
Hitchcock, Ruth Hughes: 262
Hoffheins, Jacob: 162, 164, 182, 188-89
Hollister, W. W.: 10
Hollow horn: cattle disease, *see* anthrax
Holmes, Horatio N. V.: 16
Holmes, James H.: 192-94, 206
Holmes, Julia Anna Archibald: portrait, 190; letter of, 193-215; parents, children, 192-93
Holmes Hill (OR): 16
Honey Lake (CA): 12, 295
Hope Valley (NV): 241
Horse Creek (NE): 275
Horses: *passim*; die, 53, 238; emigrant use, 137, 268; of Indians, 47, 119-23; Indians steal, 66, 97; shot, 290; stampede, 233
Hot springs: 65, 291, 293
Hotel Olympia: 80
Houses: *see* sod houses
Howe, Col. Marshall S.: 286-87
Hudspeth, Benoni M.: 288n

Hudspeth, Will: 290
Humboldt River (NV): 12, 236-38, 289-93; Desert and Sink, 239; desert wells, 239; Meadows, 238
Hundley, Alice May: 136-37, 147; ill, 154
Hundley, Lewis: 136-38, 146; ill, 154
Hundley, Margaret Ellenor: portrait, 132; diary of, 136-55; marries, 133-34
Hundley, Thomas Augustus: 134, 137, 149, 151-52; children, 134-35; ill, 153, 155

Ice Springs (WY): 281
Illinois: 16, 21, 31, 218; College, 27
Illnesses: see ague, cholera, medicine, smallpox
Independence Rock (WY): 49, 108, 185, 227, 280
Indians: atrocities of, 98, 284, 287; burials, 45-46; fear of, 233, 288; friendly, 33, 63, 96, 172; gifts for, 68, 71; graves, 146, 203; horses of, see horses; kill emigrants, 120, 236; killed by emigrants, 38; steal livestock, 61, 70-71, 268; villages, 53; Ward massacre, 120; see also tribal names; squaw wives; women
Injuries: from stampede, 178; by wagons, 168; see also deaths
Iowa: 20, 164-65, 218-19
Iowa City (IA): 163
Irrigation: 248

Jackrabbits: see rabbits
Jackson County (OR): 19-20
Johnson, Cub: 139-42, 145
Johnson, Mrs. Laura K.: 17, 23
Johnston, Albert Sidney: 250-51
Jones, Mrs. Justine: 17
Jones, Larry R.: 287n
Judson, Emeline D: 84, 129
Judson, Holden A. and Phoebe: 83, 85, 88, 93-94, 107, 112, 114, 116, 127, 129
Judson, Lucretia: 84, 88-89, 93-94, 97, 108-09, 123, 129
July Fourth: recognized, 56, 204, 225, 276

Kansas: 135, 191-92, 264-69

Kansas City (MO): 91
Kansas River: 267
Kimball, Mrs. Dortha: 136
Kimball, Elizar and Melinda: 20
Kimball, Heber C.: 247
Kimball, Henry: 27
Kimball, Ira: 27, 30
King, Walter: 85, 107, 126
King County (WA): 85
Kinnikinnik Canyon (ID): 285
Kiowa Indians: 147-49
Kirkland, Moses and Nancy: 85, 124, 126

Lander, Edward: 80
Lander, Frederick West: 11, 282n; road of, 10-11, 282
Lane County (OR): 21
Langton, Seth and Robert: 162, 170, 172, 185
Laramie Peak (WY): 46, 275, 277
Laramie River (WY): 46
Larson, Don and Lillian: 17
Lassen's Meadow (NV): 293
Laundering: 65, 92, 104, 276; passim
Lawrence (KS) Company: to CO, 191-215
Leroy (KS): 265
Lewis, John and Susanna: 17, 19, 24
Lewis (IA): 168
Lewis County (WA): 83-85
Lewis River (ID): see Snake R.
Liberty Pole (NE): 171
Lime Kiln Springs (WY): 277
Liquor and temperance: 42, 54, 57, 204
Little Arkansas River (KS): 197
Little Jordon River (IA): 168
Little Springs (WY): 283
Livestock: droves to CA, 260-61; sheep herders, 260; see also cattle, mules, oxen, sheep
Lizards: 65
Lockwood, Reuben Thurston and Mary B.: 21-22, 62; daughter Nancy, 22
Longmire, James: 126n
Loup Fork River (NE): 96, 172, 221

McCune, Matthew and Sarah: 162, 164, 181
McMenemy, Elizabeth C.: 159, 183

Maggie Creek (NV): 291n
Mail: carriers, 46, 100, 137-38, 202;
    coach, 237; stations, 237
Malheur River (OR): 71, 123
Marion County (OR): 18, 22
Marlatt, William: 22, 30, 52
Martin, Jesse Bigley: 162, 175
Medicine and doctoring: 107; calomel,
    107; cures for livestock, 67
Meeker, J.R. and Nancy: 85, 97, 103-04,
    125, 128; child Sarah, 85; Nancy death,
    105
Melons: 232; see also watermelons
Meloy, Nathan and Mary G.: 82
Methodists: 27
Mexicans: 133, 144-45, 148
Michigan: 245
Middleton, Robert: 196n
Middleton (ID): 120n
Military: on trails, 221, 226, 233
Milk and butter: 153, 265
Miller, Benjamin F. and Margaret: 19, 52
Miller, Keith L.: 82
Miltimore, Edwin A.: 287n
Mining: see gold
Mississippi River: 32
Missouri: 31, 85, 88-90, 259, 263
Missouri River: crossing of, 31, 95, 169;
    steamboat hazards, 90-92
Moccasins: 43, 103-04, 123, 147, 195,
    208
Moffett, Anita: 253
Moore, James Preston: 10-11, 259-61,
    270-71, 286, 288, 294; death, 261; ill,
    283
Moore, Martha Missouri: 10; portrait, 258;
    children, 261; death, 261; journal of,
    269-95
Mormons: H. Clapp among, 247-48;
    converts to, 135, 157-63; emigrant
    numbers, 91; fortifications, 231;
    handcarts, 158, 161, 168, 179-80; in
    TX, 134; missionaries, 46; polygamy,
    157-58; returning east, 52; toll bridge,
    113; see also polygamy
Mosquitoes: 56, 58, 102, 113, 145, 220-
    21, 274
Mount Lassen (CA): 261, 295

Mount Ranier (WA): 79
Mountain Meadows Massacre: 251-52
Mountain sheep: 140
Mousley, Ann Amanda: 158, 160, 170,
    178
Mousley, George Washington and Eliza
    W.: 160, 164-65, 169, 185-86
Mousley, Lewis Henry: 157, 187
Mousley, Margaret Jane: 160
Mousley, Martha Ellen: 160, 170, 178
Mousley, Sarah Maria: diary of, 163-89;
    marriage, children, 158; family, 160-61
Mousley, Thomas E.: 160; wife gives birth,
    187
Mousley, Titus and Ann McM.: 157, 159,
    164, 169, 183, 185
Mousley, Wilhelmina L.: 160, 170, 178
Mud Springs (NV): 295
Muddy Fork River (WY): 189, 281
Mules: 26, 43, 109-10, 141, 170; as pack
    animals, 52
Mullen, Neill D.: 82
Multnomah County (OR): 82
Murrain: see anthrax
Music: 170; see also recreation

Naches Pass (WA): 79, 82
Naches River (WA): 126
Nebraska: 270-80
Negroes: 74, 98-99
Nemaha River (NE/KS): 35
Neosho River (KS): 265-66
Nevada: 12; Carson City school, 246;
    University of, 246
Nevada State Historical Soc.: 245
New Mexico: 193, 211-13
New York City: 129
Newton (IA): 166
Nez Perce Indians: 122
Nisqually River (WA): 128
Nobles' Route (in CA): 261, 295
Northern Light (steamship): 129
Nye, James W.: 255

Oakland (CA): 217
Oberlin College (OH): 22
Oddfellows Lodge: 50
Ogden (UT): 232

Ohio: 16, 22, 79, 89, 92, 217
Oklahoma: 135, 151
Olympia (WA): 84
Omaha (NE): 170, 219
Oregon: overland parties to, 15
Oregonian: newspaper, 20
Osage Indians: 43, 153; Nation, 151
Osborne, Andrew J.: 262
Otter Creek (NE): 37
Ottumwa: in IA, 218; in KS, 266
Oxen: 128, 218; bought, 181, 185; death
    of, 53, 55, 65, 114, 278, 283; price of,
    54, 63, 68; lame, 118; Indians steal,
    149; sick, 114; traded, 112

Pacific Creek (WY): 110, 228
Pacific Spring (WY): 228
Paiute Indians: 292, 295
Palo Alto (CA): 246
Park, James P.: 162, 180
Park City (UT): 135
Pawnee Fork (KS): 150
Pawnee Indians: 41-42, 96
Peaches: 25, 71
Pelton, Ann Marie: 82
Peria, Ellatheria D.: 161, 164
Pierce County (WA): 84-85
Pies: 67, 113, 150
Pikes Peak (CO): 10, 143, 205; climbing
    of, 206-11, 213-14; gold rush, 191-215
Platte River (NE/WY): 38-49, 95, 99-108,
    171-84, 220-26, 270-80; North, 41;
    South Fork, 135, 142, 144, 272-73
Plum Creek (NE): 271
Plum Creek (WY): 47
Plums: 151-52
Polk County (OR): 21, 30, 82
Polygamy: 249
Pony Express: 9, 277
Port Angeles (WA): 81
Portneuf River (ID): 58, 186-87
Potatoes: 122, 128, 232
Powder River (OR): 75, 123
Prairie Creek (NE): 98, 174-75
Prairie schooners: *see* wagons
Pratt, Orson: 247
Presbyterian Church: Indian mission, 33
Prices: of provisions, 71; in OR, 76; in

    WA, 127
Prospect Hill (WY): 108
Provisions for the trail: 219; *see also* beef,
    flour, milk, potatoes, prices
Puget Sound (WA): 80
Pumpkin Creek (NE): 180n
Puyallup River (WA): 127

Quicksand Creek (NE): 224
Quincy (IL): 31

Rabbit Hole Springs (NV): 293
Rabbits and jackrabbits: 53, 59-60, 67,
    118; *see also* hares
Raft River (ID): 59, 288
Rafts: 138
Ragtown (NV): 239
Rain: *passim*; 198
Rainboth, Mrs. Zahna Z.: 17
Rattlesnake Creek (NE): 223
Rattlesnake Mts. (WY): 227
Rattlesnakes: 102, 203
Recreation: on trails, 90, 205, 286
Red Bluff (CA): 10
Red Buttes (WY): 47
Red River (OK/TX): 154
Reed's Creek (CA): 261
Renfro, John: 264
Reno (NV): 246
Republican River (KS/NE): 267-69
Reshaw's Bridge: 183
Rivers and creeks: crossing of, 63, 137,
    202; *see also river names*, bridges,
    ferries
Roads: dusty, 53; muddy, 166; rocky, 227;
    rough, 142; sandy, 223
Robinson, William Davis: 161-62, 164,
    186
Rock Creek: in ID, 60-61, 65; in WY, 282
Rock Spring (NV): 289
Roeder, Elizabeth Austin: *see* Austin,
    Elizabeth
Roeder, Henry: 79-80; marries Eliz.
    Austin, 80; death, 80
Rogue River (OR): Valley, 19
Rosses Creek (ID): 286
Rush Springs (NV): 289

Russell, William Green: Cherokee expedition, 143n
Sacramento (CA): 242
Saddles: 27; side saddles, 10
Sagebrush: 48, 59, 108, 283
Sagehens: 53, 60, 67, 116, 118
St. Joseph (MO): 30, 32
St. Louis (MO): 88-90
Saleratus: 40, 139, 184
Salmon: 69-70, 75, 122
Salt Lake City: 137, 157-64, 232, 247-52; Fort at, 250; Tabernacle, 247
Salt River (WY): 284-85
Salt Springs (WY): 285
Sam Cloon (ship): 88
San Francisco (CA): 217
Sandy River: Big, 139; Little, 110, 187; in WY, 53, 110, 228-29, 283
Santa Fe Trail: 145-49, 194-203; freighting on, 194-95
Santa Rosa (CA): 193
Schools: in NV, 246, 253-57; in OR, 30
Scotts Bluff (NE): 45, 104, 275
Seneca Falls (NY): 9
Service berries: 231
Shawnee Indians: 148
Sheep: 10, 61, 143, 259-61, 264-95; dogs, 260, 265; trail deaths, 260; drown, die, 272-73, 277; sold, 276
Shell Creek (NE): 220
Sherman (TX): 154
Shoshone Indians: 54, 68, 120n, 142, 289-91
Sierra Nevada: crossing of, 241-42
Sierra Seminary (NV): 246, 253-57
Sill, Dr. Eugene: 218n
Silver, Barnard S.: 159
Sioux Indians: 41-42, 179, 221, 271, 273-74, 277
Slavery: in MO, 31; in New Orleans, 133, 192
Smallpox: 180
Smith, Henry Nash: 253
Smith, John F. and Hanna: 18
Smith, John Lyman: 162, 186
Smith, Samuel and Melissa: 18
Smith's Fork (WY): 113, 284
Smoke Creek (NV): 294
Snake Indians: 50, 122

Snake (or Lewis) River (ID/OR): 115, 287-88; crossing of, 58-71, 115
Snakes: 65; *see also* rattlesnakes
Snow, Erastus: 162, 164
Snow, Mrs. Robert G.: 159
Snow: 137
Sod houses: 32, 34-35, 65
Soda Springs (ID): 57, 114
South Pass (WY): 110, 228, 283
Spring, Agnes Wright: 192
Spring Creek: in NE, 181; in WY, 283
Springfield (IL): 166
Springs: copperas, 230; *see also* hot springs
Sprouse, Will: 139
Squaw wives: 44-45, 106, 147-48, 227; Indian dress, 59
Squirrels: 38, 53
Stagecoaching: 9; stations on trails, 277, 281
Steilacoom (WA): 127
Stewart, Alexander Franklin "Frank" and Laura R.: 18, 24; marriages, 18
Stewart, Amos Kendall "Doc": 17-18, 24, 28
Stewart, Ann Elizabeth: 17
Stewart, Hanna Jane: 18
Stewart, Harriet Augusta: 15, 18
Stewart, Joel and Sarah Sutton: 15
Stewart, Melissa: 18, 24, 27, 28; letter of, 23-25
Stewart, Susan: 18
Stony Point (NV): 291
Stoves: 30, 195
Strawberries: 110, 142, 282-84
Strawberry Creek (WY): 282
Sullivan, Pauline: 17
Sulphur Creek (WY): 230
Sulphur Springs: in OR, 73; in WY, 140
Sunday observance: 31, 124, 142, 150, 155, 209, 223, 244, 259
Sutton, Asahel: 16, 19
Sutton, Harriet Augusta: 15, 28
Sutton, James McCall: 16, 18-19, 24-25, 29, 48, 66
Sutton, John Pierce: 15, 26, 28, 48; children, 15
Sutton, Laura Ann: 15, 25

Sutton, Margaret Jane: 19, 25-25
Sutton, Mary Emily: 19
Sutton, Melinda: 20, 24
Sutton, Sarah: children, husbands, 15, 17; death, 15-16, 77; letters of, 17, 23-77
Sutton, Solomon Henry: 16, 19
Sutton, Walter and Louisa: 15, 20, 26
Sweaney, Frances Bishop: 262
Sweetwater River (WY): 49-52, 109-10, 185-87, 227-28, 280-82; Strawberry branch, 110

Taos (NM): 212
Taylor, Abigail Irene: 152, 155
Taylor, George J.: 163-65, 170
Taylor, John: 163-64, 169-70, 177
Taylor, T. and Alma: 139, 143
Tehama County (CA): 260, 262
Tennessee: 16, 22
Tents: 39, 49, 71, 99, 185, 220, 271
Terry, Thomas Sirls: 163, 178, 180, 182, 189
Texas: overland party to, 133
Texas Company: 184-85
Thistle Creek (ID): 285-86
Thomas, Preston: 134, 145
Thousand Spring Valley (UT): 235, 289
Thunder, lightning: 98-100, 166, 226, 274
Thurston County (WA): 82
Tierney, Luke V.: 200n
Timber: in ID, 55, 255; in OR, 74; in Sierra (CA), 242; in UT, 135
Tipton, Meshach and Elizabeth: 22, 72-76
Trading posts: 42, 45, 47-52, 58, 106, 144, 227, 229
Trinity River (TX): 155
Trunk: abandoned, 116
Turnham, W.: 22, 33, 39, 52
Twain, Mark: see Clemens, Samuel L.
Tygh Valley (OR): 15, 77

Umatilla River (OR): 124
Utah: Deseret, 250; military to, 250-51
Utah State Historical Soc.: 159
Utah "War": 157-58, 187
Ute Indians: 148

Vacaville (CA): 245

Van Wormer, Charles and Mary: 85, 87-89, 94, 105, 107, 114, 127
Van Wormer, Frank: 118
Verdigris River (OK): 153
Vermilion (OH): 79-82, 86, 129; wagon train of, 79-130
Vina (CA): 262

Wagons: abandoned, 77; numbers of, 29, 171, 218; other conveyances, 75; repairs on, 58, 116, 138, 152, 171; upset, 63
Waldo, John B. and Avarila: 22-23, 74
Walla Walla River: 124
Walnut Creek (KS): 151-52, 200
Ward, Alexander: 120n
Warren, John Q.A.: 261
Washington Historical Soc.: 79
Washington Territory: 126-29; emigrants to, 79
Washington, Univ. of: 79
Water: passim; container for, 54; poor quality, 117; scarcity on trails, 140
Watermelons: 153
Weather: cold, 36, 53, 57-58; flood, 198; see also hail, rain, snow, thunder, winds
Weber River (UT): 137, 157, 187, 231-32
Wells, Daniel H.: 247
Whatcom County (WA): 79, 83
Whidby Island (WA): 83-74
White Horse Creek (ID): 119
White River (WA): 126
Whitsell, Henry and Margaret: 85, 118-19, 126-27
Whitworth, Rev. George: 85, 129
Whitworth College (WA): 85
Wigwams: 43, 71, 103
Wilkes, William and Elizabeth: 163, 184
Willamette Valley (OR): 21
Willow Creek: in ID, 65; in WY, 228, 282
Willow Spring (WY): 184, 226, 280
Wind River Mts. (WY): 52, 281
Winds: 268; see also weather
Wolves and coyotes: 40, 42, 95, 100, 197, 224, 279, 282, 287
Women: fear of Indians, 201; see also feminist movement, squaw wives
Women's rights: 200
Wood, James: 102

Wood: for fires, 166; lack of, 38, 116, 223; wagons used for, 123; *see also* cedar, sagebrush
Wood River (NE): 98, 221
Wright, Mary (Ebey): 85, 107; husband, 108

Yakima River: 125
Yale University, Beinecke Library: 262

Yantis, Alexander S. and Sarah: 86, 123-25
Yellow Creek (UT): 230
Yellow fever: 23
Young, Brigham: 247-49
Young, Phineas: 163, 170
Younker, J.F.: 196n, 199n

Zahniser, Aaron and Harriet: 18